CATHRYN MAHONEY

Oon'ch-illia

The Secret Human Life

of an Ancient Star Woman

Oon'ch-illia

Cathryn Mahoney

Table of Contents

Table of Contents

Table of Contents

Oon'ch-illia

Dedication

I dedicate this book to the She'masha'taa People and the 32 Ancient tribes who have guided me on my journey and allowed me to shine their light of wisdom and truth.

Cathryn Mahoney

Introduction

*My light reflects its essence within all spaces, within the
molecules of the earth itself.
I am a star - a particle of light
plucked from the darkest part of
the sky.
The hand of the great spirit steers me on a journey from
oblivion.
Sudden rapid movement disorientates me.
I crave stillness, to remain in the space of nothingness.
Beside me, another star shines as bright.
Our light merges as musical tones.
The creator breathes life into us and sets us free.
A third more brilliant light appears before us--one, from
the highest orders.
It guides and teaches within moments of light-time. We
are scooped up and placed upon a plasma planet in a
flash.
We exist in blissful silence, in incubation. Knowledge
flows through us like a calm river.
The seamless expanse of growth prepares us.*

As beings of light, we evolved as we traveled through distant galaxies and dimensions of time and space. We existed alongside various species and races from many organic and light planets. Places we once called home.

All the while, we created new realities and expanded knowledge and wisdom. Earth, the blue planet, called us.

As seasoned travelers, we wondered if it could offer us some stability. But the people of Earth drew us into their chaos and destruction through their desire for knowledge and wisdom.

With such diversity of life, the planet was a beautiful distraction. We knew it needed saving from the minority who sought to destroy the fabric of societies within all corners of the planet. From the commencement of earth's time, we became human inhabitants and visitors.

Oon'ch-illia

*Living within a human body is so awkward and
unappealing.
I strive to break free and return to pure existence.
Yet, this place called Earth is insistent.
It draws me further in.
I am tugged and beckoned to interact again and again as
a human incarnate.
Each time I return, my light vibrates a notch brighter.
But my desired path is to the bosom of the creator and
leave earth's pull.
Within a physical body, my mind is confused with human
thoughts, needs, and wants.
It fractures my sense of being in its purest form.
I long to stretch and travel unhindered, remain invisible,
and shift through time.
Yet, I accept that my calling is to help humanity continue
to exist.
When will they understand that being present with one
another is enough and to live in harmony?
When they do, the freedom I desire will be mine.*

Note for Reader

There are many versions of a shared experience. The words on these pages are my truth. They come from direct conversations that jogged recollections of events during the journey to discover my origins and abilities. Memories resurfaced after dreamwork, bodywork, and free writing exercises, allowing my consciousness and soul to speak.

I share to tell my truth, not shame or blame those who rendered harm purposefully or inadvertently. I changed the names of certain people to offer anonymity. I am grateful for the learning and development they afforded and helped me rise higher, even though it has been a long journey to piece together and step into my true self.

I offer a unique viewpoint of personal life experiences and shifting through the veils of time and space. This book may challenge your beliefs about memory recall and perceptions about what is reality and truth. It may also challenge your thinking about time, space, and sentient life forms from other planets and star systems. Please keep an open mind and know that nothing is as it seems. Many mysteries are waiting to unfold if you can let go of pre-conceptions and need proof. Know in your own heart what is true.

Thank you, dear reader, for choosing this book.

Oon'ch-illia

Prologue

The early morning light and smell of ozone send a frisson through my body. I hadn't consciously set any wheels in motion but sensed the cliff-side walk might prove eventful. I intended to be present in each earthy step and to bathe in the beauty around me in honor of Mam. It was the second Anniversary since she slipped away, and my retreat to the coast was to remember and reconnect with the happier memories of Mike. It had been eighteen years since I let him go, except for the essence of him—Mike, whose memory I secreted within my heart.

Even though I missed Mam, I was grateful that she tore away the shroud over our family secrecy. Inner clarity brought the truth of early childhood trauma and an urgency to make sense of it. As a result, I cut family ties and drifted alone. At the same time, my therapist and Mam's ethereal presence lifted me up. In the end, though, it was Mike I really needed.

One year and three days after losing Mam, the truth she had revealed hit me hard. When that bomb exploded, I struggled to survive daily, uncertain how to get through the next. It took nine months of therapy and healing.

A new life was gestating - mine. Pain, discomfort, fears, and expectations heralded my light into the world. First, Mam was my birthing partner, and then Mike took over. He stepped into his linchpin role to ground me and help me to fill in the missing pieces.

Tentative emails to each other filled the voids in our separate lives. Within weeks they developed into reams of self-reflection and the acknowledgment of pain and grief. I knew it was time to reconnect once again.

Mam weaved her magic between us as only she could. She prodded me in the direction of a spiritual medium. I was selective. The first medium I visited said, "you don't need me; you have the gift." I attempted to tune in during meditation. I was riddled with self-doubt, and even after visiting the spiritualist church, I went into self-protection mode. Mam must have been frustrated with me. I kept seeing the name of a well-known medium everywhere I looked. When I contacted her, she had a cancellation. I knew Mam had caused this meeting. Within minutes, the medium looked deep into my eyes and then cried.

"Your Mam brought you here. She's telling me about the rift in the family and why it happened. You will not have to walk alone. There is a Michael. He's coming back to you," she said through happier tears.

My grieving had taken backstage while I supported other family members. I wondered if I could step into the role of matriarch and be like Mam. She chose to open my eyes to reveal the deception she once hid. In her absence, I refused to walk in her shoes. Instead of fulfilling family expectations, I walked away. After that, my erratic life got scarier. Moments spent relaxing on the calm waves were washed away as each new surge soared me over the edge. Through it all, I sensed a familiar light in the shadows. Was it Mike? I didn't dare hope that it was.

I reflected on the circumstances of the family rift as I walked along that winding coastal path. Guilt and shame cast long shadows until the sun revealed Mam's magical presence. I bathed in her love as I looked out to sea and reveled in the warmth of the June heat. Deep breaths inhaled brine and ozone, offering an inner cleanse. The heads of the wheat bobbed 'hello' as I passed by; fields of crimson poppies amongst gold offered a lively oil painting backdrop. They triggered a pleasant memory of Mike's melodic voice: a personal recording he made on a CD to honor my love of poppies. My heart skipped a beat as I strolled along the path. In my reverie, I avoided crushing the scattered meadow flowers to preserve golden nectar for thirsty bees. Instead, I laughed as butterflies danced lazily around my feet.

Many years ago, at a cliff-side home, I severed the ties that bound Mike to me. In a releasing ceremony, I ripped and burnt his letters and cards, throwing the ashes into the wind. As I walked a different cliff-side path this time,

Oon'ch-illia

I chose his resurrection; to breathe fire into the Phoenix. I must say there was some resistance. A volcano churned within me still. Was I safe when I was stripped bare? Mike had been elusive in my times of need. The reality of our doomed relationship had fanned an inner heat, causing a reaction. I had tried fruitlessly to forget about him, to reclaim my heart and not need anyone, but it was my greatest lie. First, it was Mam's death, then the family rift that brought realization, understanding, and acceptance. I was cast adrift from my family but realized my love for Mike still burnt bright.

As the happy memories resurfaced, the years melted away, my mind shifted to our earlier trysts. I sensed Mike close and heard him whisper softly. I smelled his essence and sank into the memory of his loving embrace. I knew it was time to act once again. I dialed Mike's number. For the briefest moment I panicked, my nerves kicking in, but I knew there was no going back. I listened to the dialing tone, and then it connected. I heard his familiar voice, and my ears thudded as my mouth went dry.

"Hello, hello, is that you, Cathryn? I'm so pleased you called."

Time froze, and I remembered to breathe. I envisioned being in his arms, so strong yet tender. His voice seduced me, and nothing else mattered except hearing his voice. The years of pain and misery dissipated in his soothing words.

"Are you there?"

"Yes, I'm still here, just catching my breath...so windy up here...I'm on the cliff, looking down on Scarborough." I rushed my words to hide my nerves.

"You were so giddy," he told me later, as was he. We were as excitable children, rejoicing in the moments. How we managed to keep it light and fun, I cannot fathom. We pushed the darkness away. All else faded as we shared words, time, and space. Love flowered again on that day. Mam smiled as she passed me. Then she vanished in a shimmer of iridescent light.

We talked and laughed with each step I took. Then I paused with my camera to share aspects of the view. I recalled so many happy times as I descended toward the bay.

I panned around the beach, "Remember - our first kiss was here? I reached for your hand and placed it on my heart."

Mike recounted, "No, you put my hand upon your tit. Don't deny it, you did. I wish I was there. I'm working in my office, at home...see," as he panned his phone around the room.

"If I close my eyes, I feel I'm with you there. Walking hand in hand, enjoying such a beautiful day. I'm sad to say I've got to go."

He concluded in a whisper, "Someone's coming down the stairs. Got to go...don't want to...love talking to you...remember me."

Oon'ch-illia

I

Grounding

I experienced the physical pain of human incarnation from the onset. My other earthly existences were wiped from my mind, while my body held memories that would resurface as my feet connected to the land. I had agreed to live a life shaped by humanity through childhood and early adulthood experiences. Tested time and again to rediscover my true self and the purpose of my existence in an organic body. Human emotions became my nemesis and my savior!

1

Emergence

I exist within a pool of golden light.
As I merge deeper within it, I am lost, falling through a rainbow chasm.
My heart sings with joy and wonder as I reunite with friends from all times and places.
They lead me into an expansive light chamber where I float within a prism and merge with a violet ray.
I am within the dust motes suspended in space.
We speak a universal language in light form as one entity, reflected in water droplets that touch the land.
Each essence forms the harmony of a signature tune as we communicate our individuality.
I am an observer and participant and am mesmerized.
My consciousness expands.
My light glitters and radiates colors far off the spectrum.
My sound is mute to the human ear.
My presence is a breeze or a warm glow upon the heart.
I am ready.

Within the darkness, I floated in a state of deep peace; the only sound was a gentle heartbeat. As I drifted, my movements flowed with the water, nestled in a cocoon of safety.

My awareness perceived new sounds – hushed tones, constant high pitches, and a new sensation called pain. An insistent pressure that turned my whole world upside down. A glow hurt my eyes. It grew brighter. Then, a freak wave snatched away my safety and the pain intensified.

Tugs and twists around my bottom, one leg, the other, then each foot. I longed to return to my warm cocoon once again. But there was no going back. Eventually, my legs were pulled out from within me. One at a time, they were untwisted from each other, yet I fought back and tried to anchor. My little ankles fail to hold. Finally, I was yanked free, and my pleas went unheard. My skin burned and prickled. The sounds and light screamed and screeched. I whined, then bellowed, exhaling my distress as I gasped my first breaths.

My senses were in shock. I was an ember in search of coolness. Large hands offered that but also fear. Reality hit my consciousness. I was in physical form once again. The hands prodded, pulled, bent, twisted, and turned me. A hard, cold object seared my skin. I sensed urgency and concern. Voices encroached upon the peace I craved. I begged for solace.

Then another pair of hands held me. I whimpered and stilled as the new soft hands caressed me. I was swaddled within warmth and comfort, then lain on a sweet smell I recognized so well. The resonance I had listened to for so long – my mother's heartbeat. Then I slept.

Moments later, a new pair of hands snatched me from my deep slumber. They stole me away, yet again, onto a hard surface and another bright light. I shuddered and screamed. Pain was my constant companion. With more twists and pulls, my limbs were moved from one position to another. I was a puppet, a plaything.

"Please stop!" I screamed.

There was only one way to go: forward into this life. My last moments of dithering were to no avail. My feet were a reminder, symbolizing the complex role I agreed to play. The Creator had set this chain of events into motion. If I refused to turn the lock and step through the door of this life, I would have to repeat it all. Finally, I acquiesced. My soul was in the driver's seat, my 'star being' self, the excited traveler, while the human me would forever be the reluctant passenger.

2

Blessed

An orb shimmered and blinded me. My little fists thrashed, attempting to grab it, and my pram rocked with my movements. My eyes darted towards the dapples of light among the shade of the ancient oak, and then I stilled, listening to the voices that echoed a short distance away. I was startled by the familiar sound of a small boy's scampering feet up and down the garden, with his strange noises - "naaaoow...naaaoow", and the arm that appeared as he soared past. I wriggled, attempting to see more, but my attention was diverted by the trill of a bird from aloft its branch. I stilled again and listened. As I did, more birds arrived. They settled in the tree and waited as the human noises drifted away back to the confines of the house.

I was alone, except for my bird friends up above. The air stilled as if time had stopped. I shifted. My essence vibrated – "iee...iee...iee," as my colors changed from blue and orange to lavender and gold. Yes, I was in the body of an infant, but my soul spoke, and my consciousness expanded.

I connected with the arrival of Old One, within an aura of aqua and gold, like a sunbeam in the morning sky. Deep reverence and pure bliss filled my tiny body. His weathered hand tapped my head three times then he placed a kiss on my cheek.

"I love you, my child, and will endeavor to keep you safe," he whispered. *If an observer had been present, they would have witnessed a golden sheen around the infant and a knowing smile on her face.*

Within a gentle breeze, Old One departed. The birds sang in a chorus as the leaves danced to their merry tune. I remained still and slept.

3

Protected

The motion and warmth of my Mammy's lap lulled me into a deep sleep. We traveled for a long time, but I slept through most of the journey. My initial excitement of spending the whole day together soon waned with boredom.

"Wake up; we have to get off now and catch the next bus," Mammy murmured.

"I'm cold," I moaned while we waited for another long journey. I didn't know where we were headed, but time away from home was good enough. I sensed something astonishing yet scary was afoot, even though I wasn't yet two.

"Can you count the sheep?" Mammy asked. I soon ran out of fingers.

The bus rattled over the bumps of the country lane.

"Feel sick," I sobbed.

"Suck this sweet," Mammy said, then pointed out the window. "Look, there's a calf...it's having a drink ... from its mummy. Look...that bird...looks golden in the sun. Watch, there...it's gone...swooped over that hill."

"Where going?" I shouted to be heard above the noise. It seemed such a long way.

"To meet someone special" is all my Mammy said.

Finally, the bus stopped. Mammy lifted me down the steps, but I tripped and skinned my knee. Another lady scooped me up as I whimpered. She felt nice and squishy.

"There, there, love," she said as she tickled me under the chin. I felt happy and content, even though she was a stranger. She set me down and introduced herself to my Mammy.

Mammy was a little shy. Then I noticed a boy much bigger than me. He had a smile just like his Mammy's and said, "Hello you!"

I didn't know him, but he seemed nice. He grabbed my hand, leading me up the path while shouting, "Mum, are we going up the hill?"

He talked oddly and said, 'Mum,' not 'Mammy.' Then, he told a funny story and made me laugh. Afterward, he pulled me up the hill, but my legs couldn't keep up.

Finally, his mum shouted, "Michael, slow down: she's only a baby." I liked his name and tried to repeat it. The Mi and L felt nice on my lips, but he laughed when I made a funny face at the K sound.

"You sound like you're choking."

Then his face softened, and he pulled me eye to eye.

"Call me Mike - it's easier...can you say it?"

"Mi...ke," I repeated after him.

I was breathless when we reached the top and wished I'd gotten into my pushchair. We arrived at a waterfall. I laughed as the spray wet my face. Mammy laid blankets on the grass, and Mike's mum put our picnics out. We munched on our sandwiches as our mums talked. They seemed breathless, with an air of concern between them. I was watchful even though Mike told silly stories and pointed out beetles and butterflies. He seemed content, but I knew something strange was going on.

The wind silenced us all, and a golden light appeared in a flash of lightning. It turned into a shimmer, then into an outline of a tall man with a dark, weathered face. His smile beamed at us, and we were transfixed.

"Thank you for making such an arduous journey," he said to our parents. "You need to stay here for three more hours. Then we will know if it is safe for you to return to your homes." [1]

---

[1] Old One had requested an onerous task of our mothers that day. He had planned to take Mike and me off-world to keep us safe. The three hours was a critical time in October 1962 when the world held its breath. After a 13-day standoff, the Russians agreed to remove missiles from Cuba, and America withdrew from declaring nuclear war. Cuban Missile Crisis Causes, Timeline & Significance – HISTORY

Oon'ch-illia

They talked some more, but I got distracted by Mike. He led me by the hand back towards the path. We played hide and seek behind a tree, then a game of catch with a pebble Mike had found.

"Let's go see that man again," Mike said, but when we returned, he had gone. My stomach rolled, and my head lolled.

"Where gone?" I asked my Mammy.

"He's coming back soon, dear," she reassured me.

"I'm tired," I said as I laid down on her knee.

The man's return woke me from my slumber. It was his warmth I felt first. Then, I realized we had all nodded off. In a daze, I tried to understand his words.

"All is well now; you are safe to return to your homes …sorry for the long journey I asked you to make."
He approached, tapped lightly three times on my head, and then stroked my cheek. It felt so nice, like he was my grandad, but nothing like the one I knew. He looked deep into the eyes of each of us and said, "I love you," but I'm certain he had a twinkle in his eyes just for me.

I sensed he was about to depart. My heart began to beat fast, and I shouted, "Me, go too?"

Then I noticed the lines on Mammy's face. Her color was like a shadow across the sun. She choked on a laugh while her shoulders hunched her closer to the ground.

"I am always with you, my child…here," the man said while placing a hand on my chest. Then in a flash, he was gone.

Mike smiled at me and said, "It's okay; we'll see him again.

4

Watchful

As a toddler - my light sparked within me. My curiosity about the outside world ran deep, and I loved to explore. Within my family's garden, I sought the freedom I craved and would run wild or lose myself in the colors and sounds.

I dig deep down into the earth and pull up a worm. It wiggles free. I watch it bury its head and laugh. Mam points and says, "look, it's finding its way home...we don't want a bird to get it," as she throws a handful of soil over its receding body.

"Aww... I want to play with it," I whine.

"No, it's dirty. Come wash those hands now." Mam pleads as she scans the house and then leads me down the garden.

I pull away and run. Mam chases me and makes it fun.

"You little tinker...come here," she grabs me and tickles me. I squirm and scream.

"What's going on?" Dad shouts from the kitchen door.

"Look at the state of her. She's not coming in here like that." He frowns and then turns to walk away, slamming the door behind him.

I bite my lip and look up at Mam as her shoulders droop. She looks in the distance. Her face lost its color. I feel her far away and reach for her in my mind.

Should I become a statue like her or run again? I don't know what to do. Am I in trouble? Is Mam? She laughs. I scrunch my face, then scan hers.

"Let's get the hose out...you little minx," she whispers in a sing-song voice.

I breathe in and attempt a smile.

"Come here, you ... my little Indian." She scoops me up under her arm and marches me towards the outside tap, singing, the Grand old Duke of York. The cold water shocks

me. I run around in circles trying to escape it. I giggle as Mam tries to catch me with the spray.

A movement behind a curtain catches my eye, and I stop. He's watching and waiting, but for what?

Aged 3, the feelings in my tummy spoke loud in my head. I watched and listened and then reacted when my tummy told me to. Sometimes I hid, especially when my grandad and uncle visited our house.

I hated their slobbery kisses and whiskery chins when they lifted me and whispered, "you're my special girl." The silken hairs on my body stood erect. Their deep voices paralyzed me; their tone and pitch rarely matched their facial features. Adults were a mystery. Compared to what they did, what they said didn't add up. Some days my dad had me in fits of giggles when he chased me around the room, but next, he shouted at me and then was silent for days. I hid and remained quiet or sneaked around.

I carry my juice and biscuit from the kitchen. A clammy hand grips the glass tightly. My eyes burn into the liquid as I painfully step across the floor—my other hand fists around the edges of the biscuit. A thud within my chest keeps me in check to ensure that not even a minute crumb should fall to the ground. My mouth is dry. I attempt to hold my breath. A step closer to my destination.

I feel his fierce stare. He waits for me to falter, to fail yet again. But, instead, I continue to hold my breath. I'm a dragon that has swallowed its roar. My mind creates an inner volcano to extinguish the aggressor if he attacks.

I pass by with my treasures, but to sit requires perilous endeavors. A crouch, with arms, held tort, my insides turn to jelly as my sensors connect with his scrutiny.

My bottom touches the seat. I take a quick sip, then a nibble, like a quiet mouse. Each crumb is sucked up. My favorite TV program loses its appeal; my only thought is to finish and run. I sip and nibble until complete, aware of the rumbles that stir a few feet away.

Cathryn Mahoney

The inner furnace seeps into my cheeks. The dragon wants to roar and spit out its belly of fire, but instead, tears sting their betrayal. Into survival mode - time to hide. I grow smaller and smaller, and my desire to exist is lost. I am the waste of space that causes distress to the watchful one.

I have many fractured memories, often fun times that turned sour, where the pieces float around in the ether. Yet, this one event carved a deep hole within me, slow and insipid:

I know the adults think I am a cute four-year-old with curly hair and the freckles the sun has given me. I love running around the house without my panties; skipping up and down the room feels good. My short dress bounces, and I feel the air on my skin. My daddy laughs, and I do it more. I even jump up and down, so my dress hits me in the face. Daddy snatches me in mid-flight and bounces me upon his knee. In a fit of giggles, I shout, "again, daddy, again." I sense each movement - the bounce up, flying, then my bum landing. But the next time I return from the air, I feel pain. It shoots up into my tummy. I cry and fall to the ground. I look back at daddy and wonder what hurt me. His look frightens me, so I run off.

Daddy runs after me and laughs. "Never mind, pet...I don't know; you're so accident-prone." Then I see him shake his head and say in front of Mammy, "stop crying now, you silly girl...you just fell awkward on my knee." Mammy wipes away my tears with her apron as my brother, Alan, shouts from the back door. He points up to the sky, "come quick...look." I stand alone as they rush outside, all smiling and waving at the biplane flying across the sky.

My face is hot. I feel a single tear slide down my left cheek, and my tummy hurts. My attention returns to the soreness between my legs. Sobbing, I taste salt on my lips. I wait for Mammy to notice my absence. She still looks up into the sky, so I turn and scamper upstairs. I reach for my favorite teddy, and we hide together under the covers.

My quick reaction, or perhaps it had been an invisible force, ensured no noticeable damage was caused. But an undercurrent hung around. Mammy insisted I put on my panties before leaving my room, and I never forgot to wear them from that day on. There were no more bounces on daddy's lap. Sometimes he tickled and cuddled me, but I pulled away.

When he asked, "do you want to go out today, to the park or the seaside, just you and me?" Mammy always overheard, and daddy then went out on his own. Before he did, though, his voice was loud, and he banged about. When he returned, he was quiet, and I sneaked about, unsure if I'd done something wrong.

Sometimes, I heard my Mammy shout, but his voice was louder, and sometimes I heard her cry, or she busied herself around the house. When she finally put her head around my bedroom door, I was relieved to see her smiley face.

When she didn't check on me, I got scared, especially when daddy had been shouting and swearing for a long time then all went quiet. Then, I listened for sounds on the landing and felt an icy trickle down my back. I even stilled my breathing to listen.

When I was too afraid, and sound and movement kept me awake, safe invisible hands enfolded me in a tight embrace. The hidden presence was an old lady who shimmered around me within a rose-pink orb. She whispered into my ear, "you are never alone dear one," and drew a protective barrier around my bed. Within it, she told me stories of people who lived in a cave. I later discovered they were not fictional characters but my true family. I believed her to be a messenger from my grandma - one of the ghosts she often told me about. During the darkest of times, I was nurtured in the way I craved from my Mammy. I know she didn't mean to hold back, but my daddy frowned upon my neediness.

5

Dis-connected

Before my brother Alan started school, we were closer. However, as he grew, so did his distaste for me. I often followed him and his friends when they played in the woods. To begin with, they'd let me join in as they swung on a rope and caught tiddlers in the stream. But it wasn't long before I must have become a nuisance.

Alan shouted, "get lost - go away. We don't want girls playing." So, I wandered off, swishing my net or jumping across the stream, and the boys ran to hide from me. I pretended not to care. But an ache in my tummy urged me home. Perhaps, it was teatime, or maybe my tummy was talking to me.

So, at the age of 5, I learned to fend for myself and pretended I was happier on my own. Deep down, though, I longed to feel loved and included. Even when I sensed my invisible friends around, I felt something was lacking. Was there something wrong with me? Why didn't anyone want to play with me?

When I turned 7, I became clingy and anxious when my Mammy returned to work. On a school morning, I whimpered, "my tummy hurts." My mind also hurt, but I couldn't express that then. I worried about who would collect me from school and be at home for me. I was scared but didn't know why.

Mammy had to go to the hospital for an operation on her fingers and toes. I fought to stay awake when she wasn't there, even when my grandma stayed the night. I cocked an ear to sounds outside my bedroom door and imagined I was a bee with my antennae on full alert. When I grew tired, I hid under the covers. Then, a gentle voice and touch soothed me with a lullaby. The old lady told me stories of a brave warrior woman and said, "that is whom you will become one day. You are strong and brave and have so much to learn about your abilities, dear one. Soon you will know. Until then, it is my job to keep you safe."

As I got older, I incessantly pushed for Alan to notice me. I became an irritant, like a scratch he couldn't reach. In our teens, when the hormones of puberty kicked in, so did Alan's hate for me. The anger he suppressed at school or when dad shouted at him tipped him over the edge.

Yet, I seemed unable to shut up. My need for attention grew too great until Alan lobbed his shoe, aiming at my head, or grabbed a cushion to smother my din. Anything to get rid of his annoying kid sister.

When Mam came home, I would whine, "Maaam, Alan hit me again," or "Maaam, Alan sat on my head."

"I'll have a word with him, but what do you expect?" Mam responded. "You wind him up so much...keep away from him after school...go to your room."

Then, the feeling in my tummy grew too big. I missed Mam when she had to work, and she didn't understand that the thirty minutes alone with Alan until dad got in was a pressure cooker time. I needed some reaction, some sign I existed; even though the attention I got was painful, it was better than waiting to figure out what mood dad would be in. When he came home, my room felt like the best place to be, but there was no escaping, as I had to help prepare for tea.

I tried to become more invisible at home and school and retreat into my own world where it felt safer. Then, Mam said Alan and me could spend Saturdays at my grandma's house. Sometimes we stayed over, and Alan was nicer to me until he got bored and wanted to be out with his friends. I loved it when it was only gran and me. I could relax and felt 'special' in a nice way. Gran told me stories of her life, her past lives and her ancestor's ghosts. Her arthritic hands crocheted as she talked while her mind seemed far away.

Our walks to the shop took ages. "People once lived off

these plants and knew how to use them for medicine. Not today...they forget the way. Too quick to go to the quack nowadays," she said, picking a few leaves or a flower head along the way. Her love of nature was clear to me. When we returned to her home, she showed me how to turn them into teas.

I particularly loved it in the summer when she made homemade ice cream, cakes, and cold drinks and added some of the flowers and herbs she had picked.

Gran encouraged me to ask questions, be creative and curious, by spending time in nature. So, she sent me out to play in her wild garden, a wilderness full of life.

The garden pond was teaming with fish, frogs, newts, dragonflies, and insects of all varieties. There were fruit trees and brambles, long grass, lilac and rose bushes, and her favorite plant – the lily of the valley.

I still loved to visit gran as a teenager. One day she asked, "should we make a vegetable patch? Would you like to help?"

So, I dug and planted potatoes, carrots, and lettuce. I worked the land around it, cutting back bushes, pruning, and cutting the long grass. I lost myself in time and space. I sensed being watched and talked to the unseen beings around me, until adolescent thoughts pulled me back. My mind was too quick to block awareness of the nature spirits and light beings that guided and supported me. It was gran's stories that reminded me of the possibility of their existence. I only believed when I felt at peace, at gran's home, or alone in nature.

I could not speak of these things at home or share profound thoughts. If I did, somehow, I said something wrong. My opinions were often picked apart until I felt I didn't know my mind. Only one person knew anything of any worth in our house: Dad. He said I daydreamed too much and had an overactive imagination, and I began to believe it.

"You get carried away with your gran's stories...they're

only stories you know...maybe she's a bad influence...get into the real world," he often said.

Later, Mam whispered to me, "Don't listen to him, he's in a mood...it's okay, he won't stop you from going to gran's, you know?"

I often lost myself in spaces of time at grans and felt comforted when she talked to the energies around us. Sometimes I felt a waft of cool air or a tickle on my cheek and said to her, "gran, I just felt a tickle again."

"That's an angel kiss, like the butterfly (eyelash) kiss me and your Mam give you. An angel is always with you. Talk to them and thank them for watching over you. Sometimes it's someone in spirit, a family member who has passed over, like my dad. He visits me in my sleep."

Then, I believed I was never alone, though loneliness seemed to be my constant companion.

"No one really cares," I would whisper to myself in the darkest of moments when I felt no connection to anyone or anything. A loss of something, I'm unsure what, but it was so intense. I felt it in my difference, saw it on people's faces, and heard it in their voices. I smelled and tasted its bitterness. I didn't fit in.

Where did I belong? Was it with someone I'd never met - in a place, a time, a space? If so, why was it always so out of reach?

My life resembled a jigsaw puzzle I was desperate to construct, but the pieces were missing. So, I had to find them, one at a time. When I found more than two pieces, one slipped under the sofa or down a crack in the floor. Was someone hiding them on purpose? What if it was the mysterious hand of the Creator testing me or tutoring me for some important job?

Occasionally, pieces appeared right in front of me as if by magic, and I completed a small section of the picture, but when I inserted the next piece, it all disappeared.

Who's doing this? I wondered. Was it the little people?

Were they playing 'hide and seek' at my expense? Like when they prodded me and then ran off?

My patience and perseverance were tested repeatedly. I often gave up or chose to forget for a while and wondered if I'd prove more successful when I was older. Maybe, if I used avoidance tactics, would that be the best strategy? Like at P.E., I made excuses to avoid ball games because I was butterfingered. So yes, I sometimes attempted to opt out instead of being laughed at for being a failure.

Deep within me, no matter my age, I sensed which lessons I couldn't avoid, those that reminded me of the creator's magical hand at work. So, I accepted and tried to embrace the difficult lessons that germinated the seeds of latent knowledge and fed their natural pattern of growth. Even though the puzzle pieces remained hidden until maturity, I trusted the bigger picture would emerge in time.

6

Special

Alternate Sunday afternoons were my least favorite times when we visited my dad's parents. My dad called them 'duty visits' that we couldn't get out of. Alan and I had to be on our best behavior and quietly sit while grandad watched the cricket or the news. Grandad was like dad. He could be affectionate but often switched it off. Grandma fussed, but I didn't feel close to her like I did with my other grandma. I guess we played the role of happy families when we were there.

I have some fond memories—of times when I felt wanted or included in everyday events.

"Where's my special girl? Go get grandad's pipe and tobacco for me, pet. Out in the hall on the stand," he pointed through the door.

I liked to watch him fill and suck on the pipe until it glowed.

"Where's that girl? I need a bit of help," gran looked around the kitchen door at me. So, I popped to help my Mam set the table for our tea. It was better to be useful than staring at the TV or listening to my dad and grandad talk. I preferred to be in the kitchen with my Mam, and anyway, the quicker we had our tea, the quicker we could set out for home.

Regrettably, my dad agreed to begin another regular visit after our tea. His sister lived right across the street.

"You must go and see Joan and Joe; they're expecting you," my gran said to dad. So, we trekked across the street to see my aunt, uncle, and their two boys. Alan was happy, as Callum was the same age as him. My other cousin, Josh, was seven years older than me. I was bored with no one to play with, so I sat and listened to the adults talk as they sipped tea or something stronger.

At each visit, Josh began to hang around too. He tried

to talk to me, which seemed strange. My brother no longer bothered with me, so why would Josh? He was nearly a man, and I was only a little kid. When he asked me things, I nodded or shook my head, uncertain of what to say. He must have gotten fed up with that, so on one visit, he raised his voice and said, "I'm bored. Mam, can I put on the TV in the front room?" Then looked back at me. His Mam said, "Why not? Are you taking Cathryn with you? She doesn't want to listen to us adults talk."

"I'm okay here," I said with my eyes on the swirl within the carpet.

As I looked up, all eyes were on me. Dad said, "Go on with Josh; you'll have more fun there than here with us."

I left the room with Josh but darted upstairs to see if I could play with Alan and Callum. They sent me away. I had no choice but to follow Josh to the front room.

I was a shy, clingy eight-year-old, and I wanted to stay with my Mam, where I felt the safest and somehow sensed she needed me too. She was always quiet; dad put her down or blamed her for things, even in front of his family. Yet, she smiled sweetly and didn't respond. I felt like a mini version of her.

I was intrigued when my dad had to raise his voice to be heard over his older sister. She was loud and scary. Her voice boomed across the room. On the other hand, my uncle was quiet and tried to be funny. But he was often ignored or talked over, just like my Mam was by my dad when she did attempt to speak.

One of my uncle's odd ways was to catch me unawares for a kiss and cuddle. He rubbed his bristles across my face. It stung till I got home.

I asked Mam, "Why does Uncle Joe call me his special girl? I don't like his kisses; his bristles scratch me."

"Because you're the only girl, and they like to fuss over you," she said.

When Josh got me alone, he asked, "are you my special girl, then?"

Oon'ch-illia

He tried many ways to get me alone with him. The more he did, the more I looked for ways to avoid him.

When I went to the bathroom, beyond the kitchen, he pretended to be heading outside. He waited till I came out, then pulled me out in the yard with him or rubbed past me in the narrow kitchen. Josh followed when I went upstairs, hoping to hang out with Alan and Callum. Alan sent me on my way, then Josh pulled me into his parent's bedroom. I freed myself somehow and ran downstairs.

"Cathryn! Why are you running around?" My auntie boomed.

"Go in the front room with Josh and watch the telly," my uncle urged.

"I don't want to," I said.

"Don't be silly. Josh likes spending time with you," my dad shouted.

I pleaded to my Mam with my eyes.

"Go on then," is all she said.

So, time and again, I had no choice but to follow Josh into the front room. I sat at a distance from him while we watched TV, but I do not recall the programs we watched.

"Sit here next to me," he said while patting a cushion.

I kept my distance, but then he sidled in or laughed,

"You're so shy, aren't you?" Then he pulled me closer for a cuddle.

It was a regular occurrence for months or perhaps a couple of years, no matter how much I tried to avoid being alone with Josh. While the adults chatted next door, Josh kissed and cuddled me. Occasionally we stayed longer at my gran and grandads, then went straight home after. I breathed a sigh of relief. It might have been boring, but I was left alone to exist in my safe world.

The attention from Josh messed with my head. Why did the adults encourage me to spend time with him? Did Josh really love me and enjoy my company? I couldn't say the same of anyone else; perhaps that form of attention was better than none. I began to fantasize that Josh was my boyfriend, but my age made it wrong. I tried to bypass the bad feelings as I wanted to be someone's special girl.

At each visit when I was sent next door with Josh, it continued to puzzle me why the adults turned a blind eye. All the while, Josh got braver, and I convinced myself our petting must be normal. My thoughts and emotions were constant battlefields during my ninth and tenth years. I had hit puberty and was already doing 'adult' things.

Josh got more daring with age. His hormones must have been raging by this point. First, he started to turn the sound up on the TV and kept one ear cocked for the door. 'Cocked' is an apt term as that is what he turned his attention to. Then, unzipping his fly, he revealed it in all its glory. Shocked, I pulled away to leave the room, but he yanked me back.

"They'll be annoyed if you go back," he whispered.

I had no idea what to do.

With his hot breath on my neck, he pulled me closer and demanded, "touch it, go on, do it; you'll like it."

With one arm hooked around me, he pulled me tight. His other hand pressured my hand to rub it up and down his penis. I'm certain I zoned out and shifted in time, or maybe a noise outside the door disturbed Josh. Before I knew it, I was back next door to see my parents putting on their coats, ready to leave. I breathed a sigh of relief and pasted a smile on my lips.

"Yes, thank you. Yes, I've had a nice time, thank you." I was uncertain what I had been asked, and my thoughts were reeling.

"*How could they not know?*" I wondered. My face felt hot. Was it written all over my face? Did anyone suspect anything? That mystery still alludes to this day.

For a few months, there was some reason we didn't visit, and on our return, I attempted to be more vocal with Josh.

"No, I don't want to," I said when he asked me to go next door with him. My attempt fell flat.

The adults asked, "Why not? Don't be silly; he wants to spend time with you. He's missed you."

Oon'ch-illia

What could I say? So, I followed, doing as I was told once again when a part of me wanted to scream, *Noooo! Leave me alone.* My resistance seemed to turn Josh on. He got more daring. This time he unzipped and released his thingy, as I called it then, and pushed my head down onto it. I gagged and managed to escape to the bathroom. Or did I imagine that part? Perhaps, instead, I retreated to my safe inner world.

Not long after, Josh didn't seek me out. Had he gotten bored with me, or had it gotten too risky? He stayed in his room or was out of the house. Then during the school holidays, our visits stopped. I liked to think that someone intervened, as Josh was nowhere to be seen when we next visited.

"He's at Janet's house. He'll be sorry he missed you, but they've spent a lot of time together over the holidays," my aunt said.

Janet was another cousin like Josh in age, a girl I'd never heard of before.

"I thought you never saw them," my dad said to Uncle Joe.

"They got back in touch; we've sorted our differences now. Janet is such a pretty girl. She's good company for Josh," he said, smiling over at me.

It was a surprise and a relief that Josh's attention had gone elsewhere. But it played on my mind.

Uncle Joe often told me, "You're special because you're the only girl in our family."

With the attention gone, I felt a sense of loss. First, I fantasized that Josh wanted me as his girlfriend but realized I was too young for him. Then my anger mounted towards his parents, my parents, and even our brothers, but I never expressed it to them. Instead, I blamed myself.

I was convinced something was wrong with me, that 'specialness' they all reminded me about. Unfortunately, I had begun to equate 'special' with 'bad.'

My feelings of being 'bad' spiraled out, especially when

my brother's hate of me grew. I became even more alert at home. I heard noises at night I hadn't noticed before. I froze when I heard anyone on the landing or across from my room in the bathroom. I had dark imaginings, or were they distant memories of whispers behind my bedroom door and the sound of it being opened and closed when I was asleep? The floorboards creaked whenever I tried to sleep. I imagined a shadow of a man who grabbed me from behind. It tracked through my brain - was it real?

Then, I remembered the old woman who visited me at night. I didn't feel her presence when I grew older, but I heard her words when I woke from my frightful dreams.

"Kick out...kick your legs if they get too close."

I was prepared to fight but had no recollection if I did or was attacked at night.

In my adult years, I learned more about the old woman called Tasco. I discovered potential physical attacks, but she and my family in the tribe kept me safe. It was the emotional turmoil and constant stress response that took its toll.

Oon'ch-illia

7

Invisible

At age 12, I was a sullen teenager with an awkward body that didn't seem to fit. I wondered if I'd been beamed down from a far-flung planet. I was dazzled by the lights and struck dumb by sounds. I was on high alert, ready to run at the slightest hint of human interaction. But was I a normal teenager? I had no idea.

Fragments remain of 12-year-old me and the 3-year-old behind the sofa, setting it on fire when switching on an electric heater stored 'safely' out of reach. Or 7-year-old me, hiding under the covers when the floorboards creaked, frightened by raised male voices and a bed that groaned alongside a female's whimper.

Yes, I'm sad to confess to my regular attempts to hide or be invisible. I also had a repetitive dream of escaping through the window by stepping out onto the windowsill, flapping my arms, and then huge white wings, lifting me high into the sky. I flew far away into another dimension - returning home to my family within the cave. But when I woke from such a beautiful dream, reality hit hard, and my nightmare life continued. To survive, I attempted to blend into the background, but the more I did, the more I stood out. I became an object of scorn and a target for those with bad intent.

Insular and *introvert* were terms I soon possessed. I fell deep and gave my all when I had a new best friend. Maybe I trusted too quickly when I felt safe and wanted, but any slight hurt caused me to pull back. I kept giving and trying, enjoyed my friendships when they lasted, and learned to reject before being rejected. My anxiety around strangers and especially groups also grew. I saw them as a wolf pack who could turn any minute on the weakest one - who was likely to be - ME.

Cathryn Mahoney

Instead, I put my energy into activities I could do alone, such as riding my bike in the countryside. I loved to stop by streams and ponds or take a long ride to the closest beach. I also loved to swim as it offered the freedom I sought. Underwater was my favorite place, despite nearly drowning and being swept toward a waterfall when I was five. I've always reveled in complete immersion in a stream in search of gold or jumping the waves and feeling the shock of a strong wave.

I psyched myself up on one summer's day to escape the humdrum of the school holidays.

"Mam...I'm going out on my bike. Can I take a picnic?" I asked.

"Yes, it's a lovely day; you need to make the most of the holidays. I'm only half a day at work, though. Will you be back before me?" Mam asked as she made me some sandwiches.

Alan was still in bed, so I wanted to get out of the house before he stirred. I couldn't stand another day, just the two of us at home.

I had no idea where I was going. But, on instinct, I pedaled with purpose away from the streets of people. When I reached a tree-lined country road, my spirits lifted when I remembered riding a horse along it a year before when I had riding lessons. I stopped at a bridge and climbed down to the bank of a brook. I sat in the long grass to listen to its burble. Then, I became engrossed in the dapple of a sunbeam through leaves that danced to the tune of the breeze.

Then, I imagined my worries were blown downstream and into the flow - to be washed far away.

At age 14, seeds of self-awareness were germinating. Somehow, I knew how to use imagery to shift my state from misery to contentment. Nature was the medicine for all that ailed me, so I connected with the land and water and allowed it to do its magic. I immersed myself in sensual delight.

Oon'ch-illia

I drank in the diverse colors and sounds around me. My nose was tickled with perfumes - grasses, wheat from the nearby fields, wildflowers, and the distinctive smell of the sea.

The coast was several miles away, but its smell had me back on my bike and heading in that direction. It was the toughest cycle ride I'd ever done. Often, I considered giving up. Large wagons nearly toppled me in their wake. I lost my sense of direction when a landmark appeared in the wrong place. Yet, I continued pedaling. The smell of bacon and eggs frying may have had the same effect on someone else. For me, it was the smell of ozone and seaweed.

I stopped at a bridge to watch seals in the estuary. There was a flapping tail and flipper, then a splash, then another as they swam out to sea. I wanted to follow. The road narrowed with fast cars and trucks whizzing past, but my destination was clear. For a moment, I thought of Mam. What would she think? Would she be mad? Then my stomach rolled - what have I done? Why had I come so far? Would I make it back? Would my parents have any idea where I was if they had to come looking for me?

Since I had reached my destination, I pushed those thoughts aside. The roll in my tummy alerted me of hunger, not guilt or fear. So, I counted my pocket money and could run to chips and pop as added treats to my picnic lunch. Once I found an ideal spot on the beach, I ate while watching families at play. Seagulls swooped for tasty treats until I was done. Then, I looked at my watch. My tummy rolled again; I knew I had to go home. I dragged out the minutes, attempting to lose myself in being present. I pondered for a moment. What if I never went back?

8

Muddled

My dad's moods cast a shadow over the whole house. It was our fault he never achieved all the things he aspired to. I blamed myself most of all.

"Perhaps I should never have been born. After all, it was my fault you got arthritis," I told Mam.

"Don't say that you silly girl. How could it be your fault?" She hugged me tight, but deep down, I knew I was right. How often had I heard whispered conversations behind closed doors? I knew the stress of my birth had brought about inflammation in my Mam's body.

"It wasn't your fault," she explained. "I had an ovary removed a few months after Alan was born. I didn't know if I'd have another child, but I was pregnant with you a few months later. It was like a miracle."

But I couldn't be budged. The whispers behind closed doors and my dad's moods told me something different. My birth had been the catalyst for Rheumatoid Arthritis to take hold in Mam's body. There was no doubt in my mind that it was my fault.

Despite that, it felt so good to be in her arms, briefly reassured. But, as is typical of me, I could not let it lie. I looked up at her and asked, "Well, is it cos I'm accident-prone...and messy, or cos I get in the way?" I needed to find a reason to blame myself, even though I knew I was those things because of dad's constant huffs and puffs, his search for the tiniest crumb on the carpet, or finding fault at every turn. I guess it would have made any child nervous. However, that child was me, so it was my fault. My stubborn streak had me determined to blame myself.

Mam shook her head and held me tighter. I felt her sadness deep within her love for me.

Oon'ch-illia

Wrapped in her warm embrace, I am lifted to outer space, to a father who shines a light upon me and places me on a pedestal within the sky.

He tells me, "The eyes of your soul are always on vigil above the village and can see into many times and places. Your body is a vehicle to experience the physical plane on the blue-white planet they call earth. You exist without it. You are light, the same as me. You have done much good on earth. You are always with us as 'eyes in the sky' - our protector and guide."

Then he says: "your earthly father is one of many trials you must overcome. Remain strong, my child; I am always with you in here."

Old One hits his right fist toward his heart three times and nods. "It will take time for you to grow and know yourself. Have patience, child. It will be your companion along the way." His smile lit a fire within me. Then he was gone.

On my return, somehow, time had moved on, and I was face to face with an angry dad at the kitchen table.

"Phew, straight back into it then," I muttered quietly.

"Eat it all up now; we had to eat what we were given when there were rations after the war," he ranted as I picked at my food.

The rice pudding arrived next. It seemed an enormous bowlful, far too much for a little person, and yuck at that. It made me gag.

Dad shouted, "eat it up...it'll put hairs on your chest."

Shocked, I envisioned dark hairs on my white chest.

"I don't want hairs on my chest," I sniffled and stared at my bowl. I wondered if they'd be curly, as he often said, "crusts make your hair curl."

Then I wanted to shout, *"well, guess what, Sherlock? I've always had curly hair since I was born."*

He professed intelligence, but I often thought he was just plain stupid. Yet, he repeatedly said I was stupid.

That belief was strengthened every time he called me

stupid, with his tuts and sighs at something he professed I'd done wrong, or he had taken offense to my presence. I could no longer think for myself as he always told me what to think and do.

"You are too quiet and sensitive," he would say. But how was I supposed to get heard? My confidence and self-belief were at rock bottom.

It was my gran who encouraged me to know my own mind and to trust my own instincts.

She passed on the following philosophy: "you must forgive but never forget when someone wrongs you."

I kept to that philosophy throughout my life. If I didn't forget, I could avoid making the same mistakes and tune up my bullshitter's antennae. So, I forgave and let go of the hurt, even though it sometimes took months and years. With maturity, I learned I was only hurting myself and didn't want to perpetuate it - being stuck in the same loop.

I also remember gran once telling me, "Your auntie Janet keeps going on about me going to church with them. I don't need any bricks and mortar church to pray to my God; I can do it right here," as she pointed at her chest and then around the room.

"God loves us no matter what," said my gran. "We are given chances to atone for our bad actions when we pass over, as it will determine future paths for the soul to grow. Similar experiences may be repeated until the lesson is learned. Unfortunately, some people insist on doing it again and again because they are too dumb or bloody-minded to get it right. Their soul won't progress until they learn to do better."

At home, my other grandma figure, Tasco, continued to watch over me and teach me how to harness energy from repressed anger. I wasn't consciously aware of what I was learning or how, but I did gain some control of my immediate environment. Subconsciously, I dimmed my light and channeled that energy into thought forms, such as imagining a bubble of protection around me or a brick wall between me and another person. It served me well when I sensed someone might harm me. I tracked the movements and intentions of others, just as the warriors in the tribe learned to track an animal when hunting. But my strategy when threatened was usually to hide.

9

Targeted

At senior school, I was able to remain invisible for the first two years. I knuckled down to my work and, most of the time, floated or sneaked around. I felt lost without my best friend from primary school. There were no familiar faces, so I grew more insular.

The size and layout of the larger school took some getting used to, and the noise and behavior of other kids put me on edge. But I tried to blend into the background and stay focused. I excelled in Maths, English, History, and Geography with the encouragement of my form tutor, Mr. Jay. But many of my classes had disruptive pupils who ran roughshod over the teachers.

In the early 1970s, my comprehensive school trialed a behavioral management approach rather than corporal punishment. But the pupils got wise to the teachers' struggles to discipline them without the threat of a cane or ruler. That resulted in some of my classes becoming battlegrounds with no clear boundaries or structure.

By the third year, my studies and sense of security took a backward dive when I became a target of bullies. I attempted to hide within my work and withdraw from my classmates. But I had been noticed and, from then on, stood out.

Our new math teacher, Mr. Bell, who the rowdy kids called "Smelly Belly," was young and newly qualified. When he got stressed, which was often, he sweated a lot. The smell of BO riled the kids up.
"Mr. Bell, you stink, Smelly Belly."

He handed out the work, then found any excuse to leave the classroom or hide away, pretending to look for something in the storeroom. When he left, chaos erupted. It was the quiet kids like me who suffered. One day, the ringleader's bile turned towards me, and her hangers-on joined in the fun.

"Look at her, egg head; I wonder if it'll crack. Grab her. Let's draw a crack on her egg head." Karen yelled to her cronies.

One of the rowdies pinned my head to the desk while Karen doodled on my forehead. She then tapped hard on the crack line she had drawn.

"It's hard-boiled, won't crack, ha ha!"

Mr. Bell returned, and the room hushed, but as soon as his back was turned, pencils were arrowed at my head. I became their plaything. I attempted to focus on my math sheet, but unshed tears misted my vision. I lowered my head and hid my face with an arm, but my aggressors were on the wrong side since I was left-handed. I turned away from them, pretending to read. I checked Mr. Bell wasn't watching and closed my eyes for a moment, hoping that when I reopened them, I would be somewhere else, perhaps in the countryside. I reveled in my thoughts for moments, but reality soon hit when Karen shouted,

"Mr. Bell, Cathryn threw a pencil at me." She knew I tried to hide and refused me that comfort.

I looked up at Mr. Bell, who walked toward me and said, "don't do that again." Then he went back into the stationary cupboard, and Karen reached across, took my pen, and scribbled upon my arm.

They taunted me for days and weeks on end. My name in class became, Egghead. Karen and her cronies threw paper and pencil arrows at my head after the crack had been drawn back on for the umpteenth time.

"Leave it on; don't you dare wash it off," Karen said as she drew swear words on my arms when Mr. Bell's back was turned.

Despite my suffering, I pitied Mr. Bell but also wanted to shout at him to take control. At least when they taunted him, I was left alone but could not concentrate on my sums or any tests. When maths was once my favorite subject, it became my worst. Yet, Mr. Bell was too engaged in his own troubles to recognize any of mine.

Cathryn Mahoney

My report cards stated, "Cathryn needs to try harder. She becomes easily distracted."

"You, Mr. Bell, are covering your own ass," I wanted to shout, but he was the teacher and, therefore, must have been right, or so my dad thought when he gave me a bollocking for not being top of the class.

The bullying moved out of the classroom. My warrior instinct kicked in, and I scanned the periphery wherever I went, putting my barriers up. Yet, I was kidding myself. I wasn't a warrior, not really. I was unable to fight back - helplessness took center stage. I froze or hid.

My aggressors were more formidable warriors because they searched me out and always found me. They sneaked up from behind or hid behind the gym building door when I had swimming lessons. My favorite sport was stolen from me when fear took hold.

Karen's foot tripped me up, her hand came out of nowhere to grab my hair, or she got her friends to hold me down. Then her pen appeared. She wrote bitch, slag, slapper, bore, and eggy on my head and arms and raked at me with her nails.

"I'll break that egg, just watch me," she shouted and laughed with her friends.

I was constantly on my guard at school and home, and I was desperate. Once, I saw Alan leave the school alone and sought his help.

He shouted, "go away, stupid idiot, don't embarrass me in front of my friends." Then he walked away to join his friends playing footy.

When I got home, my dad saw the scratches and writing on my forehead and arms.

"What have you been up to?" he asked.

"Nothing. I need the toilet," I replied and ran upstairs to wash it off.

Then I heard Alan and my dad talking.

Dad shouted, "Cathryn, come down here. I hear you got into a fight. What happened? What have you been doing?"

"Nothing, they pick on me; I don't know why."

"What are you saying...you getting bullied? What's brought that on?"

"I don't know, do I? They write on my head - say I'm an egghead because my forehead is big. So, I try to hide it with my fringe."

My face was pulsing with heat. I didn't want to talk about it, but it had been drummed into me to tell the truth.

"Ah, right! Well, you got to hit them where it hurts. Bash them on the bridge of the nose. That'll soon stop them. Like this." He demonstrated close to my face.

"I don't think I can; wouldn't I get in trouble anyway? Can I go back to my bedroom and do my homework before tea?" I pleaded.

When I was 14, my saving grace was my feet. For most of my childhood, I attended foot manipulation therapy and wore special shoes, which of course, made me stand out among my peers. With my feet fully grown, the doctor suggested a final procedure to make life easier as an adult.

The end of my third school year came early because I went to the hospital for an operation, and then I had a week to recuperate at home before the summer holidays began. I couldn't have been happier. My big toes were straightened, and the operation had been preferable to a run-in with the school bullies. Corks protected the pins in my toes as the bones set, but I could hobble about and sit in the garden. I listened to music and read Jackie Magazine while my brother was still in school, and my parents were working. It was heaven. Those few weeks were some of my happiest childhood memories. I could relax and revel in the freedom from over-vigilance at school and home.

When I returned to school for my fourth year, Karen and her cronies seemed to have vanished. I scouted the corridors and behind doors. I scanned classrooms as I entered, but they were nowhere to be found. After several weeks of hesitation, I relaxed and focused on my studies.

In fourth year, we chose our 'options' - preferences other than the mandatory English and Maths. I was with different pupils in all my subjects and was left in peace.

I also made a new best friend, Dee. Over the next two years, we went everywhere together and were of the age to have some freedom. We spent evenings and weekends at the local leisure center, mostly at the skating rink, on disco nights. Or we went swimming or hung out. We eyed up young men while they played squash or tennis and avoided my dad at the lawn bowling club. We walked the periphery or stayed near the tennis courts in the park, away from gangs who hung out at the swings. We were happiest, just the two of us. We didn't need anyone else.

10

First Love

I was relieved to leave school, but my dad insisted I continue my education. The downside was Dee got a job, and we drifted apart.

I stayed at the sixth form and reveled in the freedom of studying three subjects I enjoyed - English, Geography, and Human Biology. My social life also improved, and I got a new best friend, Anna. She lived in the countryside and was an only child. Her family had a smallholding with a vegetable plot and chickens, and I was included in all their activities like I was one of their own. They even took me on holiday to Scotland, and I was more surprised my dad let me go. Anna's dad, John, worked at my dad's factory. He had a professional role, so my dad thought he was the bee's knees, as my gran would say. However, I also thought a lot of him. He was kind and funny and talked to me. He even listened to what I had to say as if I was interesting and intelligent.

But there was a subtle shift in our relationship. "Do you want to come and feed the chickens with me?" John asked one day. In the chicken coop, he pulled me towards him for a long hug. I felt his hot breath on my neck, and then he kissed me on the mouth. I pulled away, shocked.

"It's okay; just thanking you for helping and listening to me talk," he said.

When I stepped back into the kitchen, his wife Jane asked, "did you enjoy that...did you get some eggs?"

"Yes, four. I enjoyed helping, thank you." I smiled and then searched for Anna so that Jane didn't see the heat rise into my cheeks.

The next evening, when John came home from work, I was in the sitting room watching the TV with Anna and Jane.

"It's good to see you making yourself quite at home

here...you look comfortable in my favorite chair," John said while looking over my head. He then reached down with his hand and swept it up my thigh onto my arm.

I froze and kept my eyes on the TV. I could sense John looking over at his wife and daughter to check they were watching the TV, and then he moved his fingers from my arm to caress my breast. He pulled back on my quick intake of breath.

Jane turned towards me. "Are you okay, Cathryn?" she asked.

I felt desirable. Even though I was 16, I was almost a woman and enjoyed the attention. That is until the guilt kicked in. Jane had poor health, and I felt loyal to her and Anna. I didn't want to lose my sense of belonging to them. It was more desirable than teenage fantasy. So, I stayed away from John. I pulled away from his kisses and wandering hands when he thought no one was looking.

Within weeks life events stopped the regular visits. Maybe, Tasco had blocked them, or Jane had intervened. But perhaps it was because I fell in love with Ged. Soon after we met, my Mam took me to the birth control clinic to put me on the pill.

"Better safe than sorry," she said without any further discussion.

I spent nearly every evening with Ged. First, cuddling up on his parent's sofa when they went to bed. Then, we progressed to his bedroom when they were out. My first 'real' relationship had begun. But, after only a couple of months, Ged called it off.

He said, "There's someone else I like; she's more fun. You're too serious and full on."

I ran home in hysterics and shot through the house.

"Stop running...what's up with ya," my dad shouted.

"Leave me alone...I don't care; I want to die," I shouted back.

"Come here, you silly girl. Tell me what's wrong."

I stood in the kitchen with my arms folded and snot and tears soaking my face.

Oon'ch-illia

"Leave me alone. I want to kill myself...Ged's packed me in...says I'm boring. He's found someone better." I said through gulps and sniffs.

"You'll get over it - it happens to us all. First love's always the worst. He's not worth all this." Dad suggested.

A few months later when I left sixth form, dad said, "you need a trade. You must learn something that pays well. You can only be someone if you do well for yourself ... so you must study hard and get a good job."

That became dad's regular mantra. When Alan turned 16, dad had pushed him to take an apprenticeship at ICI, the local factory where dad worked. For me, it was the local technical college.

When dad grew up, children left home or had to bring in a wage packet to support the family. But he told us, "You've got more choices than I had. I wanted to go to college."

With the right subject grades from the sixth form, I enrolled in a medical secretarial course. It seemed a good fit only because I liked human biology and was good at English.

While still 17, I pretended to be 18 and got a barmaid job to earn money. I'm sure they suspected, but I was only a few months away, so they turned a blind eye. Then, one night, I served Dave and was smitten by his charm. He was gorgeous, with dark curly locks and smoldering eyes. We threw ourselves into the relationship. I couldn't get enough of him; it was like an obsession. First, he bought me gifts and walked me home after work. Then, I stayed at his all night, night after night, and consented to sexual experimentation to please him.

When I left college, I was at a loose end. Dave was in the RAF stationed 200 miles away. My parents went on holiday to Spain, but I stayed home and looked for work. At each interview I was told, "we need someone with more experience."

I disliked being in the house alone with Alan, so I went with a friend to Scarborough for the August Bank Holiday weekend. That Saturday night, I talked to Dave on the phone.

He was in London visiting his cousin but said, "why don't you come here instead of going back home? I'll be here till Tuesday - go on, I dare you, get on a train and come here."

So, instead of boarding the return train for home, I said goodbye to my friend at the station on Sunday afternoon and boarded the London Kings Cross train. That decision mapped out my early adult life.

11

Independence

Dave's cousin, Amy, had moved to London many years previous and worked as a manager at the high-end department store Selfridges. She lived with her partner, Noel, an Irish man, and they welcomed me into their home and hearts.

Dave returned to the RAF two days after I arrived, so I planned to go home. But at breakfast, Amy asked me, "why don't you stay for the week? Come into work with me on the tube today, and then you can sign up with a couple of temp agencies. You might not be able to get a job back home, but they're crying out for people here."

"Why not? I've got nothing to get back for; I guess it's worth a try," I said.

The first agency I walked into was keen to sign me up and offered me a position to commence the following day. I pushed the dark clouds away and embraced the light. Someone wanted me. They thought I had what it took to be a secretary, even without experience. So, I accepted, and after two days, my new employer offered me a full-time secure job. It was in the typing pool for the Obstetrics and Gynaecological Department. I typed up the dictated clinical notes for the Queen's Gynaecologist within his NHS team.

I was astounded that he arrived in the team room on the first Friday with cream cakes, a Friday tradition. It was my first meeting with him, and he was so down to earth. I also met his Registrar, Roger, a couple of house doctors, and some nurses from the ward. I had become a multidisciplinary team member, not just a typist listening to their voices.

That evening, I phoned my parents, who had returned home from their holiday. "Hi, it's me. Have you had a nice time?" I asked.

"Where are you? Why did you go to London? It's that Dave, isn't it? Your dad's upset that you up and went." Mam said.

"I'm coming home tomorrow, but I've got a job, so I must be back Sunday night. I need some clothes and things. I'll tell you about it when I see you, okay?" I ended the call with, "I'm sorry, Mam. Love you."

I returned to London relieved after a fraught weekend. Luckily, my parents had overcome their shock and were pleased I got a job. The fact that I was working for the Queen's Gynaecologist was a bonus since it gave my dad something to boast about. However, I had to remind him that I did not work in the doctor's private practice but in the NHS team and would rarely come into contact with him. When I did, he was the Consultant of the medical team I worked for, and that was all. His Registrar, Roger, was the doctor I had most dealings with.

My office manager was scary. She was a tiny woman from Nepal and married to a Gurka. I wondered if she was one too. She was the doctor's gatekeeper and ruled her team of secretaries, not with fear, but with a sense of responsibility, as if each audio tape we handled was a newborn baby. Yet, she had a soft side and took me under her wing. When we were alone, she acted like my gran.

As I look back to those times, I sense something familiar about her that I was too immature to notice then. It was her protective and nurturing nature but with a no-nonsense attitude. It was Tasco, the old lady who soothed me when my night fears took hold.

After two months of settling into my new London life, Dave arrived for a weekend visit. I had moved into a tiny bedsit in Acton, down the road from Amy and Noel.

When the new week started, and I was preparing to leave for work, Dave said, "I've got some leave to take, so I thought I'd stay a bit longer. I'll go back next week."

I was surprised, as I suspected the RAF would need more leave notice. Dave stayed at Amy and Noel's flat, but we spent the evenings together. After spending a second weekend at my bedsit and no sign of him leaving, I questioned him.

"I've gone AWOL, I can't stand it there, but they're looking for me," he said.

Later that week, Amy convinced Dave to hand himself in. "Noel doesn't want the police knocking on our door," she said.

Dave returned to his barracks and was locked up for two weeks; then, they kicked him out. One evening, he turned up at my door saying, "we can be a proper couple now. I'm not going back up north, and I'm not staying at Amy's; Noel doesn't want me there. I'll get a job, maybe at a hospital like you. It can't be that difficult."

I was a naive 19-year-old and a soft touch, mainly where Dave was concerned. So, I asked my landlord for a larger bedsit so we could live together. Within a week, Dave had gotten a job, went to work, and came home around the same time as me. At the month's end, I asked him to contribute to the rent and bills, but he had no money. The same happened the following month, and I struggled to pay for everything. He promised he would have some money the following month, but he didn't.

I confided in a friend at work. She was suspicious when I told her, "Dave's doing well and to get a technician job at Hammersmith Hospital without any experience."

Behind my back, she talked to someone she knew at Hammersmith Hospital to ask if Dave was a new starter. Then, the next day on coffee break, she said, "Cathryn, you know Dave doesn't work at the Hammersmith, don't you?"

"He says he does, but he tells me different things. He goes out when I do and comes back after me. The other day though, someone at our digs said she had seen him a couple of times come back after I had gone out."

That night I challenged him.

"Well, I tried to get a job," he shouted. "I'm not perfect like you. Anyway, I met someone, an American girl. She said I could go there. She's going to send me her address when she gets back."

I shouted back, "but I'm paying the bills, and we are meant to be a couple. You've been leading me on, saying you'll be paid soon, and you're off enjoying yourself and chatting up other lasses."

I was on a roll, so he shut me up by pushing me, then slapping me across the head.

"Shut the fuck up, going on at me all the time," he spat.

At least I had gotten the truth from him, but he made out like it was all my fault that he couldn't get a job. He hadn't even tried. Instead of being out at work all day, he hung around with members of the Krishna society.

When I told my friend the next day, she planted the seeds that Dave was a compulsive liar. I couldn't trust anything he said and grew scared of him, but I was more fearful of him leaving me. A week later, I discovered I was pregnant. Naively, I was excited and hopeful it would be the glue, as people often say, to mend our relationship. Dave was overjoyed and promised to get a job to support us.

Yet, within days, my Mam convinced me not to trust him. She said, "Dave doesn't have it in him to support you. Can you survive on your own down there with a baby? You know coming home isn't an option. Your dad won't have a baby in the house."

Dave's moods became erratic. Finally, he showed me a letter from the other girl. "Look, she wants me to go over there. It will be better for me than staying here."

I was ten weeks pregnant when my Mam convinced me to have an abortion and to tell Dave to leave.

But, when I asked him to go, he became tearful and begged to stay, "I want us to be a family; I love you, I've got nowhere to go, you can't make me go, I want our baby, you can't kill it, I'll stop you, this is all your fault, listening to your Mam. What does she know? You're ruining my life."

Oon'ch-illia

Mam turned up the next day. "I've got a return ticket and only three hours. I've just come to get Dave to leave."

Then she said to him, "Come on, pack up your things, you're going back home. I've got you a ticket on the same train."

I watched in shock as Mam helped Dave to pack. He meekly obliged, then left with these parting words, "if you kill my baby, I'm going to come after you."

I felt abandoned and wandered around the shared bedsit feeling empty inside, apart from my awareness of the growing fetus within me, whose life I was about to take. I felt guilty and then got worried. Would Dave be true to his word? Later that week, I faced an abortion on my own, with Dave's words rattling around my head and the vision of my Mam pulling him away from me.

Some years later, I was able to talk to my Mam about the events of that day.

"Mam, I've struggled to forgive you for what you did that day. I know you had to take Dave away from me, and I'm proud that you could do that. It was such a surprise. But then, to leave me to deal with everything alone. How could you do that?"

"I had to do it; I felt responsible in some way. I always knew Dave was a compulsive liar. His Mam worked in our shop for a while, and he got a Saturday job. He was a right Walter Mitty!"

"Well, why didn't you tell me? I wouldn't have gone through all that," I screamed at her.

"You wouldn't have listened...you would have stuck your heels in more, wouldn't you?" she said.

"But you took Dave home, leaving me to get on with it. How could you do that? First, get rid of him, then tell me to get rid of the baby and leave me to get on with it. Do you know what it was like? I heard women giving birth and babies crying while I was waiting for the operation. I could feel the nurses and the doctor judging me. I already felt guilty. It was horrible after, too. If it wasn't for Amy keeping an eye on me, I don't know how I'd have coped.

How could you just leave me?"

I pleaded with her for answers, but she just shook her head and said, "I'm so sorry."

It was gran's letters that helped me to forgive my Mam. She reminded me I was hurting myself more and had to move on. So, I began to enjoy life and found the freedom I craved. I made new friends, danced the night away, and flirted with a musician. London life was appealing and uncomplicated for a short while. But then, I had a shift. I craved love more than independence.

12

Married

At a hospital social do, I met Dan, who was a safe bet after my mistakes. Sixteen years my senior, he wanted to settle down, and I wanted stability and security. I turned my back on the warning signs and threw myself into the whirlwind romance. Dan had longed for children, and I fantasized the baby within me had survived the abortion. Instead, I imagined it was hibernating, ready for another man's seed to give it life.

On a week's vacation, I drunkenly proposed to Dan, and then a few weeks later, I discovered I was pregnant again. That time around, I ignored my friend's warnings. She had dug up some dirt on Dan, but I brushed it to one side. I chose to believe she was jealous of my happiness and my love for Dan would overcome any obstacles. So, I moved into his bedsit, and we made our wedding plans.

We got married three months before my 21st Birthday when I was 17 weeks pregnant. We had a small wedding party of family and two of Dan's friends, who were our witnesses. Following a celebratory meal bought by my parents, we cut the cake and had a buffet tea in our dingy bedsit. Then, Dan whisked me away for our honeymoon night, spent in a budget London hotel, followed by a mid-week break in North Wales.

A few days before the wedding, Dan passed his driving test and bought a car. With a family to support, having wheels seemed important, but the Alfa Romeo was more about impressing than practicality.

Halfway through the honeymoon, the low-slung car hit several bumps in a slate mine car park. Then, we endured two night-time journeys to and from a garage in Birmingham with headlights that flickered on and off as Dan negotiated the sharp country roads.

On our return to London, with further repairs needed, we began a nightmare saga. As the list of car repairs grew, Dan turned to his amateur law studies.

The next thing I discovered was the man who sold us the car had collapsed from a suspected heart attack. During his recovery, he accused Dan of causing it, what with all the stress.

"The crazy man won't leave me alone - shouting and swearing at me, blaming me for selling a dodgy car."

After several tense months, the case was settled out of court, and Dan was warned about the consequences of his aggressive attitude. Was this an omen for our married life, I wondered.

In 1982, my son Simon was born, and we moved from London to a house in the Essex suburbs. As a housewife and mother, I took my roles seriously. However, money was tight, and Dan had a two-hour journey morning and night for his job in London. I attempted to take on a part-time job to supplement our finances, but Dan accused me of abandoning Simon and running after another man.

It was a secretarial job for a Health & Safety advisor working out of his home. The man visited us in our own home to discuss the role. He offered to collect and drop me off after the three-hour typing stints two evenings a week and on a Saturday morning. I agreed to a trial run, and the man arranged to collect me the next Saturday morning.

When I prepared to leave, Dan shouted up the stairs. "If you go with him, I'm going out too. Simon will be left home alone."

He seemed to mean it, so I rang the man, catching him as he set off. I said, "I'm so sorry, I've changed my mind. I can't leave my baby. I'm sorry to mess you about."

Our daughter, Beth, was born just two years later to complete our family, but the cracks had begun to show. So, I decided to get a job at Mcdonald's to supplement the family income. I thought, *"Dan can't have a problem with that."* It was evening work at first. Then, I agreed to stay till closing 2-3 nights a week, which meant cleaning all the equipment until the early hours.

One night when Dan collected me from work, he saw me laughing with my male workmates. They were only kids, well, late teens, and I felt much older since I was a mum of two.

Dan ranted at me on the way home, "I see your true colors showing, flirting again with any male willing to talk to you. Next thing, you'll be opening your legs for them all."

"What on earth are you saying? Do you even hear yourself? I was only having a laugh. It's innocent fun, and they're kids. It helps get us through the night, especially when cleaning all the grease and grime," I shouted back.

The following week, one of my co-workers, a 19-year-old lad, offered me a lift home in the early hours when the trains had stopped running. I was grateful, as I didn't want Dan getting the children out of bed to collect me late at night. But the accusations came.

"You're a slut; a slag. You need to keep your legs shut. Is Simon even mine?"

I grew wary that Dan was revealing a darker side. It was my Mam's daily phone calls that kept my sanity. Again, I replayed my gran's words in my mind. "Forgive, but never forget." I did that repeatedly but vowed to set a point of no return. Before that time arrived, there was another solution. Dan was offered voluntary redundancy, so I encouraged him to take it to have a new start.

In 1987, we moved back home, closer to my parents, which was both a godsend and a curse. I found full-time employment as a Medical Secretary in the Medical Physics Department. Dan was offered a job at my dad's company but turned it down. So instead, he became a self-employed odd-job man, and then we remortgaged the house so he could buy into a franchise as a driving instructor.

Cathryn Mahoney

I found the 9-5 routine mundane, and the constant balancing act of work and home life sucked my life force. I was always at the beck and call of someone. I felt an inner drive to learn something new, but I didn't know what. When I interacted with my colleagues, I listened to them talk about their different jobs, and they shared their personal lives with me. Most of them were men, so I had to be mindful of who and what I talked about when I got home at the end of the day. Dan often quizzed me, so I didn't tell him when I had a lunchtime walk alone with Martin; instead, it was a group of us.

It was safe to talk about my friend, Angela, though. She worked in the Mould Room, where she made casts for patients undergoing radiotherapy for cancer of the head or throat. A mask was made to protect the patient from the radiotherapy beam directed to specific locations. I was more interested in the person, and how they coped with it rather than the technical details, so I liked to ask Angela lots of questions. It allowed her to offload since she dealt with many frightened and tearful people. It started me thinking about exploring a patient support role rather than being a secretary.

Dan could do the school run at home, or the children occasionally went to a childminder, and my Mam helped in the school holidays. As our children grew, they preferred to play with their friends or go to activities, so my quality time with them dwindled. The weekends were a blur of ferrying them around between shopping, housework and visiting my parents.

I played all the parts scripted for me, with constant costume changes. However, it felt like I was wrapped in an invisibility cloak.

I am a speck of light
A firefly in search of my mate.
My broken pieces jangle.
I'm frozen deep
I am lost - within the recesses of a forgotten place.

Oon'ch-illia

"Stop being so miserable," Dan whispered into my ear. "What's the matter with you?"

I was a silent observer of my family at play. With the shutters up, I was lost in the inner reverie of another time and place. With a false smile and a half-hearted laugh, I looked for excuses to complete some important tasks that couldn't be delayed. I immersed my mind and body in my housewife role within my domain and maintained a hectic life with no time for Mam to play. How I ached to lose myself. To become child-like and join in my children's games. To shake off my self-imposed grown-up rules and responsibilities.

"I must stay in control" was my inner mantra, my iron shield and suit of armor to keep the dark ones at bay.

I went through the motions, meeting the expectations of my multiple roles without being fully present. Still, I remained open to the messages left for me, often hidden in discreet locations along the path of my life's journey.

On the immediate horizon loomed the day of my major discovery, which would take all I had ever known away from me, including my children. All because of my desire to know me, to make sense of the otherworldly mysteries that flittered unseen around me.

An evening school prospectus landed on the doormat.

"Maybe it offers a chance to learn something new," I wondered.

But how to attend evening classes while balancing the demands of young children and a full-time job? Where did my search for self fit into it all? Dan had the luxury to pick and choose his hours and collect the children from school, but my time with them was limited. Mum-guilt nibbled away from inside at the thought of doing something just for me, but each box I existed in caged me further. I longed to break free.

Something inside me clicked one day. I couldn't ignore the drive I felt for a new challenge. It blared in my head - *the time is now!* Finally, maybe, I had picked up one of the clues left for me at a pivotal location and had to discover what lay ahead on my path. So, I pulled the prospectus from its hidey-hole underneath the phone book and scanned the Autumn term classes. My instinct proved right - the perfect subject jumped off the page - 'Self-Hypnosis for Beginners.' The classes were held one evening a week at the college next door to the hospital where I worked.

I convinced Dan that the subject would somehow help me, even both of us. I'm uncertain how I convinced him to approve, but I did. There was some trade-off, however. The evening tea-time routine was the first thing to go. Even though I rushed home from work, sticks were poked at any opportunity to slow my haste. I acted quickly and caught them with my biddable arm to add to the pile of fuel, ready to set fire to my dreams.

"Why am I doing this? Is it fair to leave the children when I barely see them during the week?"

It ran as a tune on a constant loop in my mind, and tiny shards of glass jangled within my head when it was time to walk out the door. I almost ran but then choked. Perhaps, it was the mushy leftovers from the children's tea. It tickled my throat, and my eyes watered.

Then, a woodpecker hammered into my brain, *"you can't go."* But another voice in my head urged me, *"get out the door."*

It was my Mam's voice, even though she lived fifteen miles away. As my encourager, she chased away the storm clouds and replaced them with a cool breeze. Ripples of light soothed me. Then I saw a dark image - it was a large bag of the shit I insisted on carrying. I turned it into a balloon that drifted away with the breeze.

I intended to gain new knowledge and find some freedom. That desire had already caused a shift in me.

When I arrived at the self-hypnosis class, it was to a small group with two teachers. We learned about trance states, imagery, and manifestation techniques. I was excited and felt relaxed because this seemed right up my street. We first practiced a visualization exercise to help us have a good night's sleep, and I couldn't believe how simple it was.

On my return home, I expected an interrogation from Dan, but it never came. My absence seemed like no big deal, so I breathed a sigh of relief, then slept through the night.

I got tense before leaving for class each week. My nerves battled with my desire to learn and grow, and despite snide remarks from Dan, I had begun to feel good about myself.

We practiced a new visualization technique halfway through the course. The teacher asked us to put our feet flat on the floor, relax our hands on our laps, then close our eyes and focus on deep breathing as he guided us into a trance state.

Then he said, "as I count down imaginary steps from 1 to 10, feel yourself sinking deeper into a pre-sleep state with each number. Then, notice you are walking down a country lane. Connect with all you see, hear, smell and sense around you, feeling safe and content. Imagine a wide-open field ahead and a hot air balloon in the middle of the field. Notice the colors, sounds, and sensations you feel as you approach it. Someone you know and trust is waiting to take you on a journey. Their job is to keep you safe. They help you into the basket and ask where you want to go. This is your journey—a time to release all the things that hold you back in life. As you lift into the air, you notice a writing pad and pen on the floor beside you. Enjoy the journey, but on the way, write down all the things you wish to release from your life, then throw them over the basket, however you choose."

I enjoyed the journey across golden fields alight with the evening sun and looked down on watercourses meandering into the distance. I wrote a few sentences about what was preventing me from living the life I chose. Then, I ripped up the pieces of paper and threw them into the wind. Doing so with much enthusiasm. As I watched the wind whisk them away, my children came to mind, and they disappeared too.

One of the things I released was feeling trapped and not having control over my life. It wasn't my children's fault, but they were why I stayed with Dan. I panicked and brought myself back out of the trance state, then ran to the toilets to compose myself. I felt sick. My guts spoke. I knew that someday I would have to let my children go. But I reasoned with myself, that could never happen, not until they were adults. When I returned to the room, the group shared their experiences, but I kept quiet.

I spoke to the teacher after class. He reassured me and showed me a technique to help put things into perspective. It calmed me, but I wasn't convinced by his reassurances, as a sense of foreboding stayed with me. I remained apprehensive and avoided going into a deep trance state from then on in. Was it a premonition?

13

Purpose

The exhilaration I experienced during the day kept me wakeful throughout the night. My body buzzed, and my mind ran through the finer details of stepping into the therapist role while practicing a childhood regression exercise. I met the challenges my client had presented to me. After counting her down into a deeper trance state, I used the prompts given during the lesson.

"OK, Lesley, while your whole body continues to relax, I would like your subconscious mind to drift back in time to a time when you felt the feelings you described earlier, the fear you described. Take yourself back to the first time you felt that as a child."

I watched Lesley's non-verbal cues and could see the movement behind her eyelids and the change in color on her face. Then she grimaced and took a deep breath.

"You are safe now; I am here. What is happening? Can you tell me what you see, hear and feel?"

Lesley pulled herself up on her seat with her head to her knees and her arms wrapped around them.

"Lesley, you are safe. What is happening now? I am here with you."

She jumped up and moved towards me; she screamed, "no, you can't make me, no, I won't."

I was scared, but my intuition and compassion kicked in. "It's okay, Lesley, you're safe now; say what you need to say or shout, but it's important to keep you and me safe."

Lesley started shouting at an invisible person beside me. Then she sat down and sobbed. It was heartbreaking to watch. I had learned not to comfort but remind her of my presence and that it was my job to keep her safe.

"Thank you, Lesley, for sharing with me. Is there anything else you need to say to that person?"

Her sobs had eased, and she whispered, "no, I want to sleep now."

"Rest now; go to your safe, quiet place, Lesley. I will leave you there for a few minutes. When you next hear my voice, I will ask you to come back to full conscious awareness."

I encouraged Lesley out of the trance state by using a more commanding voice. "Lesley, it is now time to come back to full conscious awareness, into the present time, and back into the room at the Hypnotherapy center."

I counted her back out, with more emphasis on the words, and then, "three, two, one, you are back now with me, here in this room, open your eyes, stretch, and take a deep breath. Put your feet flat on the floor and ground yourself here and now. Well done, Lesley, welcome back."

I gave Lesley time to ground herself and become fully aware of her surroundings. The noises of other people talking, the light from the windows, and an approaching instructor checking up on us.

When asked how the session had gone, Lesley said, "I can't believe I did it. I felt so held and safe and was able to face my uncle. I've never done that before. I wanted to attack him but knew it wasn't safe to do, but I could yell and make him feel small like I did. Cathryn was great. She was with me every step of the way as if she knew what was happening, what I needed, and when I needed it. I've felt stuck for so long. I think I've shifted it. I feel empowered and alive. Thanks, Cathryn."

Lesley reached out and hugged me as the instructor walked away, giving us time to talk more about Lesley's first childhood regression experience.

I recall, afterward, feeling ten feet tall. Energy coursed through me through the dark, still hours of the night. It triggered memories of service to others as a healer, seer, and teacher. Then I dozed. When I woke, there was a sense of knowing something profound, but only the previous day's memories flooded back. I jumped out of bed, desperate for air and space to think. It felt like an electric shock had fired my synapses back to life.

My soul shrieked: *"Yes...at last! She has realized her potential."*

Let's rewind to that realization. It was halfway through the first week of an intensive Hypnotherapy course in Scarborough, North Yorkshire. Mam lent me the money for the course, and Dan somehow had let me loose, yet I was sure he'd make me pay for it in some way.

After we had worked together, Lesley approached later that day, "I can't believe how powerful that exercise was. I feel so different, and I'm certain it's something to do with you. You were the right person to help me. I felt that you knew me, even the younger me; you were there every step of the way."

That same evening, I joined a small group of fellow students in one of the local bars. I didn't want the day to end as I was on such a high. Mike was there, which I confess was one of the reasons I went along, as well as to share my success of the day. Everyone appeared to have enjoyed the regression exercise, as the air was charged with wonder, awe, and success. We had learned so much in such a short time, and friendships developed through sharing personal stories. Therapy training can lead to deep exploration, so bonds form quickly. For some people, it can also lead to romantic attachments.

That notion was furthest from my mind. Instead, I felt content and proud of myself, which unleashed a bubbly and talkative side of me, an unusual occurrence without a glass of wine for courage. Somehow, my confidence and self-esteem soared in the company of people who really saw me.

They all beamed at me as I announced, "I now know my purpose in life. It is to help people in this way; it feels so natural. I can't believe I can really be a therapist. It feels like an amazing new life on the horizon. I must remember today and follow it through. I know I can do it."

I also knew something else was fledging. A profound knowing deep in my gut that I was in the company of someone special, who felt safe and familiar, with whom I didn't need to pretend to be someone I wasn't.

Mike's presence was like a soothing balm to my soul. Our eyes met across the training room on the first day, and we sought each other out from then on. An invisible thread pulled us closer each day, and I was curious about him. He was gentle, softly spoken, and encouraged others in the group to share experiences. He was also a joker who knew when to lighten the mood when it dipped. I felt safe in his presence yet pondered on the frisson between us.

I was surprised when he told me, "I already work as a therapist, but it's good to learn more."

The magnetism was unmistakable, and I wondered if his need to learn wasn't about the training but something personal.

I made it clear that I was married and not looking for complications.

"Me too," is all he said.

He walked me back to my B&B so we could chat some more. I sensed light waves spiral around us the longer we were together, and that night, my sleep was disturbed by images. It felt like the rainbow current of light waves had been injected into my veins. I woke with the sunrise after a short, fitful sleep. Then, the dawn chorus invited me out for a walk.

I retraced the steps I had walked with Mike the prior evening, still soaked in his sense and smell. Then, I took the cliff-side footpath to a lookout over the sea. Wildlife skittered around me as the early morning sun sparkled upon the white caps of the waves. I reflected on the previous day. The rainbow of light waves flowed and shimmered within my aura, and I connected with the colors of the natural world.

A peacefulness wrapped its gentle arms around me. The sun rose and warmed the land, and the air was crystal clear – it was a perfect early spring morning. I marveled at the diamonds that dazzled upon the sea, then consciously breathed in the ozone and brine as it wafted on the cool breeze. It filled my lungs and surged through my veins. Then, as I focused on a wispy cloud within an azure sky, a wave crashed below, and then, silence.

A robin sang to me from a nearby branch, its beady eyes expecting a tasty crumb. As it flew off, my eyes fell upon the daffodils and crocuses, which danced in tune with the breeze. Their hues reflected the sunlight. Then, the heady scents of cherry blossom petals captivated me as they swirled above my head, mingled with damp grass and wildflowers. I attempted to find expressions to match the beauty all around. Finally, I unlocked my inhibitions and set my true self free.

The deep peace and joy within me became an inner smile, and I laughed out loud. I felt an impulse to sing and dance but struggled to allow movement and voice. I was like a child desperate to play all day, but schoolwork invaded the space. My adult rules inhibited my inner child's curiosity and sense of wonder. A too familiar fact where rules and regulations crash the party, and I call time on the pure bliss of being at one with nature.

"No one is around, but perhaps they can hear me?" my nagging voice said. It was my cue to go, but I allowed myself a moment longer before I did. I grounded myself and became immersed in my natural surroundings.

The colors brighten.
Light and shade dance through the trees.
I shrink and view the world from a fairy's perspective.
The vibrancy of the grass absorbs me.
I sink deep within the earth
amongst the grains of sand and clay.
Within the delve of a pebble,
a dewdrop is an iridescent lake.
A blackbird towers over me with a wry expression
but passes me over for a tasty worm.

Cathryn Mahoney

Then, a butterfly landed on my knee, and I broke from my reverie. I looked out to sea and breathed in the ozone. On the next exhale, I released doubt and inhaled self-belief.

14

Divorce

I stood and listened. "Why are you saying that?" My guts twisted. They tightened like a coiled spring.

"I have to get out," "I must get out," a little voice in my head pleaded.

"In my day, you had to stick together, no matter what. You have to work it out," Dad said. Mam squirmed behind him.

Why was he the peacemaker? I couldn't believe it. *"You have an ally now,"* I thought, while Dan lapped it up since he was the injured party.

"I have to get out," grew louder in my head. The spring tightened like a vice on my heart.

Then, I spat out, "I have to go."

"What?" they said in unison, stunned.

"I have to go...I need to think."

Then I was out the door and, in the car, my foot hard on the accelerator as I drove down the street.

"Let them decide between themselves. Whatever they say, I'm not listening, just like they're not listening to me," I muttered and tried to control the shakes.

I couldn't believe what I had done. I drove, unsure where I was going. The guilt kicked in, but I kicked it back out again and drove on.

I soon realized where I was headed. After parking, I climbed over the stile into familiar woodland. It was a warm summer evening. I was grateful; the children had already been tucked in for the night before my parents' unexpected arrival. Dad had been all high and mighty when he appeared with a mission to fulfill. He only thought of himself, ensuring I didn't land on him with the children in tow. Just like that last time when I'd considered a return home pregnant. That idea was soon squashed.

Cathryn Mahoney

Walking along the woodland path, I reflected to myself and sobbed. With each step, the coiled spring relaxed, and the words came out.

"Fucking hell, what am I going to do. Bloody dad, who does he think he is? I bet Dan loved the attention. They're against me, even Mam. Fuck, fuck - bastards!" I stamped about.

There wasn't another soul around, but I still worried about being heard. The words needed their release into the air to prevent me from going mad. I shouted no louder than my spoken voice but wanted to bay like a wolf.

I reached the waterfall I'd headed towards. Then, I abruptly stopped, reliving the last time I was there. It had been one of the most joyous moments of my life. A glorious few hours Mike and I had snatched. He'd taken my hand, and we skidded down the muddy bank toward the stream. The spray from the falls dampened and cooled the charged atmosphere between us. Stolen time together, with no thought for those we betrayed. It was pushed to the back of our minds. Yet, we could not deny our strong bond and the deep love we felt. It wasn't a sordid affair as our spouses thought it to be. We had re-found each other after such a long time apart, much longer than we realized at that time.

As I pondered by the waterfall, I sensed Mike's essence had drawn me there in my time of need. I imagined his strong arms soothing me, reassuring me that everything would be okay. I knew distance wasn't a barrier between us. His love would keep me strong.

Our meetings, no matter how brief and far apart, were set to remind me how strong our connection was. It was up to me to walk my rightful path and still do my best for my children. My parents grew up believing you had no choice but to stay together once you were married. Pretending to be happy and living a lie wasn't acceptable to me. I had already put my own needs and mental health on the line, but was there any other option?

Oon'ch-illia

Mike and I lived parallel lives, both unhappily married with two children. While sharing aspects of our lives, we identified times and places where we could have met but passed on by.

"Why didn't we find each other sooner? We wouldn't have married the wrong people," I said to Mike once.

"It wasn't meant to be...we've met now; that's all that counts," Mike reasoned.

I stared at him pensively and said aloud, "perhaps, it's still not the right time...there are too many reasons we cannot be together."

I walked on alone, past the waterfall, trying to figure out what to do. I knew I was with the wrong man, yet the one I wanted to be with couldn't be with me. The children were too young to uproot. Who would do the uprooting? Not me. I knew Mike wouldn't do that to his children, either.

It was too late to 'work at the marriage' as my dad had advised. It was already broken. There was no amount of fixing left. Dan tried to force me to love him, but I could not reciprocate. The separation couldn't be avoided. If we stayed together, someone, or all of us, may suffer a worse fate.

My thoughts continued to flitter. I tried to walk out my anguish. Which path to take? Grief overcame me when I recalled a happier moment with Mike in the same spot. I craved his touch. Each essence of joy I captured in my memories was snatched away in a puff of steam.

I reached the end of the path and debated whether to keep walking up to the moor and never return. Images of my children and Mam popped into my mind. Guilt kicked in. I had walked out on them and left Mam to deal with things in my absence. I worried my children had heard the commotion in the hallway and knew I had stormed out. I didn't want them to be upset because of me, but what if that had already happened?

These new thoughts permeated my brain and forced a quick return to my car. I fought cold tendrils that seeped deep into my bones as I drove. All the way home, I found it impossible to know what I would say. I had never done anything like this before. I felt like a naughty child. How could I have done that? Yet, I was also pleased that I had rebelled for once. Mike's ethereal presence made my heart skip a beat then calmness stilled me. Somehow, I found the confidence to face whatever awaited me.

When I walked through the door, my parents had left, and the children were still asleep in their beds, totally unaware.

Dan grunted, "you heard what your dad thinks," then he walked upstairs, "I'm going to bed now you're back."

For the next few days, it was as if nothing happened. When I next spoke to my Mam, she said they had left soon after me. They decided not to interfere. I felt bemused and still uncertain of my next move. The ball was in my court.

Frustrations forced the matter. Dan attempted to exert control to overcome my rejection of him. My 'guilt' button blared red when he projected his hurt back onto me and attempted to undermine me at every turn. His beliefs came from the same generation as my dad's.

"I'm your husband; for better or worse - you can't leave me," he told me as he forced his affections onto me.

I saw him as two characters: Jekyll and Hyde. His moods frightened me. He goaded me, whispering in my ear, "you're mental. You need locking up."

I had caused his change in behavior towards me. One day it was, "I'm depressed. It's your fault I'm like this, cos you don't love me; you're driving me mad." The next, "it's the antidepressants; they're making me be like this," when he apologized for lashing out.

"I'm your husband...don't turn your back on me...you don't love him. He's hypnotized you...you're so stupid, you're a fucking daft cunt," was a usual rant.

"Who is he? Tell me his name...I'll find out...then we'll see, won't we," he threatened.

What was the catalyst for me to leave? The increased

threats? The black eye? The bruised ribs? The red mark around my throat? All those, but most of all, the effect on the children. I had to protect them. They had begun to witness some of our arguments. Dan's mental health and its impact on them were of grave concern. Beth had tried to be a barrier between us, to protect us from each other. Simon was quiet and withdrawn. Ultimately, after several weeks of escalation, I had no choice but to put on my big girl pants and leave.

At times I wished I loved Dan more or had never met Mike. Dan was a good dad and a loyal husband. He was great when life was smooth. But the damage had been done. There was no going back. I couldn't love Dan like I loved Mike. Maybe, I had fooled myself into thinking I loved him from the beginning. I'm sure I did, but his insecurity and insinuations had eroded what we had. And, in his emotional state, I couldn't trust his ability to protect the children. My only option was to take them with me when I left.

It was a mistake to turn up at my parent's house. I should have known that wouldn't work. My dad reiterated his belief about sticking it out. He didn't want us there and told me to take the children home, "you've made your bed, lie in it," was his response in my time of need. Mam felt helpless but tried to make us feel at home. After the first night, the tension got too much.

I really needed my parent's help, but my dad wouldn't budge. The children were bewildered and wanted to go home. I swayed. Could I do this to them? I was tempted to go back. No wonder so many women do, I thought. The dilemma tore me in two. Was I being fair to the children? I couldn't leave them alone with their dad, but I couldn't go back.

A friend offered us a couple of rooms in her home. It was a temporary measure until I could find somewhere else to live. I had so much to organize, and I was like a rabbit in headlights.

Mam worried about us moving further away, and the

children cried when I said, "we're not going home."

Dan went ballistic when I told him, "We're going to a friend's house. I need thinking time." Even though I knew I had left for good.

I walked out of the family courtroom, totally shocked. *"What just happened? Who was that woman the judge was talking about?"* I wondered.

My Mam asked if I was alright. I just stared at her and asked, "What do I do now?"

In the eyes of the judge, I was an unfaithful wife, a woman who selfishly put her own needs before those of her children. However, I was also a confident woman with a good job and big ideas.

His concluding statement was, "You are both capable of caring for the children, but they will have more security and be more settled with their father in their own home."

I heard the subtext: "He puts their needs first and has no other distractions."

The court welfare officer had stressed her concerns. She told the judge: "The children want to stay together."

He agreed that they should. But she also told him: "The children seem scared not to live with dad as he has told them if they don't, he will move away."

He didn't seem to hear that part, or when I told him of the times, I had called the police out and had been advised to seek an injunction. But I had refused to force Dan out of his home when I was the one who had strayed, and I didn't have the foresight to ask for the police reports. My solicitor didn't represent me well. Perhaps he knew I deserved all I got.

The judge wasn't interested when I said I left because I thought it was best for the children. I was an unfaithful wife, first and foremost. I later discovered the judge had a history of favoring the dad in custody cases. He believed in a father's rights – no matter what. In some ways, I agreed with the judge. I didn't want my children living separately from each other, and I knew it was best for them to be in the family home, close to their schools and friends. But the reason I had taken them away in the first place was overlooked.

The judge ruled that Mr. Surtees was a loving father who was genuinely stunned and reeling from the break-up of his marriage to the woman he still loved. He wanted to be reunited with his children and provide for them more than anything. The judge briefly acknowledged he may not have responded to the break-up appropriately at times, but that was understandable.

I panicked outside the courtroom. I was due to collect the children from school but was no longer allowed to. I had dropped them off earlier that day, reassuring them I would see them later. I hadn't wanted to worry them about the what ifs, but now, their dad would be collecting them. How would they feel now, especially Beth, who was frightened of his moods?

"How will she cope?" I asked my Mam. I had to return home without them and pack up their belongings for him to collect. When would I see them again – I had no idea. He had promised regular contact – but could his word be trusted?

"I'll take everything away from you. You wait and see," Dan had threatened,

I dreaded getting back to my friend's house. The three of us had been living there for a year since the divorce. There had been such upheaval when court dates were adjourned, and on the third attempt, I got the wrong judge. I knew my choices had gotten me to where I was, but the thought of packing my children's clothes and toys tore my heart in two. There were empty spaces within our two shared rooms. The essence of each child was already fading. Dan had now taken everything away from me. I knew he would meet our children's needs the best he could. It was their emotional well-being I worried about. He would use them as pawns. It was a waiting game. What was his next move?

I took the opportunity to better myself while I didn't

have complete responsibility for the children. At work, an Oncologist encouraged me to use Hypnotherapy with cancer patients and staff. Another physician was raising money for a Holistic Cancer Centre, but I discovered they would only allow clinical staff to work there. It was time to take advantage of my independence, so I served my notice and became a full-time student at the university.

"A Degree in Psychology would certainly provide the credentials needed," I thought.

After eighteen months, Simon returned to live with me, but Beth remained with her dad. I balanced my time as a single parent with studies and work. It was easier without the previous turmoil and Dan's moods to contend with, but it didn't stop his attempts to influence me, just as I'd expected.

When Simon reached sixteen and attended college, I kept focus on my professional and personal development. Once I was on the right track, the growth opportunities came thick and fast.

Mike played a distant role in my life, with intermittent contact. Despite our strong feelings, we continued to live separate lives. It never seemed the right time for our children and us to consider a relationship. We lived on opposite sides of the country. He was still married and, unbeknownst to me, had just had a third child. He often worked away from home and felt guilty being away from his children. I was balancing work, training, and quality time with my children. I had no intention of unsettling them any further.

Oon'ch-illia

II

Meaning

Meeting Mike turned my life around and upside down. First, it gave my truth the confidence to peep out from around corners. Secondly, Mam's death revealed family secrets that led me on a journey of therapy and healing. Thirdly, when I re-opened my heart to Mike, he led me home to my real family, our collective, and our tribe. They gave us spirit quest experiences and travels that revealed ancient mysteries. There were tests of patience and endurance at every turn, including wedding and honeymoon adventures.

15

Career

The luxurious soak within lavender-infused bubbles eased the tightness out of my limbs while I sweated out the toxins from winter's long confinement. The howling menace had threatened the entire foundation of my existence. I now embraced the arrival of spring to aid my recovery from sleepless nights, and while I wallowed in peace, the sun warmed the land outside. Early sunrise brought growth, awe, and wonder. New beginnings – what surprises would I discover in my fourth decade as I adjusted to my new place? A new home that echoed both death and resurrection.

When the next century began, my new home was a cliffside farm cottage overlooking the North Sea where I could quite easily have become a hermit, just like the old man who had lived in the cave below me in 1754.

In that other time, I often sought him out while others gave his cave a wide berth. His wisdom soothed my soul after I'd subjected myself to attack outside the Spitfire alehouse for being the dotty old witch who harangued them.

"That dirty firewater will be the death of you. How can I heal you with my herbs when you pour that poison down your throat."

They spat vile and swiped at me with a cane or bottle. Yet, the next day they came to my woodland hideout like dogs with their tails between their legs. A good show they put on in public with the drink in them. But they soon asked for forgiveness when my light touched them. Open-hearted, I remained, as I have throughout the ages.

After three years of study, in 1997, I received my 2:1 Psychology Degree. I signed up as a volunteer telephone counselor at Rape Crisis and trained as a bereavement counselor with a local hospice. Within two months, Rape Crisis employed me as a full-time counselor. I also facilitated support groups and mentored volunteers.

I wanted to make a difference, to help other women and children. I was deeply concerned about the lack of recognition of the impact of emotional abuse. At the time, it was only assessed within neglect cases. So I became involved in inter-agency training to raise people's awareness of the emotional impact of sexual and domestic abuse. I networked with social workers, the police, and teachers.

With my counseling and training career launched, I invested in additional courses. Several times that year, I traveled to Suffolk, 250 miles from home, to train as an Inner Child Therapist.

As the year 2000 heralded the new millennium, it brought many changes. Simon was at university. Beth attended college locally but still lived with her dad. At the same time as moving to my cliffside home, I resigned from my job at Rape Crisis. Being a charity, they had funding issues. In addition, there was the threat of redundancies in the run-up to Christmas.

I told my manager, "I want to build my private Inner Child Therapy practice, so I want to cut my hours to part-time. Would that help with some of the finances? It could suit us both."

"I'm not sure; I'll have to take it to the management committee. I'll get back to you," was my manager's reply.

A week later, I received a letter from the management committee informing me that my request for part-time hours had been rejected.

"We are concerned you are planning to poach clients and set up in competition with this organization," was the condensed version.

When I asked my manager about it, she said the Chairperson had made the decision and sent the letter. I knew then it was my manager who had questioned my loyalty. I had no intention of poaching clients but saw the unstable financial climate as a reason to move on.

By the end of another week, I served my notice. After I left, I realized my manager had either felt threatened or jealous that I was setting up independently. Everyone's job was on the line, and I had jumped ship before I was pushed.

It was an exciting and scary time since my fresh start meant no regular income. To top it off, Simon and his new girlfriend, Chloe, arrived for the Christmas holiday. I was looking forward to seeing Simon but wasn't ready for company. I had never met Chloe and felt under pressure before they arrived. What were her expectations?

It was a wet and windy Christmas eve, and the light had faded when they drove up. Chloe rushed in with bags of presents, mostly hers, and left the car door wide open. The wind whipped it back and buckled it - how careless could she be? Simon and I attempted to close it but to no avail. I mumbled and ranted when Simon told me he had to go to work on Christmas morning.

"You can't drive out in that; it's not safe. You'll have to park against the hedge out of the wind. I don't know what we're going to do."

I could see Simon was worried, but he said, "I better go see how Chloe is. She was upset because you snapped at her. She didn't do it on purpose."

After pacing the room, I knew I would have to drive Simon the 80-mile round trip, so he could get to work. But I needed petrol. So, at 6 pm on Christmas eve, I drove around for an hour but everywhere had closed.

When I returned, Simon asked, "Do you have anything to eat? We're both starving."

"What do you think I've been doing? I didn't choose to drive the streets to get petrol. I had enough to go to gran and grandad's tomorrow but not to take you into work. Couldn't you have found something to eat, now I have to prepare something. I'm bloody knackered."

My guardian angel must have been listening in. On Christmas morning, Simon received a phone call. When he hung up, he said, "Mam, I don't have to go to work; they have enough staff. Isn't that lucky?"

"Well, at least we don't have to worry about that. Just focus on our Christmas dinner. Happy Christmas, by the way!"

Chloe had invaded my newly acquired space. At every turn, she was in my seat or leaving cups around. The warm welcome and motherly fuss were in scant supply. Within a few days, I changed into a rhino. I stamped and snorted around the house. Lo, behold anyone who got in my way.

The future looked grim. My house guests brought with them the harsh reality of the challenges I had taken on. Concerned, Simon listened to my rants but was out of his depth. He thought it was best to take his girlfriend back to their digs to let me sort out my mess.

Something inside keeps me moving on.
Driving down dark alleys, around sharp bends,
then long, straight roads.
Each destination shines bright,
then is obscured from sight.
I stop periodically at resting places and interesting sites.
Pleasant interludes that are pivotal.
They offer glimmers of light.
Each moment of enlightenment reveals a new part of me.
My nervous system fires and flickers.
Charging hidden potential.

So it was. The decade of my forties brought moments of darkness and then glimmers of light. I continued with private therapy and teaching work. I also worked part-time for organizations such as Women's Aid, Mind, and Social Services. When work went quiet, I teetered towards becoming a silent recluse at my cliffside home. There, I enjoyed early morning walks and pottering in my garden.

In the winter, it was a different story. As I wrapped up in several layers, the wind howled through the cracks in doors and walls. My only companion was a mouse. It took a regular path from the front door to the back of the house. It sneaked between my feet as I rested by the fireside.

I prayed for daylight as the gales wrapped a whirlwind of fear around the house. My fears took me down a path of destruction to join forces with the elements. Bundled up in my layers, I hid under the duvet on the camp bed I had set up in the back room. The kitchen with an open fire and the attached downstairs bathroom was my living room, dining area, and even bedroom on stormy nights. I curled up in the fetal position begging for mercy. Every time a gust blasted the house, my heart pounded back. The beat in my ears failed to disguise the sounds from outside, even with industrial earplugs. My mouth dried, and my lips stuck together. Then I needed the bathroom. So, I dashed into the cold past the dancing shadows while sidestepping spiders and beetles.

As I battled for control of my sanity, I imagined the house and car lifted in a tornado and deposited on the rocks below. Or, roof tiles were strewn around, and the car was on its side.

"Why did I choose to live here?" I muttered to myself as I paced up and down.

I never settled for more than thirty minutes at a time on windy nights, only ever managing to sleep when dawn approached. Each gust sent me checking - looking out of windows or dashing to the bathroom, then hiding again. I attempted deep breathing to calm myself, but the next gust brought another wave of adrenalin, and my feet were out of bed. I lived in fear of destruction. Instead, every morning after a storm, only branches were lying around. The worst that happened was when I saw a bush uplifted, like a sagebrush in the desert.

The reassurances I gave myself worked in daylight, but my fears resurfaced in the dead of night. "Maybe this time, the cliff will collapse."

I wondered if my fears were wishful thinking - to take

Oon'ch-illia

my life when I was too cowardly to jump off the cliff.

I celebrated my 40th with a new friend, Chris. After enjoying a lovely meal in a local restaurant, I invited him to stay for the night. I banked up the fire, lit candles, and filled our wine glasses. Chris then suggested we do some candle gazing. We sat on the floor and gazed into a flame with soft eyes. Immediately, we both felt a breeze waft between us. The flame rose and flickered and nearly went out.

"Did you feel that?" Chris asked. "There's a young girl here...can you see her?"

I watched him scan the room. "No...only the candle flicker," I replied.

"She wants to talk to you...should I tell you what she is saying...she's pretty insistent." He told me.

Then, I sensed her presence and began conversing with her, with Chris as the interpreter.

She said, "Many people will come to you. They need your help to pass to the light. I can help you. They are stuck and need you to move them on."

The cottage I lived in was built around 1730. The farm manager of the clifftop farm originally occupied it. It sits behind a crossroads of farm tracks from the farm to the cliff edge. At 365 feet above sea level, the fields rise above the cottage towards Hob Hill, the highest cliff rise. The path descends in the opposite direction through the fields towards the old Victorian town of Saltburn-by-the-Sea.

The cliffs once housed a Roman signaling station. Its watchtowers protected locals against the threat of Anglo-Saxon raids until the invaders overran it in the fourth century A.D.

So many people have lost their lives over the cliff edge throughout the centuries through murder, accident, and suicide. There are still a few reported each year, usually suicides. Two boys lost their lives when taking selfies on an unstable part of the cliff. A recovered mobile phone provided the evidence.

Cathryn Mahoney

I was hesitant about what the young girl had asked of me. I closed my eyes and tuned in. As soon as I did, I sensed pain in my chest. Then I felt the presence of a middle-aged man. He was holding his chest. I knew he was dying of a heart attack.

I visualized a white light around the man and said aloud, "your loved ones are waiting; see the angel of light approach. They are here to take you into the light. You are safe and free now."

I watched the man walk toward the light, then took a deep breath to ground myself.

Chris said, "The little girl says you did well. Can you help a few more people? They, too, are ready to go into the light. They have been trapped for a long time."

For, what must have been forty minutes but felt like hours, the people came thick and fast. One after another, I helped them pass into the light. Briefly, I sensed the health condition that took them and felt their pain and shock. I wrapped them in my light and sent them on their way. Most smiled. Others looked surprised or dazzled. Yet, I could sense relief and release from all of them. But then, our visitor said: "You must stop now and rest."

We moved into the kitchen for a hot drink. It wasn't long before Chris suggested we gaze into the flames of the open fire. We both felt a full sensory charge. I could smell my grandad's pipe smoke, hear clear voices, and see vivid images in the flames. Chris saw people from his past and appeared to be drawn to a particular energy. At this point, there was one man who kept close to me. I can still describe him. He was a professional man in his sixties, well dressed and with a calm of authority about him. I sensed he was a mathematician or scientist and had a lot to teach me. He was balding and wore round glasses. I placed him to be from the late 1800s. I sensed he was my spirit guide and was there to magnify my light.

Darkness descends over Chris. His eyes scan images and then pulls sensations inwards. A flash of anger ignites within him. It has been repressed for too long. There's a

87

presence that longs for revenge. I look into his eyes and feel overwhelmed by the strength of the darkness. My spirit guide stands behind me. I'm illuminated as if an overhead 100-watt light bulb has been switched on. Chris gasps and says:

"Your light is blinding me...stand by the wall, and I'll describe it to you."

As I do, my light pulses and fills the room. For now, it stops the darkness in its tracks or at least subdues it. Chris seems content. His excitement about seeing the power of my light has overshadowed the darkness he attracted. The evil presence has disappeared, but where does it lurk?

"I think we need some rest. Good night, Chris," I said hastily as he retired to his room. There was this sudden need to think and create space between us.

The next morning Chris said, "I had the best night's sleep ever."

"That's good. I'm pleased you slept well. I was restless after all that excitement last night." I replied.

In fact, I never slept. Instead, I remained hyper-alert, fearful that the darkness he had brought into my home would swallow me. The time to drive Chris home couldn't have come any sooner.

I visited Chris at his own home twice more after that. He seemed content with a sort of newfound power, and I couldn't maintain eye contact. I could see the darkness lurking within him. How could I be in the company of someone who attracted the dark ones? It was too risky, so I turned away. As I put on my coat to leave, he showed me a picture of a teenage boy.

"I really fancy him. I prefer younger ones," he said.

I looked at the innocent face in the picture and nearly gagged. I should have challenged him; perhaps I did. But, I only remember my haste in walking away. Later, I fell into my natural pattern. I allowed distance to grow and time to take care of matters.

Cathryn Mahoney

For several weeks I was more open to seeing spirit people everywhere I went. The young girl stayed with me as a companion and guide. I talked openly to her when I drove to work and back. One time I soaked in the bath with the door open. I could see spirit people queued up outside the back door.

I shouted, "go away, leave me alone."

I believe my companion shooed them away. Then, I began having a repetitive dream and worried it would come true. I didn't want any premonitions. Perhaps, I was going mad. I wanted to put a stop to it, and someone must have been listening. My little friend disappeared, and I didn't see any more dead people. Perhaps it was my spirit guide who had acted on my behalf. I sensed my higher senses were blocked for my protection, and the brief 'awakening' was a little nudge. It was a taster of what could be, and I cherished the experience.

Oon'ch-illia

16

Re-kindled Love

How many times had he declared his love for me? It hurt so much the distance and the separations. The pull to be together was so strong. Our meetings were brief, stolen hours that passed too soon. I was always waiting; he was always late. Often, I sat in my car and wondered if he would turn up or had changed his mind.

My thoughts whirred. *"What the fuck am I doing here waiting for you once again...I shouldn't be here. What am I thinking of? No good will come of it."* I berated myself, then saw him, harassed and eager to see me.

As soon as his arms encircled me, elation took away doubt. My worries turned into willow wisps.

"This is belonging – I know it to be true," I told myself as I focused on the precious moments together. Our love remained strong despite everything that kept us apart – we had to make do with the stolen hours.

Lunch, a drive, a walk hand in hand, sometimes more. We soon filled our brief hours talking about our wishes and dreams. We both reveled in the simple things we shared. Mike's jokes and funny stories always lightened the mood. I remember the touch of his lips and fingers, looking for comfort, re-connecting of body, mind, and soul. We longed for the freedom to express our love to the world without the companions of heaviness and despair that accompanied our secret assignations. We continued to reassure each other that - our love would always burn strong.

After several years of infrequent contact, we had a reunion in the summer of 2001. It was the first time Mike was able to turn up at my door. Looking back, I realize it was the same year as my 40th birthday.

Significant events seem to happen every decade.

Cathryn Mahoney

I was hopeful that Mike's visit to my home signified the beginning of our relationship. I paced the rooms waiting for him to arrive, I pushed doubt to one side. He chose to travel a long way to spend just one day with me, but would I be able to let him leave?

We shared sweet memories as we walked the cliff path among wheat fields of poppies that bobbed recognition in the breeze. Mike reminded me of another time we laid together among hundreds of my favorite flowers, hidden from sight. I stopped him so we could admire the view. Hand in hand, we stood, transfixed by the aquamarine sea, and the breeze captured our essence; our signature tune entwined with the land. Mike caught the image of the backdrop of white caps dazzled by playful sunbeams, a moment for prosperity.

I pointed to the trig point on Huntcliff, "I've sat up there at five in the morning...on a sunrise walk. It was glorious."

Then I confessed, "I've dared myself to jump on the days I felt lost...I've walked this cliff path...and looked over...then wondered, what if I end it now?"

Mike blanched. I reassured him, "they were daft thoughts that soon flitted away."

Secretly, I knew those cliffs had seen the end of one of my previous lives. Sometimes, I wondered if my times of darkness would lead to madness, and I would choose to end my pain.

The mood lightened when Mike took my hand and ran. We skipped and squealed like children down to the bay. Kicking our shoes off, with sand and pebbles between our toes, we splashed into the waves. We banished anguish; only joy survived.

We retired to eat at the local smugglers' watering hole, but, as always, we wanted to be alone. After a rushed lunch, we followed the stony path back up the cliff, so keen for the privacy of my home. Holding one another tight, we wished away the sad goodbyes. Time together was precious. To be in one another's arms in silence.

Oon'ch-illia

Whispering the things, we longed to do if time would allow. We avoided leaving the sitting room. He may have stayed if I had taken his hand towards the bedroom. I knew he was torn. The inevitable separation could not be avoided, even if we tried.

He promised, "in time, things will change."

I felt doubt in his voice, so I acted nonchalantly.

"Let's just enjoy what we've got," I said, knowing that was all we could ask for, even though it broke my heart. Of course, I did want to beg him to stay.

All I could say was, "okay," when he announced it was time to depart.

"I really must go now...it's a long journey ahead...and the rush hour...I promised...the kids...to see them before bed." He told me between kisses.

We clung together, then I pushed him away when he said, "I promise...I won't leave it so long next time."

"Don't make promises," I asked. Pasting on a smile, I waved him off. Little pieces of me broke away. My heart was whipped away as a silent passenger. It sought refuge within his car. I wasn't just saying goodbye to him, but also to my heart.

An empty shell wandered from room to room until I knew he was safely home. Tears soaked my skin. I wanted to wail, but that wasn't my thing. I had to accept he was really gone. Life must resume as it was before. A solitary figure within a clifftop home. Miss Independent, with only myself for company. I pottered out into the evening sun. Absorbed in de-heading roses and watering to fill time and empty spaces.

Communication grew sparse. Mike's promise was not realized. His messages appeased.

I listened to the devil on my shoulder, *"he was using you...he doesn't really care – he'll never leave them...you don't figure in his life at all!"* I began to believe that to be true. I had to take control, to abandon my love for him. To reclaim my heart and mind.

His explanations were excuses in my hardened mind.

Cathryn Mahoney

"My family needs me...my wife was car-jacked...can't cope alone...I just can't...would be unfair...to leave the children with her...even for a day. They need me."

What to say? "I understand. I'm sorry to hear that."

Our next communication was a year later.

"I've been unwell and getting tests. Haven't been able to travel. Don't want you seeing me like this anyway." It seemed like another lame excuse.

"I love you...I want to take care of you," I told him.

Too many reasons. His health, his family, and then work got in the way of even talking to each other. My compassion waned. It could not replace how bereft I felt.

I shouted, "what about me – I'm totally alone – I'm not coping either – life is shite."

It was only the wind that heard my words. I wouldn't confess them to Mike. A friend told me to let him go, to use a releasing ritual. So I burnt letters and photographs and bagged the ashes up. Then I walked to our favorite spot overlooking the sea.

I shouted out into the breeze: "You are gone now - you cannot break my heart ever again."

I imagined Mike floating in the waves. It wasn't me who had jumped that day. Memories of our special times were exiled to an eerie grave where many tortured souls had gone. Yet, some memories I chose to hold tight.

A small part of me knew I would open my heart if Mike appeared along the track. That never happened. The days became weeks, and the weeks turned into months, which turned into years. In time, I convinced myself I'd let him go, but my soul knew otherwise, and my intuition kept the ember alight.

17

Remembrance

It was a favorite place we headed to. A walk along a hillside with a bird's eye view of our town below. A place I wished to take flight from. To lift my wings and soar in the thermals like the paragliders, a mix of blue, red, and yellow sails.

Many times, have I dreamed- a flap of my arms morphs into the wings of a graceful swan flying across the surface of a lake.

I had felt the physical presence of wings during an angel workshop. A deep pressure in my shoulder blades as I flexed them for what seemed like the first time - a conscious memory of having wings. Then, I fell into a dream state and collapsed onto the floor in the middle of a group meditation session. Wings of a white dove that, within a single breath, were those of Archangel Ariel, then the Goddess, Isis. All three merged into one.

My feet stayed firm, planted on the cliffside, unlike my Mam's. We scattered her ashes within a fissure caused by an earthquake perhaps thousands of years ago. Now, it is a spectacular rush of water in wintertime. During summertime, it is a babbling brook hidden by overgrown bracken and heather.

For me, it was a sacred, ancient place and an overlook toward familiar land. I didn't know it then, but it offered a view of my first marital home with Mike. A temporary place where we would wait patiently for our together home – a healing retreat – where our ashes would be scattered within the grounds.

Several months after we had scattered my Mam's ashes, I returned with Beth to remember happier family times. After our walk, we went for lunch at the on-site café built into the hillside. This had been a favorite place of Mam's, especially when she could not walk and take in the view. At least she could sit outside, warm herself in the sun, and overhear the adventures of walkers, cyclists, and paragliders.

While we sat reminiscing, Beth giggled.

"What are you laughing at?" I asked.

She gazed over her shoulder and giggled again. "Stop tickling me," she said.

I didn't really need to ask, but I did. "Who's tickling you? Grandma, isn't it...I've felt her too."

We both tuned in deeper and could sense her glide between us and kiss us on the head. A warm fuzziness wrapped around us as her arms pulled us in for a hug. We sat there with grins on our faces. The spell was broken by other customers, then we felt conspicuous. Mam saw this as her cue to slip away. Her presence had lifted our hearts, and our mother-daughter time was enriched.

As I sink into my repetitive dream, I effortlessly shift from a walk to a hover above the ground. My arms scoop forwards through the air. Then, whoosh, giant wings scoop me up several inches, and the pain within my muscles and tendons is gone. With each whoosh, I rise higher, hover, and glide like a hawk, my eyes scanning for prey - for a soul seeking guidance, a gentle touch, or a word of encouragement. For them, magic may be at play, but for me, my truest essence is a simple, soothing touch. My joy is in being, to experience the effortless motion. Yet, I never lose the awe. As if I have just discovered my ability to fly every single time. It's like being born again, without knowledge of all the other times I've existed on earth.

When I wake from such a dream, I sense that if I scoop the air with my arms, I will be inches above the ground. Then I imagine gliding effortlessly from place to place, an observer of life. It feels so real. No wonder, as a child, I stood at my window contemplating flight. I dug deep to find the courage to step onto the window frame.

"Perhaps, I won't fall to my death, but really, really, fly," I told myself. I never put it to the test.

Oon'ch-illia

During one of my hypnotherapy training courses, I came across a fellow student with amazing powers. He could hypnotize with eye contact. One evening he led several of us into a trance. We all had unique experiences. He struggled to bring me back, but I heard his voice from a distance. It beckoned me. His insistence sent a shock wave into me. My body jumped an inch off the bed, yet I remained in a state of euphoria.

Finally, he asked me, "did you enjoy your journey around the moon...you seem to like it there?"

I couldn't answer. It resonated, but all I remembered was a feeling of deep peace.

My friend Nancy brought him to my home a few months later. He had regressed her to the time of Jesus. She believed there could be a comparable link between her friends, including me. While skeptical, I agreed to the regression. Perhaps, I blocked it because it felt forced. I did regress to the era but did not see or speak to Jesus. My many lifetimes didn't seem to include one then. I have an affinity with Mary Magdalene and have felt her deep love for Jesus, but I believe I connected with her divine feminine energy, not with any human beings at that time.

Over several months, I had spontaneous regressions when I was with Nancy. I felt safe with her because she was an excellent therapist. I worked through themes of fearing men, feeling betrayed, and being ostracised. In one of the regressions, I was a young girl who had jumped off the cliff at Saltburn. I had run away from a man who threatened to hurt me. In another session, I was a warrior stabbed in the back by a comrade. I continued through some similar scenes related to that. It helped me to make sense of my trust issues.

My comprehension of feeling ostracised came about unexpectedly. For many of my adult years, I felt a sensation across my right wrist as if I had slashed it. I discovered an attempt to take my own life had proven successful in another life when my tribe had ostracised me. My crime was carrying the child of another woman's man. I gave birth in the desert but couldn't feed my child or myself. I suffocated the child and then killed myself. After the regression, the sensation in my wrist had gone. It has never returned.

Awareness of my true nature has grown over the years through sensory recall. I began to experience a constant buzz in my ears. Just as you may tune the car radio to pick up your favorite channel, I was tuning in to different frequencies. It became more acute when spending time around my feathered friends in a dream state.

In harmony with the buzz within my head, the birds raise their vibration. We meet at a crossroads of mutual appreciation. They signal their intent, then silence. As I focus in, they watch and wait. The buzz intensifies and then stops. Did I imagine the secondary sound? The high pitch signaled sudden movement. It seemed to emit out of my right ear.

They flock, within arm's reach, and then fly off in all directions. Within the stillness, my heartbeat sings, "fly free – sing loud."

Muscles tense as thoughts crash my desire. I scrape my self-belief across the ground. My instinct to fly free with the birds and sing loud has been squashed. Don't be stupid; you can't fly. Your dreams are not reality. Those times the air held you within the gentle breeze, and when the stars flashed past, and the moon was only a touch away, the skies turned purple and red when you were suspended in space. That was a pleasant dream.

Whoosh, I fall hard back into an awkward, heavy body. The mist of dread descends as the incessant mind chatter returns. So, unlike the birds, who squabble like children, with a moment to fight over, then silence.

Where had I gone? The human steps back indoors after a moment lost in reverie. Or had I become at one with my feathered friends?

18

Restoration

Sally called my name. I followed her out of the waiting area towards her small therapy room on the second floor. My guts twisted as I sat. Would I reveal more to her today? We had been getting acquainted, but I sensed the time had come to delve deep. She knew I liked to be in control, so she had taken it slow. I confessed I had given other therapists a hard time, with my need to be one step ahead.

Something must have prompted Sally to ask about my relationship with my dad. I took her cue to speak,

"I always got things wrong; I was accident-prone. Like when I dropped my drink, he boxed..."

Sally stopped me mid-sentence. "He did what?"

I wondered for a moment what she had referred to. Had I even said anything? I looked at my lap and then repeated myself.

"He boxed my ears." When I looked up, her lips were pursed, and her eyes glistened.

"I can't remember what happened. I saw the mess on the floor, then my ear hurt, and I cried," I said.

Sally did not speak, so I followed up with, "well, I must have deserved it, mustn't I?"

"I really can't understand why you would have...Do you think that is acceptable behavior for a parent?" she asked.

I shrugged my shoulders and had no idea what to say next. "He didn't do it that often," was all I could say.

"If you saw him do that to another child, how would you feel?" she asked.

She seemed upset for me, at least for the younger me. I absorbed this turn of events. But then, I wanted to make excuses for him but knew it was futile. She wasn't having any of it; she could see right through me.

"Have you had problems with your ears?" Sally asked.

"I guess I have a few times, but that could have been ear infections." As I said it, I thought about the irregular noise in my ears.

That session was a turning point when I woke up to the actuality of my early years. I could finally express to another person the messages my body had revealed. Sally had a nurturing approach and enabled me to be the child again.

She understood when I said, "I felt like a sponge who took everyone's "shite" and absorbed it all. I had felt guilty for just existing."

She opened my eyes to the belief I'd carried that I was a naughty child who deserved such punishment, and everything bad that had happened was my fault.

I felt safe with Sally to let my younger self continue to speak. My heart quickened a beat and then another. The words were on the tip of my tongue, and then I spat them out.

"There's something else..." I confessed.

Sally asked me to carry on. "It's big ... I don't know where to start," I stuttered.

"Time is getting short; do you feel you could tell me next week when we have the full hour?" She asked.

My stomach did a free-fall dive. I would have to park it deep inside for another week. There was every chance I would lose the courage and avoid the subject once again, but I knew she was right.

It had taken me months to commit to therapy. I had tried to push down the darkness that seeped through my bones, made my skin crawl, and kept me awake at night. The unusual body sensations, nausea, headaches, and constant restlessness had me pacing the rooms of my little house. I later learned they were symptoms of Post-Traumatic Stress and had begun to tip me over the edge. I grew concerned about my ability to help my clients. How could I when I was going through similar issues?

Oon'ch-illia

Six months previous, I had traveled to the Isle of Skye for a mid-week break, a journey of nine hours each way. I spent the first Anniversary of my Mam's death alone on a private retreat. It was a well-deserved luxury, but at times it was torturous. With nowhere to hide, the grief attempted to swallow me whole and spit my guts out. I drove and walked to keep my body and mind focused. To escape the incessant playback that plagued me every day. I attended a cranial osteopathy session.

The practitioner asked many questions, particularly, "Have you ever had whiplash or any problems with your ears?"

"No, I've never had whiplash," I replied as a distant memory popped into my mind, then disappeared again.

I told him, "I had ear infections as a child."

I felt much better afterward and did the exercises he suggested; then, I explored the island again. One positive thing I achieved was writing and sending letters to my children. I told them how proud I was of them, just as my Mam would have done. I had planned they would receive the letters on their gran's Anniversary the following day. I arrived home that next day to attend a family gathering and was pleased my children had received their letters.

A week later, I received a phone call from my dad, and somehow his voice triggered a memory so deep and scary that I was floored. The nightmare began from that day on.

I drew images that came to my mind. Then I scribbled words that did not compute in my brain. I hid them away. During the nights that followed, I filled many pages. My subconscious mind spoke desperately to me, but I didn't want to accept what it said.

I responded, *"it's your imagination; you're making it up."* But the drawings and words continued to express all I saw and felt during the dead hours of the night.

Was I mad? Doubt instigated a tentative discussion with my Clinical Supervisor. We agreed I would explore therapy options. By this point, I knew there was no other choice. I felt adrift, concerned my work would suffer. My family knew something was wrong. They asked awkward questions, so I withdrew even more. I led them to believe it was menopausal symptoms that had turned me odd. Finally, I could no longer keep up any pretense.

My next therapy session approached. Waves of panic overwhelmed me, but I respected Sally and couldn't stand her up. On hearing my name, I almost ran. Instead, my footsteps got stuck in treacle as I climbed the stairs. I was unable to look at Sally. Instead, I stared at a speck of fluff on the floor and tried to shrink within it.

"How are you?" she asked.

"Okay" was all I could say.

"You seem nervous...is it because of what we are going to talk about today?" Sally inquired.

"I'm not sure now...perhaps another time," I offered.

I don't know what happened then. Sally must have recapped from the previous session. I was on the floor as tight as a tennis ball. Then, by some magic, cushions and a blanket appeared.

I try to disappear into the corner of the wall. I creep and whimper, and my arms and legs entwine tighter around my body and head.

"Go away...leave me alone," I beg.

Hesitant, I peep out.

Sally asks, "how are you doing...would you like to lie on the cushions and wrap yourself in the blanket?" She then backs off.

I sidle closer, and she wraps the blanket around me.

"There now...you're safe here with me," she croons. Sally backs off again as I tighten up and attempt to merge with the cushions.

"Can you tell me what is happening?" Sally asks. My legs twitch, ready to run, but instead, I retreat further. I sob and gulp the air around me. Words fail me. I feel so small, and Sally senses that.

"How's little Cathryn doing?" She asks.

"Don't know?" I reply. I begin to rock and try to sleep.

Oon'ch-illia

She leaves me with an occasional word of comfort and reassures me that I am safe.

I sense time passes by. My adult self comes to the rescue. I raise my head and test the water with a tentative "Is my time up now?"

"It's okay, we have a bit longer yet...but do you feel ready to sit back on the chair," Sally asks.

I know this is the cue to bring things to some conclusion. My face feels hot, so I avert my eyes. Sally reassures me about confidentiality and offers me time alone in another room before I go home. I then realize my face is wet, and my body shakes.

"We do not have to talk about it...but I know something significant has just happened," Sally says to acknowledge the gravity of the situation.

I nod my head in agreement with Sally, who then asks: "do you know how old you were?"

"3 or 4," I hazard at a guess. "Someone was going to hurt me."

The adrenaline pulsed through my veins. I needed to move, to let it go. Sally did a grounding exercise with me and then got me a cup of tea. I sat in the adjacent room as she went for her next client. I heard their murmurs through the wall and felt like an intruder. It was time to go. I did as Sally suggested and took deep breaths when my body hit the air. Distracted, I drove home. Then managed to avoid any awkward questions from Beth.

"I've got a migraine; I'm off to bed," I told her as soon as I walked through the door.

The next session followed days of restlessness, with more writing and drawing to give voice to the sensations of my younger self. I noticed a pattern in my scribbling. Sally asked me to bring them to continuing sessions so we could explore them together. We began to build the pieces of the jigsaw.

On each revelation, I then questioned it and told Sally, "That can't be true."

She encouraged me to see what stared me in the face. She was a skillful mirror to my subconscious mind that lay bare in front of her. My younger self started to trust my adult self and allowed words to form. Sally took me to the playroom. I used small figures in a sand tray to depict scenes from my childhood. I expressed shards of memory and the pain locked in my body. One figure attacked another, and then a third figure came to help. It helped me make sense of the drawings and sensations in my body. Repressed anger began to express itself. As the words flowed, the tone grew louder and more insistent the more courageous I felt.

I shouted: "Go Away...Stop it...Leave me Alone!"

The male figure in the sand threatened to hurt the little girl, but she stood up for herself. I found my voice.

It took a long time to even believe it myself. The conflict inside tore me apart. I continued with my therapy but also had cellular healing sessions with David, who had come highly recommended by my friend, Nancy. It helped release the uncomfortable body sensations that expressed themselves in jerking movements. My legs kicked out, and my skin tingled. Healing was gradual until the pain and the associated blockages to memories held tight within me were acknowledged.

A pivotal moment was halfway through one of my healing sessions. An aura of pure white light merged with David. I sensed it was my mother's energy. He confirmed that was true. Maternal love filled the room. The healing was profound and peaceful.

Suddenly, David said, "Your Mam has asked me to say these words to you: **I believe you.**"

Those were the words I needed to hear, and the floodgates opened. The patches of stickiness within my aura dissipated in an instant. I felt free of the self-imposed prison. The one I had forced myself to return to, day after day. If Mam believed me, then I hadn't made it up. It was time to believe in myself.

Oon'ch-illia

In the last few years of her life, Mam had been a Reiki healer, despite the agony of Arthritis and Osteoporosis. She always cared for others and never asked for anything for herself.

I tried to tell her about Josh a few years before she passed away.

"Mam, I need to tell you something...it happened to me when I was younger...I was made to do something...I didn't like it."

Her response shocked me. Her sadness was palpable. Without asking who did what, she had surmised it was inappropriate sexual activity and then asked, "It wasn't your dad, was it?"

I felt so awkward. He had gone for a walk. "Of course, not ... why would you ask that?" I said as I heard my dad come through the front door.

The conversation rattled around inside me. She hadn't expanded on it but was pleased it wasn't dad.

A few weeks later, I thought I would test the water by also telling my dad about Josh. It was his family, after all, and they no longer talked, but I had no idea why.

I said, "You know when we used to go to Aunt Joan's, and I went with Josh? He made me touch him, you know, down there," I gestured with my head.

"It happens with some families, you know, in certain cultures," was all he said.

"What? Well, it shouldn't have happened in ours," I just shook my head, stunned.

"Well, why didn't you say something? We didn't know, did we?" he asked rhetorically, then changed the subject.

I couldn't believe what I had heard, so I got up to make some tea.

From that moment on, things didn't sit right with me. Over the next few months, questions about my childhood bubbled up.

Finally, one day I asked my parents, "why are there no family photos when I was between the ages of four and my teens?"

"We didn't take any...didn't have a decent camera," was my dad's brusque reply.

On a New Zealand tour with my parents, an aunt, and her friend, I was chosen as the designated driver and 'dogsbody.' The rebellious teenager within me reared her ugly head. I had a stand-up verbal fight with my dad. I cannot recall the words, but it stopped when Mam got upset. I then challenged her for being so passive with my dad.

"Why do you let him bully you, and you still protect him? You should stand up to him and stand up for me too!"

I supported women and children through domestic violence and abuse. Yet, it had taken a long time to find the courage to challenge behavior within my own home when I was married and longer-term with my parents. Looking back, I realize the argument with dad and then Mam helped release the suppressed memories. After Mam passed away, I was free to express the truth.

I'm always grateful that I made peace with her in her final weeks. We had talked through the New Zealand trip and reached a mutual understanding. Post-death, I could release any pent-up anger during my therapy sessions. I knew without a doubt that Mam watched and listened. She guided me to see things in a new light. Her presence at the healing session confirmed all I knew to be true.

Oon'ch-illia

19

Reunited

My call to Mike on the 2nd Anniversary of Mam's death took place on June 23rd, 2010. It remains etched in my memory bank. Such a glorious midsummer's day as I walked along the cliff. We talked for an hour until I met the crowds on Scarborough's North Bay and sat upon the sand among the families' building sandcastles.

I looked out to sea and reminisced, still hearing Mike's voice in my head. *"Remember me,"* he'd said.

A touchpaper set fire to my insides as the memories flooded back. I was desperate for love and compassion, understanding and support; that is why I had reached out tentatively to Mike. I soon found he was just as hungry for my contact; his time of waiting and searching had ended.

Regular phone contact began, in addition to the reams of emails. Then Mike said he was staying in Scarborough for a few nights in July. He often planned time away from his chaotic family life so that he could complete work projects.

"But, why Scarborough?" I asked him.

"Why do you think? So, I can feel close to you," he said.

I knew I had to go see him. Scarborough was only 90 minutes away, somewhere I had often taken the children for a day trip. So, we planned our meeting, and I booked a day out of work. I sailed up and down the hills rather than drove as my lightness lifted the car. However, when I parked up along the promenade, I panicked.

"What am I doing? So many years have passed us by. What if we are too different now?" I mused.

Despite having second thoughts, I strode towards our designated meeting place. On the opposite side of the bridge, I saw Mike stroll towards me. I imagined myself in the likeness of Micky Mouse when he fell in love, and his heart bounced out of his chest. My mouth went dry, so I breathed in the ozone to steady myself. Then we were face to face. I portrayed nonchalance and babbled some nonsense about my journey. Mike said, "I'm nervous but so happy to see you again. Come here." He wrapped me in a bear hug and kissed me on the forehead. I had arrived back home.

We spent a lovely but awkward day together. Then, I went back to Mike's hotel room for a drink before I set off for home. I kept my distance and announced, "I only want to be friends, nothing more. You are still married and have your work and clients; I also have mine. So let's not complicate things."

Mike simply nodded in agreement and then walked me to my car. After giving him a peck on the cheek and a promise I would keep in touch, I got in the car. My body felt heavy, so I focused on starting the engine and staying upbeat. Then, Mike kneeled, reached through the open window, and kissed me hard on the lips.

I melted into his kiss and thought, *this is what I've been missing; it feels so right. I can't just be friends.*

We looked deep into each other's eyes; words weren't needed.

"Let me know when you're back home," Mike said as he waved me off.

We met again at another hotel near Scarborough only a month later. I drove to meet him after work and stayed over, returning to work the following morning. Then, we arranged to meet at the same hotel six weeks later. It had begun.

The day that Mike arranged a weekend visit to my home was an event that I never imagined would happen. I had a brief panic when I recalled the time, I waited for him at my little cliffside cottage almost ten years ago. When he never returned, I had ripped and burned his letters and released the ashes into the wind.

Oon'ch-illia

"Oh no! what am I doing – am I setting myself up for heartache?" I thought. My friends' warnings blared like foghorns in my head. They didn't want to see me hurt.

When Mike arrived, I was in a state of shock. He had done as promised - driven cross country to spend a weekend with me at the bungalow I had moved into. I had a meal waiting, and we stayed up talking most of the night. We cuddled up in bed till lunchtime, followed by an afternoon walk and a film night. Yet, the long goodbye the following day was a wrench for us both.

Mike's hidden love notes left their mark and kept the flame of hope alive. He promised to return in a fortnight and said it would be a regular occurrence, but it seemed too good to be true. Yet, on alternate weekends he arrived, sometimes late at night after a day's work, and once, he surprised me by arriving for breakfast. One of our favorite songs is *"I drove all night"* by Cyndi Lauper. He proved he would do just that to get to me, which he did, when he then drove every weekend during the worst winter we'd had for a decade.

In the Spring of 2011, Mike did three things that proved his commitment to me. Firstly, he asked his wife for a divorce. They had lived separate lives for years, but it seemed easier to stay together. He announced, "do you know that I searched for you and returned to Saltburn a few times, but you had left. I can't lose you. I won't let you go ever again."

Secondly, he booked a Mediterranean cruise for my 50th birthday and, thirdly, invited me to accompany him to the Queen's Garden Party instead of his wife. He was honored for his service to the public with his innovative health solution audio programs.

On the night of my 50th Birthday, April 29th, 2011, I discovered how deep my connection with Mike went, with an event that became etched in my mind. While he slept peacefully, I remained wide awake until the early hours. As the clock ticked by, Mike grew restless and mumbled a few words in a strange language. I thought he was dreaming. His eyes opened, he looked at me, and then he spoke in stilted Old English. The energy around us felt charged. I was certain an angelic presence was in Mike's body.

He introduced himself. It felt peaceful, and I accepted open-heartedly what he said to me:

"You would have named me Michael, but I go by a different name...one difficult for your mouth to sound."

His next words sent me dizzy, "I entered the body of the baby that did not see this world...I drew close to leave my resonance, to remind you of us, your people. It is time to let go of the guilt and sadness you still carry."

My time spent talking to Michael was such a beautiful experience. He brought much love and peace of mind. He reiterated that our deep connection had been reignited. I had carried the life within me for twelve weeks. It had not developed in physical terms but had brought the essence of 'Michael' and the tribe wrapped in that life spark. As I write this, I now realize my deep grief was wrapped up in that spark of recognition of my true family—the sense of loss of enforced separation and the guilt for ending a life.

Michael told me: "You have no idea how deeply I...all of us...love you. You will soon know us as your family. I may not be in body form in this lifetime, but I will still be with you...we will meet many times."

He then told me a bit about his life as a warrior within the tribe. As soon as he left Mike's body, I wondered if he had been Archangel Michael despite all he had said. His energy felt pure.

When Mike woke the following day, I told him about the visit. He had no recollection but said, "You seem lit up...I'm pleased you have been given reassurance and comfort."

Many similar and more surreal experiences began to happen. Often during the early hours, but then any time of day. They soon became a way of life for us.

After our first meeting in 1991, Mike sensed he knew me as soon as he looked into my eyes. He remembers seeing my eyes in his bedroom wallpaper when he was six, around the same time Gemel first appeared to him. Throughout childhood, Mike witnessed death and saw ghosts. He had visions and premonitions, which became a natural part of his life. He presumed everyone saw and dreamed the same way. It was not until his early teens that he discovered this was not the case.

After my first visit from Michael, others in our tribal family asked to visit. We gradually discovered new personalities who had much knowledge to impart. It was a time to trust and expand our minds. But even though they brought much joy, our endurance limits were sometimes tested.

20

Re-awakened

I tossed and turned again while Mike snored beside me. Had I made a huge mistake moving in with him? The constant rumble from the street hummed in my head. My need to pace fought with the desire not to wake anyone within the house. My restless legs were eager to feel the floorboards beneath my feet, but the thought of their creaks and groans held me still and silent.

The battle raged in my head. *"I need to move. I need to get out."*

Then, Mike's breathing shifted, and I held my breath. Finally, a calmness descended and soothed me. I watched Mike for movement and then heard a deep, gentle voice beckon me close.

The light hadn't seeped through the curtains, so I put my face against Mike's and heard the soft tones of the strange, yet familiar language Michael had spoken in. But this voice had a commanding tone. It tingled through my veins. My heart raced, and my stomach lurched as I scrambled for a name and what to say. Then he reached for me - three distinct pats on my head. After a moment, words in my own tongue caressed me. "I love you, my child."

I felt an inner smile from deep within my heart lift me. Then, I lay still while his hands placed colors around my back and head.

"Thank you...I love you too," I replied to the aura of aqua and golden light around Mike's head.

"You are never alone - stay strong, child," he said as his words faded with the golden light that evaporated away.

Mike's breathing quickened, his body twitched, and then he snored.

For a moment, I floated out the window onto a cloud.

Oon'ch-illia

"There's no chance of sleeping now. Who was that?" I whispered into Mike's ear.

Mike's body twitched, then stilled. Another voice, a child's voice, was hesitant. "Old One's been...I can feel his light."

"Is that who it was?" I asked, even though intuitively I knew. Yet hadn't dared hope I was right until I was told so.

"I'm pleased he made contact. You know it's me, don't you?" Jheneeka asked. "I won't stay long...don't want to disturb him," she said of Mike.

It disconcerted but excited me when visits happened while Mike remained oblivious. Occasionally, he had a snatch of a dream but nothing more. When he awoke, I told him the details of who had visited and what had been said.

Initially, Jheneeka visited most regularly. Sneaking in during the early mornings as it was easier when Mike was asleep. After a while, she turned up at random, at any time of the day. Usually, at mealtimes or while Mike and I were out walking.

On one such walk, a slight skip in Mike's step, and a blank' momentary look on his face, signaled an arrival. The subversive glance in my direction alerted me that Jheneeka had entered Mike's body. His outer shell was relaxed, childlike, and feminine. Her speech was soft and hesitant as she stuttered over some words. Jheneeka was excitable. Her chatter was rapid and interchangeable from her own language to ours. As I conversed with the body of Mike, I engaged with my young visitor.

"How are you, mummy? How is daddy?" she asked.

I had given permission to be addressed this way, as that is how she perceived our relationship. So, I welcomed her and told her about our day. She waited for me to stop speaking but fidgeted and twirled on the spot. She had been given the gift of orator for the tribe and was eager to impart some precious wisdom.

"Old One has said I can tell you...you and 'him' (Mike) will do much good work together. He will not have to work the way he does now. You will have a nice home, and people will seek you out. You'll both heal and teach." She beamed at me after her serious speech.

Then, she danced along the pavement, humming to herself, content.

"Jheneeka, remember Mike," I called out, anxious to keep her in check for his sake.

"Sorry, but you must pretend to be Mike; he wouldn't do that. What if someone sees him doing that? He'd be mortified." She was remorseful and fearful.

"Have I put 'him' in danger?" she asked.

I said, "you know he's frightened of making a fool of himself publicly...he doesn't want to be put in a specimen jar."

Jheneeka soon learned to take her job seriously, to protect both Mike and me. She was just a child and, at that time, unworldly of our ways. I needed to stay one step ahead to manage the time for the three of us. And Jheneeka grew wary of someone seeing her. She tuned into Mike's feelings and saw the image in his mind of being stuffed into a specimen jar. I had to remind her that Mike liked to exaggerate for effect, even in his own mind.

My need to keep watch on Jheneeka's actions stilted her evident joy and pleasure. It blocked her spontaneity. My mind was forever in conflict as I scanned the outside world for judgment or harm that could befall both her and Mike. I balanced the needs of Jheneeka with Mike's and my own. I loved our times together, but I struggled to tell her when it was time to leave. The time constraints and balancing act frustrated me.

Jheneeka came to learn about our world and to teach me about hers. I worried that our world would corrupt her. Instead, she learned of the many pitfalls that could influence our lives and hers. Her thirst for learning more continued; it seemed only weeks before she had mastered our language and Mike's mannerisms and speech. She was able to pretend to be him if someone approached.

I wanted to encourage the child she was to be free to express herself openly, but I couldn't. Unlike my child clients, whom I encouraged to express their natural ways, with Jheneeka and the other youngsters that followed in her wake, I had to keep a tight reign. They had to grow up quickly and adopt the roles they had chosen to take. For Jheneeka, it was the gatekeeper and protector of Mike and me. I worried our environment was unforgiving, or was that just my perception of the world from childhood experiences? I felt I had to put limitations on Jheneeka and instill some of our fears in her. But most of the time, she rose above them.

As an aside, Jheneeka taught me that she was a star being in a native child's body. There were time differences too. An hour of our time was equal to several of theirs. Sometimes the time gaps were more significant. It was challenging to compare age and maturity on those scales. Jheneeka translated everything into our time and our language to help me understand. There was so much to learn, but the wisdom her elders imparted was offered in analogies. They insisted on making me work things out for myself.

I was clueless about how Jheneeka and others from the tribe accessed Mike's body. However, I knew Mike had agreed to this, as had members of the tribe. So, it was of mutual benefit to them and the star people. *(This will be explained in more detail in a later chapter!)*

The interactions were stimulating but also took me out of my comfort zone. One day a new presence appeared like a whirling dervish. I was glad Mike's kids were out of the house.

Mike opened his eyes. I sensed a visitor, but it wasn't Jheneeka. Instead, the eyes scanned my face with awe and shock and listened to me speak.

"Hello, who are you?" I asked.

Silence, then the 'presence' ripped the bedsheets off, looked down at Mike's body, gasped, and then giggled. She had noticed she was in a body with a penis. Wide-eyed, she scanned my face and then the whole room. Still, she did not speak and was startled when I did.

I asked, "do you want to look around?" Then, I reached for her hand. She stared at it, but she grabbed hold as I moved off the bed towards the door.

On the landing, I explained to her the objects as we passed. Her hand touched each one. Then, she repeated after me in broken English. "Door," "light switch," as I switched on then off.

In a flash, she was off, down the stairs. Concerned she could dart out the front door into the street, I followed close behind. She stopped dead in front of the hall mirror and giggled at her profile. Then she jumped away and back again, then peered behind the mirror.

"What do you see? Can you see yourself?" I asked, but she ran into the sitting room. There, she touched pictures and ornaments, lifted sofa cushions, switched lights on and off several times, and then twirled on the spot.

A lorry braked hard on the street, and she froze, so I pointed out at the traffic and passers-by. I reassured her they were unable to get in the house. Then, as her initial shock dissipated, she climbed into the window to wave outside.

Then, she ran again. I feared I would see her waving from the other side of the window, so I ran to stop her. She was by the mirror, standing sideways and peering into it, and then she laughed and jumped back.

"Can you see yourself now?" I asked. She nodded and giggled.

The many distractions in the kitchen became her next target: a water tap, more electric switches, and a different window to look through. I then attempted to explain how all the appliances worked, and how we got hot water, gas and electricity. She switched everything on and off while I gave a running commentary to keep her focused and engaged. Her frantic dash around the room made me dizzy, so I diverted her to the conservatory and opened the outside door. That stopped the little minx in her tracks. She smelled the air, breathed it in, and put one foot over the step.

The traffic noise from the street startled her. It seemed loud, even to me. So, she hid behind the sofa cushions. I reassured her, and after a while, she cuddled into me.

"Can you see the birds in the trees...and smell those flowers," I asked as I pointed outside the open door.

I explained to the visitor, "our garden is a safe place if you can ignore the noise on the other side of the house."

She kept cowering, so I closed the door. "It's cold, and Mike is only in his pants. We had better get him back into bed," I said.

After a while, I guided her back upstairs. She peered into all the rooms before I insisted, we return Mike to his warm bed. The reality of this strange new world tumbled around her, so I urged her to return to the tribe.

"You have so much to share with your friends when you get back," I advised.

"Love' ou, White Bird ... Tank 'oo," she said.

"That's okay; I've enjoyed your visit," I replied rather too quickly, but my relief she was leaving passed her by.

As an afterthought, I said: "Hope to see you again."

She was gone. And Mike's eyes closed as he rolled over towards me. I held him as he awakened.

"Is everything okay?" he asked, scrunching his face to stifle a yawn.

He sat up straight, looked at me long and hard, and asked, "what's happened? Who's just been here?" The unknown quality of the visit jangled him.

"I'll let you wake up; I just need to check something," I replied.

I went around to check nothing was disturbed or left on or switched off that I hadn't noticed our visitor touch. I also checked the front door was still locked.

Cathryn Mahoney

The new visitor disorientated me. So, I vowed to share my concerns with Jheneeka on her next visit. I reassured Mike that all was well and explained little of my experience. I left out the bit about him nearly being out in the street in just his pants and barely his dignity.

I grew wary of new visitors since the 'wild child' incident, as I later called it. But then we had random visits when Mike and I spent a few days in London. The first was a warrior who had somehow slipped through. He wanted to meet me, and things got a bit too familiar. I freaked out and called for Jheneeka. The warrior was abruptly dragged away.

A day later, the matriarch of the tribe, Sashma, visited to apologize. It was her first visit. She was timid. I was excited when she explained who she was - the wife of 'Michael,' the first warrior who visited me on my 50th birthday. I showed her the city lights through the large picture window of the hotel bedroom and frightened her when I opened a window - what with the constant noise. She has often reminded me since, with a glint in her eye:

"I'm still in therapy from the trauma of that day."

Jheneeka shared my concerns with Old One about the random unexpected visitors. Her gatekeeper role became official. She set rules for the tribe. No one was allowed to visit me without her say-so. They could only arrive after she and I agreed first. Then they were announced.

After each visit, Jheneeka returned to ask: "Was that okay for you? Did they respect you?"

21

Lessons

A mist blew in from the east and, with it, a brewing wind. Salty tears spread white lace across my exposed skin. The tide turned, crashing the shingle higher up onto the beach, and foam rolled in like a tumbleweed across a prairie. It flipped across the expanse of exposed sand that turned into a mini tornado.

Jheneeka whooped with delight, whereas I turned my back and longed to retreat. Her joy became infectious, and I laughed into the frigid wind as she ran towards the sea, chasing bubbles of light, her senses on overdrive.

It was her first experience of sand whipped up by the wind and the ocean spray so cool and damp. She licked the salt from her lips, mesmerized by the crash of wash against rocks. She stood stock-still as tiny creatures scuttled back with the waves. Then her feet padded with exaggerated steps over shells and seaweed. The elements were wild. They turned an enthralled girl into a screaming banshee. The air snatched her cries and deposited them downwind of a few hardy souls.

I was captivated as Jheneeka ran around in circles. Her untethered display of color dazzled me with a light show of pure joy. Suddenly, she wrapped tight around my torso, thanking me for allowing her such an experience. Anyone watching may have witnessed a man embrace a woman to protect her from the lashing sand. Yet, they could not see Jheneeka, who showered me in pure love.

I felt honored to share and witness this 'first' with Jheneeka. Even though I couldn't be fully present. As the ever-vigilant parent, I remained in control. It was my job to keep Jheneeka in check and temper her excitement for safety's sake and decorum, all at the expense of my own enjoyment.

The fierceness of the dance of the sand sent me in search of shelter, but Jheneeka thought otherwise. She scampered off down the beach. She drew a symbol in the wet sand when I caught up with her in a battle against the wind. I realized she had broken away from her own excitement to teach me something as a reminder that latent knowledge was buried deep within me.

Jheneeka pointed and asked, "Do you know what it is?"

"It looks familiar...is it a symbol for peace or energy?" I muffled with my face zipped within my hood.

"The 'OM' symbol...it's the vibration of the universe." She announced.

Then she explained, "you know the sound...sound it out...go on...louder...I can't hear for the wind...louder."

We intoned together, swaying with the vibration that resonated through our bodies, into the sand, and into the air. It sang within the wind and tingled within the salty spray. I felt a deep connection with the Earth and all life forms.

Looking back, I fully appreciate that it was no accident the elements were electrifying that day. They energized Jheneeka's words and her actions. Moreover, the sensory experience captured through my energetic connection with Jheneeka on that day has intensified since such memories are stored within our light bodies.

I have often felt worried about not remembering such experiences, but now I understand that learning through doing and observing seals the energy within. I have been reassured many times that it is never lost. Each time it is recovered, there is deeper immersion. My memories are stored away as candid snapshots of moments of learning. On many outdoor excursions, the elements played their role. They reignite my synapses to bring forth stored knowledge and wisdom held within the cells of my body and the annals of my soul memory. Archived files are then relocated as 'live' in a more accessible filing cabinet. Ready for me to share with others when appropriate.

Oon'ch-illia

During those early days, Jheneeka was my teacher. She helped me to trust my innate wisdom. Following such lessons, in snatches of time, such as on the windy beach, I would return home to research information I had been given. So, I began collating journal notes. They consisted of the day's story, research, and personal observations.

I had learned from my previous lifetimes that people struggle to take my word for things. But, with modern technology, I could now find snippets of research to back up the knowledge and ancient wisdom my tribe shared with me. And, in time, I began to recall them for myself.

On our beach adventure, I called time on Jheneeka. I reigned in her childlike wonder when she ran ahead.

"We need to get warm; Mike is cold - it's time to go," I urged. The guilt about restricting her enjoyment stabbed me in the chest.

"It's bloody freezing." I stamped out with my feet to get her attention.

I rarely have regrets, but I did on these occasions. I felt like a party pooper. With a heavy heart, I had to keep the three of us safe. Jheneeka was just a child, and Mike was somewhere else while his body was at our mercy. I hated to put a damper on a child's enjoyment, but the time for play was over. We had to navigate the dunes. I imagined them eager to swallow us whole, and the trees beyond were intent on smacking us in the face as we crossed their path.

Jheneeka stepped into her role as gatekeeper and protector. She sensed our fatigue and took my concerns seriously while at the same time giving me some needed perspective. The walk back to the car was difficult, but she gave us some energy to battle the sandblasting and shedding branches. She reassured me when I panicked as darkness descended and the pine trees loomed overhead. She had learned of my fear of the wind during the dark hours. In daylight, I embraced its power.

Cathryn Mahoney

The rain came and lashed us for good measure. Jheneeka was hyper-alert to my labored steps within the quickening mud. I'm sure she sped up time. Before I knew it, we had arrived back at the abandoned car park. Our car invited us into its bosom. Soon we were stripped out of wet clothing and seated with the heat on full blast, with a flask of tea in hand.

Jheneeka checked us over and asked, "Can I come for food?"

We had planned to stop for a meal on our way home.

"You'll have to ask Mike," I told her.

I watched as Mike's eyes closed, and Jheneeka slipped away momentarily. His body was unattended under my watchful gaze.

No sooner than she was gone, Mike's eyes opened, and Jheneeka announced, "Daddy said okay - I can stay...go for food." So, we went to get our fill, as Mike likes to say.

22

Healing Abilities

After I moved from my windblown cliffside cottage to my bungalow, I studied and practiced Angelic Reiki. It seemed the most natural route for me to become a healer, especially since I had connected with the energies of Isis and Archangel Ariel a few years prior. Yet, counseling and teaching work continued to be my mainstay once I moved to Warrington.

I studied various healing modalities and updated my Hypnotherapy and Past Life Regression skills. I combined talking therapies with healing, using crystals, light, and sound. But my forte continued to be inner child therapy and child and family counseling. I believe my practice would have grown on recommendations alone, but I felt pulled back home. With the birth of my grandson, Jack, and longing to be close to the North Yorkshire moors and coast, the pull was too great.

On my return, I began working at a healing center in Saltburn by the Sea, where I offered energy healing and group meditation sessions. But I struggled to advertise my spiritual work and share the experiences and learning Mike and I were having with our tribe.

Then we decided to plan our wedding. At the same time, Jheneeka started telling me about the mountains and lakes around their cave home. The more she piqued my interest, the more information she provided with names and locations of places we may wish to visit. The seed had been sown that we could visit North America for our honeymoon.

23

Transitions

In my room with a view, I witness the texture of new buds on darkened trees. My eyes catch a kingfisher as it dives in a flash of electric blue and orange. Then a long-tailed tit appears. It pecks an insistent sign language at the window: "let me in." I turn towards a glow of amber that hovers by the door.

Mike's now asleep; "how long do I have to leave him this time?" I wonder.

The panic that caused a sudden rush of bile to lodge in my throat has subsided. The amber glow reads my thoughts and draws close to me. I feel his warmth. Another bird tap-taps away. It's letting me know I'm not alone. My restless legs twitch. I turn back to the outside world and lose my thoughts in the flow of the stream.

It's time to check on Mike. I'm sure all is fine. I've heard the creaks and groans of the caravan move under Isame's weight. Our safe pair of hands came to the rescue once again.

Dread still lurks within my shadows, fanning my doubts – what if he isn't okay this time? What if his breathing has finally stopped? How many times can we do this? Be at the mercy of God.

For a while, Mike and I lived between his house in Warrington and our caravan in North Yorkshire. When the house was sold, we lived together in the caravan for a few months until after our wedding in 2017. Then, we moved to a rental property in a nearby town, keeping the caravan for weekend breaks.

One day we were on our way there and decided to stop for lunch. We were both tired, and I was irritable, not sure what I wanted to do that day. An argument ensued before we parked up. For a change, it was me who stormed off.

Oon'ch-illia

After a short while, I returned to the car, but Mike had disappeared. It took several attempts to contact him by phone. When he answered, we agreed to meet at the café. I arrived first and sat at the last vacant table. When Mike came, he appeared disheveled and went straight to the bathroom. When he reappeared, we ordered food, but I noticed his body shaking while he conversed with the waiter. He had cobwebs on his coat. As we ate, I reached for his hand. I could see he was just about holding it together. I let him finish his lunch before I asked where he'd been.

Mike enlightened me: "I was trapped in a building across the street...I thought I'd never escape."

I was intrigued but kept him calm. "Maybe we should talk about it when we get to the caravan," I suggested.

Mike told me the story when we were settled there: "I slipped into another time. The building was derelict; it was above one of the shops. Someone had locked me into a small attic space...I panicked...couldn't breathe, and was trapped for ages... Finally, I barged my way out. The energy there was evil. I thought I'd be stuck there forever."

I asked Dulaa, my new protector, if he could tell us what had happened.

He appeared before us and said to Mike: "Gemel came to help you get out, or you would have been lost there."

He then told us both: "It was a portal. It moves across the area. Many people in other times and some dogs have got lost and have never been seen again. It seems to have returned after some time."

Then he said directly to me about Mike: "His anger and thoughts of harming himself had caused him to slip into the energy vibration of the portal. It had sucked him in, and he was stuck there."

We were advised for a while after that to keep clear of the area. The portal movement was inconsistent, and Mike remained vulnerable. In time, Gemel studied the portal and moved it out to sea. Months later, it vanished.

Cathryn Mahoney

As Mike and I got to know each other, he recounted many stories as a child when he was visited by the tall 'Indian' named Gemel. He could describe him in detail and remembered many aspects of their time together. Gemel often appeared at the foot of Mike's bed and told stories of his life as a warrior.

"You too will be a warrior one day," he announced to Mike, who jumped up and down on his bed excited at the prospect.

Gemel's job was to guide Mike through his childhood and keep him safe, especially from himself. He often got into scrapes as an adventurous and mischievous child. He ventured out at all hours to work with a local farmer and a milkman. When out with his friends, they shot and roasted rabbits and pigeons over an open fire. Sometimes they sifted through a rubbish pile in search of treasure. It was a dangerous pursuit, but they were oblivious.

Later, Mike would realize the health implications. The rubble he shifted through was left there from buildings that had once been a TB hospital and a dismantled American airbase.

Gemel was impressed with Mike's caring attitude and willingness to help people. He always had a smile on his face and a cheery chat. His ambition was to be either a vicar or a clown. He wanted to help those in need, make them laugh, and lift their spirits. Instead, he became a Hypnotherapist.

"I guess I've preached a bit and made them laugh, eventually," Mike once told me after a full day of client sessions.

After hearing about Gemel in Mike's life, I was curious and jealous that I had no such 'special friend.' I certainly didn't have any vivid recollections. Only fleeting feelings and images of the little people and a 'grandma' figure. My strongest memories were of, feeling alone in the world and invisible. I understand now that it was due to the many lifetimes of being insular to protect myself from harmful people that my barriers also prevented me from seeing and hearing those guiding me.

When Gemel first visited, I was delighted. However, I soon discovered he wasn't just Mike's special friend; he was special to me too. He had been the leader of the tribe before Jheneeka, but he was more of an encourager, just like Mike.

Gemel visited me every full moon. His purpose was to remind me of our deep connection. During our chats, I discovered he had rarely been far away from me in this lifetime and most others. I found it difficult to describe the subtle difference I felt with Gemel initially, but as we became reacquainted, I understood what it was. I got a similar feeling of belonging, deep love, and respect, like I did with Old One. A coming home. Each time he merged with Mike; our bond strengthened. I now describe it as a brother vibration, whereas Old One is a father. They had returned to me at the same time when my father and brother in this lifetime ostracised me.

24

Origins

For several months, Jheneeka visited me once a week to tell me my origin story. I discovered my first home planet was called Skilarkia, but it had been destroyed by its own sun. I then learned that my original name was Oon'ch-illia. The tribe calls me White Bird or Eyes in Sky, but ancient ones call me- Oon'ch – my sound resonance, followed by Illia - my personal expression.

Telling my story was challenging for Jheneeka. The information was relayed to her telepathically from Gemel, with the gritty details laid bare. She was afforded little time to digest and translate the words into English in a tangible way. I chronicled her words for hours until my back and head ached. Mike was sent far away from his body, so he was not affected in any way.

The three main characters, who I called *The Other Three Musketeers*: Oon'ch-illia (Me), Tomaz (Mike), and Gemel, travelled with our collective, the Shee'masha'taa People, through galaxies, solar systems, and black holes in a fleet of craft. And through energy systems from one dimension to another.

Various planets became home for short periods, and friendships were formed with their inhabitants and other transient star tribes. Sometimes, we made enemies. One such group stalked us. We had fierce battles with them on several occasions, which resulted in the loss of many lives. But we re-formed with allies who joined us along the way.

Over eons of time travel, we developed new skills and abilities, and our technology became more sophisticated. Our collective kept records of developments, including observations of technology used by our enemies.

Then we discovered the blue and white planet called

Earth. We observed and explored the planet until we integrated with humans within many lifetimes and places.

My journey began in North Yorkshire, England, in 954 AD. I then traveled backward and forwards in time. Then in Egypt, 1480 BC, I merged with Princess Meritaten and Tomaz (Mike) with Prince Niul when they fell ill with the plague. We aided their survival, but they were exiled soon after. We remained with them through their epic journey from Egypt by sea to Europe and finally to Ireland, where a bloody battle with the Tuatha de Danann ended their lives. I share more of this story in Chapter 55 (*Queen of Scots*).

Old One and certain others in our collective arrived at Roanoke Island in 1583. They merged with a local tribe and befriended the first European settlers. Then, they set out on foot on an epic voyage across North America. It was completed when they arrived in the Rocky Mountains of Canada in 1785.

During their travels, they reformed with other tribes, chiefly the Blackfoot. They became involved in battles to instill peace, save lives, and offer healing, knowledge, and wisdom.

As the collective progressed with its mission, they also advanced. Their individual and combined light grew in strength. Some tribes perceived them as gods, and others were fearful of them. They discovered new ways to use the earth and the solar system to shift between times on and off-world and returned with many stories to share.

Jheneeka explained that I had been witness to many historical events. I have lived many lifetimes in Europe, Africa, and North America and journeyed off-world to other planets. Our collective has formed connections with Ancient Star Nations, and they observe our travels with interest. Old One has allied with their leaders; 32 ancients are working together benevolently, helping when they see a great need.

Cathryn Mahoney

I found the story mind-boggling. I imagined writing about characters in a film, not about Mike, Gemel, and myself. If it wasn't for the experiences I'd already had with the tribe, I may have believed my dad, like I did as a child, that I have an overactive imagination. But, as I wrote Jheneeka's words, I knew deep in my heart the stories were real. Vivid images and memories resurfaced. I had to distance myself while writing. I knew if I connected with my emotions, I would come unstuck.

Suddenly, the writing came to a stop. There were still many parts of the jigsaw to piece together, but that was it for now. Jheneeka was sent on a critical mission, and it was months before she returned. Gemel accompanied her on the task, but Old One had to rescue them both from certain death. Their light was almost extinguished, and the native bodies they merged with had remained resting in the village but didn't fare well without their star being companions.

Tribal members who offer to be hosts for the star beings are often close to death or have a health condition. It's rather like being given a golden ticket to have extra time to do good deeds. The hosts always have a choice of how much involvement they have in earthly and off-world activities.

When the star beings returned to the village, Isame placed them in healing chambers for the length of a moon cycle. When they recovered, merging with their human counterparts took further recuperation.

My concern for Jheneeka and Gemel replaced my need to continue writing. After Jheneeka had recuperated from her near-death experience, she struggled to hear more of my origin story. She returned to it briefly, and it was split into two, with the first part focusing on the long, arduous journey that eventually brought us to Earth. The second documented the grueling journey across Africa. Then, by sea into Europe, and across land and sea into Ireland, ultimately ending in the slaughter on Irish soil. So many lives ended in violence, time and again, have been our experience.

The two manuscripts remain incomplete. So instead, I began this book as an introduction to my origins and the journey Mike, Gemel, the tribe, and I have been on together ever since, particularly highlighting my purpose in this current life.

25

Two Become One

Picture the grand country house surrounded by woods and parkland. The perfect wedding venue. When we decided to get married 25 years after our first meeting, it was going to be a quiet affair or while on another cruise, or so we thought.

Our first cruise, a week after my 50th birthday, was our first holiday as a couple. Just a year later, we went on another Mediterranean cruise and dined with a couple who were married on board. They had four friends with them who were their only guests at the ceremony, but they celebrated their nuptials surrounded by thousands of people on the ship.

We were engaged on that cruise and bought my ring onboard. When we first announced our engagement, it was at a family birthday party the day we arrived home. It ended in tears and tantrums when Mike's ex-wife stormed off. His daughters were distraught. Perhaps our timing was a bit off! They thought us selfish, but we were like excited children. Sadly, our exuberance had impeded our judgment. Why on earth would they be happy for us?

Our working life and events in our children's lives pushed wedding plans to the back of our minds. My time was split between Beth with a newborn son and my life with Mike in Warrington, so when a friend suggested we buy the caravan, I convinced Mike it was a good idea. I had felt in the way staying at Beth's house, and Mike was also back and forwards since we had taken on the challenge of several 'spirit quests' in North Yorkshire. So the caravan became our weekend retreat and also a place for grandma bonding. But it wasn't long before it became our home.

Mike rediscovered his past roots in North Yorkshire on our' spirit quest' walks. He had merged with local men as my protector when I worked as a healer, seer, and teacher up on the moors during previous lifetimes. We were drawn to standing stones, streams, and certain trees where we had planted our essence in those other times.

Mike's house was put on the market, and after traveling to and fro for a further three months, he moved into the caravan with me on July 12th 2017. His furniture went into storage, and we adjusted to the cramped space in our first joint home. However, since it was classed as a holiday home, we had to provide proof of permanent residence. We had until the following April to find another home.

Despite that, our wedding plans were in full flow. And our idea of a quiet affair turned into the wedding of the year. We were never married in other lifetimes, so why not? I had usually been the other woman. Or, one of us was off-world while the other had a short life or merged with another human on Earth.

We had been drawn to the grand country house a year before making our wedding plans. It is now the well-established Guisborough Hall Hotel, the former home of Lord and Lady Guisborough, after whom the local town is named. It was our favorite venue for lunch or afternoon tea.

During our visits, Mike often saw a young girl with auburn hair watching us. She appeared around corners, leaning over a terrace above our heads or waving through a leaded window as we drove away. Her confidence grew at each visit.

One day Mike announced, "she's standing beside you, watching you eat."

"Would she like to join us?" I asked.
Mike encouraged the child forward and asked her name.

"I'm Charlotte. This is my home...I live here with my mummy and daddy...have you seen my picture in the other room?"

After our meal, we went into the drawing room.

Mike pointed at the wall of pictures and said, "There she is, and she has the same dress on. Aren't you pretty?" He turned to Charlotte, who smiled and nodded.

We soon learned that Barbara, one of the youngest girls in the tribe, had befriended Charlotte and became a regular visitor at the hall. She encouraged Charlotte to interact with us when we next visited for Sunday lunch. The young lady we first saw was a lively child. We suspected Barbara's influence there. Charlotte chatted as we ate, then became restless. She danced and ran around other people's tables. It unsettled us – our eyes were everywhere. So, Mike called her back and asked if she wanted to step into his body. Her antics had been a ruse.

Mike closed his eyes briefly, and there was a shudder. His eyes opened, and her aura of disbelief and uneasiness hit me.

With a giggle, Charlotte looked around, picked up the cutlery, and asked, "May I?"

She ate with decorum. Barbara had taught her to pretend to be Mike, and I was surprised by how well she impersonated him when the waiter approached with our dessert.

Charlotte relaxed and told me about her family and life in the hall.

"The gardener, Scottie, he's my best friend; I help him when I'm allowed. I don't like my lessons...my governess is stern."

Then she told me. "My home is in France. Daddy sent us here to keep safe."

It didn't seem the right time to ask about that, so I asked, "do other people in the hotel see you?"

"One or two may have, but my mummy insists I stay away. Sometimes in the garden or corridors, I may have been seen."

Charlotte explained she stayed mainly in her own time but stepped in and out. She told me, "Guests sometimes see my grandmother. She is known as the white lady."

Oon'ch-illia

From then on, we got to know more about Charlotte. She became firm friends with Barbara. We are convinced they both encouraged us to get married at Guisborough Hall.

We visited the vicar to set up the wedding date and discuss our intentions for the day.

"That's it; you're in the diary for Friday, September 29th, 2017, at 11am. So where are you having your Wedding Breakfast?" Alice asked.

She was pleased we attended her church since buying the caravan. We were part of the church community. I joined the choir and attended confirmation classes, so it was our natural choice for our marriage ceremony.

"We are thinking of Guisborough Hall. We are going there next," I said automatically, surprising myself with this revelation and hearing Mike's gasp.

As we returned to the car, Mike looked at me and said, "Why not? Let's go there now for lunch."

As we ate, we told Charlotte our news. Her excitement for us was infectious, so we stopped at the reception desk to make an appointment with the Wedding Planner. The following week it was all arranged, and the financial costs hit us full-on.

Mike got swept along in my wake. He had enough to deal with - moving home and concluding therapy work with clients. Then, the stress and dust from packing the house up brought on a bout of Pneumonia.

After a week of rest, the dining area became his office while I focused on the wedding and honeymoon plans. It helped me avoid the reality of our situation while Mike reeled from the new turn of events, too many in a short time. My spontaneity made him dizzy - I had so many ideas for working together as healers and teachers and future travel plans, but Mike's home and work life had been in Warrington. He needed time to settle and adjust to leaving all he knew for the love of one woman. What had he let himself in for? We were both nervous but kept our feelings in check.

Cathryn Mahoney

Significant hiccups rather than disasters affected the wedding plans. Firstly, my maid of honor stepped back from her role and from being a part of my life. Then Mike's son, his best man, heralded the next hurdle to overcome. His wife gave birth prematurely to their daughter the day before our wedding. He and his two sisters arrived early on our wedding day. Mike and I didn't sleep a wink. While Mike waited to congratulate the new dad, I awaited a major disaster.

Before breakfast, I sought Mike out and blustered: "I don't know if I can do this...too many things have gone wrong. What were we thinking of? It's just as I expected. We should be focused on helping our kids...it's their time for weddings and babies...why on earth are we having a big wedding...I don't think I can do this."

Mike went pale, "Don't do this to me...I'm knackered … I wanted to spend time with my son...he's just become a father...for fucks sake."

I soothed him and calmed down after breakfast. Then, we went our separate ways into the whirlwind of getting ready. After the painstaking make-up application, my hair was curled while the photographer paced the room, wanting me to get dressed for the bridal photo shoot. I kept calm and wondered again why I was doing this.

I told myself that we had made a mutual decision, and it was important for both of us. We deserved a traditional wedding and reception in a beautiful historic building. It wasn't any old building but the home of a special little girl. Someone we had a previous connection with. Our family and friends knew nothing of this. We could only spend time with Charlotte while our photos were taken in areas of the house and gardens that she chose for us to visit.

Our tribe were all present during the ceremony and the speeches, and we acknowledged their presence when we could. I was sad that they were unknown to our other guests, as they were also family and friends. If anyone besides us had been able to see the tribe that day, the room would have been full instead of a third full.

The day was magical. The rain stopped as I stepped out of the car to enter the church. Light streamed onto us through the stained-glass window as we were blessed after saying our vows. Mike stumbled over his words; overcome with emotion that I was finally his wife.

"We both look bloody gorgeous," Mike whispered when we had a few moments to ourselves.

It wasn't just about us, though. Everything we had done had been in honor of others. Our shared words reflected that, and we hoped it would not be lost on our guests. Our union was more significant than anyone realized, but we knew, and so did our tribe. Two people became one powerful unit that day. The wedding was the starting point. I stood up and announced our intentions, reading Mike's speech as well as my own. It wasn't about the words but the vibration they were wrapped in. Everything I had chosen for the day had a meaning. The colors of my flowers were yellow and purple. The hymns we sang, and the speeches, all signified to those present how important our union was. The historic building set the scene for what was to come.

Old One and Gemel wrote a bonding reading for us, which my friend David read during the church service:

The Creator's Love
All the worlds the creator made with his will.
None are greater than the other.
The mountains and valleys rejoice at his name,
singing echoes deep and high.
From the deep waters of the oceans to wide open
plains, his works are known.
From the smallest, unseen in creation
to the mightiest place, his name is known.
As the corn soaks up the sunshine, the mountains
embrace the cold of peak snow, and the rivers run to the
lakes and oceans, so our destiny is fulfilled.
Love and mercy abound from the creator

of all that is. None are lost or forgotten.
By his will and command, we are protected, guarded,
and guided, kept safe in light and body.
From the moment we are created to the moment this life
ends, we are watched over.
In between times, we are loved,
receive love and give love.
Becoming one, two share with the other.
Bonded together in love and promise for all days.
The creator loves all the works of his will forever.
When the sun is no more; when the moon is gone; when
the stars no longer shine, his will remains; bringing
together lives and souls, bound by the promise we are
reminded of this day, the creator loves us all today,
tomorrow, and for all seasons.

We set off on our mini honeymoon to Fife in Scotland two days after our wedding. I had chosen the destination, with a surprise in store for Mike. Rest was also needed, so we didn't travel too far when we got there.

As we drove along a country road looking for our Guest House, Mike paled and slowed the car down to a crawl.

"What's wrong...are you okay?" I asked, scanning his face, then outside to see if I had missed anything.

"I must go slow behind this horse and cart. Can't you see them?" Mike asked me when he realized I didn't.

"No, I can't see anything except the road. You must be seeing them in their time. It's safe to carry on," I assured him.

As Mike sighed and shook his head, I lifted my eyes from the map and pointed ahead, "only half a mile and then a left turn into the Guest House." It had been a long drive. Mike is more likely to slip between times when he's tired, and it unsettles us if it happens when he's driving. Nevertheless, an early night was on the cards.

I couldn't wait to see Mike's response to his surprise. He had no idea why I had chosen the North-East coast of

Scotland. The next morning, as we drove to a small coastal town, he soon found out.

For the second time in two days, Mike went pale and gasped. This time, on seeing the road sign: *Lower Largo - Birthplace of Robinson Crusoe.*

We drove down the street along the harbor to the car park. Mike attempted to keep his emotions in check. I could almost hear his heartbeat as he looked around. We stepped out of the car right onto the beach. As we looked around the bay, flickers of recognition passed over Mike's face. He resembled someone who had lost their memory, and snippets sneaked back.

"Would you like to walk along the street?" I asked, then pointed toward the houses that fronted the beach. After a few yards, Mike stopped outside a terraced house with a bright red door.

"This is familiar. There's something about it...I've been here before," Mike told me.

"That's interesting...should we walk on and see if you feel pulled anywhere else?" I suggested.

After reaching a crossroads, we continued left towards The Crusoe Hotel. We couldn't resist stepping inside and decided to have some lunch while we were there.

"I've been here before. It's different now, of course," Mike said over our meal.

His attention was taken by artifacts hung around the room. All of them connected with maritime history when Navel Lieutenant Alexander Selkirk left the Scottish shores with his Captain, Admiral Sir Andrew Wood, on a long voyage. Alexander failed to return home and, for many years, was presumed dead. He had jumped overboard following a fight with the captain. Daniel Defoe wrote his novel 'Robinson Crusoe' based on Alexander's survival on a desert island.

The waitress saw our interest. She informed us, "If you go down that corridor and through a door, it takes you into another room. It has information and artifacts connected to Alexander and the Crusoe version of the story."

Mike seemed bemused by all he witnessed within the room. The fictional character he knew and loved as a child was him in another lifetime. It seemed too fanciful to be true. We left the hotel and wandered around the town. Mike was drawn to several places he recognized. Emotions and sensations were strong. On Main Street, we saw the life-size statue of Alexander Selkirk and the plaque near his childhood home. Then we returned to the harbor to view the signpost that points to Juan Fernandez Islands. Some 7,500 miles in the distance was where Selkirk lived for more than four years as a castaway.

Mike felt the strongest pull to another area of the bay. We walked along the sand, and then he stopped and pointed north.

"See the rocks up there? I can see myself there. I was anxious to return to my island. I couldn't settle back into life here. I went to those rocks to think…to get away from people. All the attention when I got back frightened me…I was so used to my own company. I left a few weeks after I'd got back…went to London for a while…to seek another voyage."

He felt homesick for the island home and the peace he had there. The emotional pull grew deeper the longer we stayed on the beach.

Mike was flooded with it. "Let's go. I've had enough."

We got in the car and drove the country lanes, so Mike could breathe and clear the cobwebs of his past away.

I had kept the trip a secret and had no idea how he would react. I wondered if it had been a good idea. Our only previous knowledge of his connection to Alexander had been through a past life regression. I transcribed Mike's words as he described the experiences of that life while in a trance. At the time, he didn't know the name of the Scottish town, only had a sense of where it was. In the regression, he spent most of the time on the island until his rescue and had come to terms with his life there.

Mike needed rest after the shock, so I kept our next excursion for the following day. It was to the ancient site of Dunino Den, a mystical holy well. It is hidden down a quiet country lane, with a deceptive drop beyond the church graveyard and no indication that a mysterious cavern lies deep within the ground.

Upon arriving, we negotiated the ancient staircase down the side of the 15-foot rock face. We were greeted by a burn meandering through a wooded oasis. Visitors view the site as a gateway to the Otherworld. Ribbons and messages hang as tokens of remembrance from the trees. The crevices of the sandstone wall were filled with coins to honor the spirits of the sacred site. Many believe if a coin is removed, it will bring bad luck. [2]

We immersed ourselves in the peaceful energy and ancient vibe.

"Mike...I need to walk in the water...go upstream... see those rocks," I said as I took off my footwear.

We waded and slipped across stone and moss around a bend in the burn, away from prying eyes. A small cave greeted us. It had a ledge just big enough to sit on. As we settled, a familiar feeling flitted between us.

I asked Dulaa, "have we been here before?"

"Yes, a long time ago. You were traveling with your new husband to his land. You were young and in love. You rested and spoke to the spirits here. Look inwards at the rocks and see what you feel, then turn around and stand in the water. Not just you, both of you."

The energy around us pulsed where we stood. Then, Dulaa asked: "Do you feel a higher presence, and that of the spirits of the water and the earth beings here with us now?"

---

[2] Dunino Den - Our History in a Nutshell | Order of Bards, Ovates & Druids (druidry.org)

Cathryn Mahoney

We tuned in to the spirit entities and felt the peaceful connection with the earth and our presence there at other times. I then felt the energy of the regal woman I once merged with. I sensed her feet in the water and reveled in her joy.

I spoke to the spirits, "Thank you for being here with us and reminding us of our connection to the land, the people, and all beings who reside or visit this place," I felt my essence soak into the water and lap onto the land.

We then picked our way back across the rocks to the glen. When we reached the grassy bank, Dulaa told me, "Meena was always with you."

He referred to a young woman we met on our way to Dunino Den. She was from another time and of Pictish origin. She asked to join us for the rest of our time in Scotland. Of course, we were happy to have her company, and Dulaa was smitten with her.

I learned that in a previous life, I had merged with Agnes, Maud FitzAlan, daughter of John de Baliol, King of Scotland. Agnes married Baron FitzAlan in 1297. When they visited Dunino Den, they were on their honeymoon. Meena was Agne's lady's maid.

After discovering this information, Dulaa said, "You will learn more about that time and other times you spent in Scotland. Meena will also be by your side again."

Mike had a vague recollection of visiting Dunino Den with me in another lifetime and traveling further north. When he was Alexander Selkirk, we had a brief love affair during a journey to London. I was a young milkmaid, but I died days after we met. In London, Alexander met and fell in love with an innkeeper before he joined another seafaring voyage. He died at sea.

It was understandable that Mike had mixed feelings about visiting Scotland. He was pleased I had helped him lay the ghost of Alexander Selkirk to rest. However, there were still many triggers in relation to battles and death in other lifetimes in Scotland. We would discover more on future journeys if he chose to take them.

26

Transatlantic Travels

A week after returning from Scotland, we moved to our permanent home and adjusted to our new surroundings. By the end of the year, we had utilized quiet time at the caravan to plan our first big adventure to North America. Jheneeka helped me plan the route. We were retracing the journey our tribe had taken on foot. For them, it took two hundred years; for us, we planned six weeks of travel by car and plane.

Six months later, we set out on our adventures. The destinations we chose were important historic sites or where our tribe had significant interactions with other tribes or European settlers. The journey commenced from Roanoke Island in North Carolina. Afterward, we traveled across ten states and flew to Alberta, Canada, to visit the mountains where our tribe settled.

As soon as we returned from America and recovered, I planned our second trip with locations in Oregon, Idaho, and North California on the agenda. This time it was a four-week journey that began thirteen months later. This time, to areas where our tribe had befriended the Nez Perce, Salish, and other tribes of those territories.

Jheneeka and the tribe had given little guidance on the purpose of our visit to specific locations. That was revealed when we were there, and we became immersed in the emotional impact of the conditions the tribes were subjected to. The hardships they faced while battling to keep their lands during the European invasion for us brought physical pain, heartache, and anger. There were also moments of unadulterated joy when we met elders, such as Old Chief Joseph and Chief Smohalla, in their spirit forms.

These stories are shared in Part 4 of this book, and my previously published travelogues. [3]

---

[3] After 189 Miles Turn Left: Treading the Path of the Peaceful Warriors 'A Travel Journal with a Difference': Amazon.co.uk: Mahoney, Cathryn, Mahoney, Michael: 9798645845735: Books

Exploring Ancient Wisdom: Between a Rock and a Highway!: Amazon.co.uk: Mahoney, Cathryn: 9798743181841: Books

Oon'ch-illia

27

Locked Down

It took far longer to recover from our second Transatlantic journey, and Mike vowed never again. I felt homesick and began planning the next trip until the pandemic put a hold on plans - to Mike's relief. That began three years of frustration and feeling stuck.

The tribe advised me to assimilate my learning to date, rest, and write. My inability to be visible deepened and I became protective of Mike and the tribe. I felt it wasn't safe to share our experiences. As I discovered my identity, I struggled emotionally. Who would believe me anyway? I would come across as another crackpot guru in the making.

I kept abreast of themes discussed in spiritual groups but grew frustrated attempting to find common ground to share our experiences, so I pulled away from the typical new-age beliefs. People made assumptions when I tried to describe our experiences. I had to find a way to explain the difference: it wasn't channeling or soul walk-ins.

While I thought it was important to keep abreast of the spiritual climate, Mike didn't want to be influenced by it. Instead, he wanted to remain a pure vessel. So, I felt alone, with my need to research and share knowledge and wisdom. I had to find a way to be true to myself and my role.

I shared my frustrations with Old One and Gemel who had been visiting monthly since our wedding. They were helping me piece the jigsaw together but made me work hard. They bounced back questions and used analogies in their teachings.

My frustrations deepened during the first lockdown and was often tearful at our meetings. I looked for answers but wasn't given any, so I became more disillusioned.

Two years prior, I had stopped working with clients and groups due to our travels, but now I was stuck at home and was uncertain about what direction to take.

A mutual decision was reached to stop the visits from the tribe, which caused sadness and some relief, but a shift was needed as Mike, and I coped with the new turn of events affecting the world. The tribe also had issues to contend with, including a time shift and meetings with other ancient races. We were all getting on with life, but I felt bereft.

I had agreed to press the pause button because I felt I had nothing to offer the tribe. It seemed like we all went through the motions of living in separate worlds. We had different needs and priorities - for us - it was just to survive each day and hope things would change. Mike was still worn down by his experiences in America, and it had become increasingly painful and disorientating for him to allow tribe members to use his body.

Then, we had to cope with dwindling finances and little contact with family and friends. It all took its toll. It was a time of consolidating all we had learned and a time to rest and live our regular lives separately. I was also worried that the tribe would be affected by the virus and its impact on humanity, and I wanted to protect them at all costs.

Despite my healing and spiritual work stalling during 2018-2022, my learning continued. During sessions with Isame, he asked me questions like, "what color is this? Where does it need to go?" Nine times out of ten, I got it right. He brought concoctions made from stones, plants, and herbs which he mixed with colored lights plucked from the air. Then, they were placed deep into my body to heal organs, muscles, and joints.

I participated in my own healing while Isame mixed the specific colors to help realign my feet and back. When he finished, he checked the energy in my body and aura. Often, he said, "close your eyes; tell me when you feel a vibration."

Oon'ch-illia

I was able to tell him when I felt his hand close to my feet or head. The distance grew as my energy expanded after each healing.

Isame is seven-foot, three, and broad in stature. He has the gentlest hands that can inflict pain but to good effect, and he can look deep within the cells of the body to see where healing is required.

As the tribe's medicine man, he is always on call, so I'm grateful when he visits me.
"I can have some rest when I'm here," he says while lying beside me after my healing session.

In the village, someone often needs him, or he is called away off-world to help other species of organic and light beings. He also travels to different worlds to collect solids, ingredients, and plant materials not found on Earth that can help with his healing. Then his helpers make potions, poultices, and dressings for him.

Isame has delivered many babies, probably realigned hundreds of broken bones, and mended broken hearts. One of his favorite activities is to submerge the children under a cascading waterfall at the healing pools. They have often recounted tales of being held over his head like an umbrella to protect him from the shower of water, then thrown into the pool. Even though it's a fun activity for all concerned, Isame tells me, "the waters lift mood and strengthen their light. Yes, we all benefit from it."

Even the leader of the tribe, Jheneeka, finds time to relax and allow Isame to manhandle her in such a way. Despite her responsibilities, I don't believe she will ever be too old to play. She benefits from the stress releaser, and it strengthens bonds.

Throughout 2020 and 2021, Isame was my mainstay. He visited on a weekly basis to top up my and Mike's energy and kept a check on our mental health. Any interactions we had with other tribal members were in their light form, without merging into Mike's body. They came briefly as a wisp that transfigured into a hazy outline.

Dulaa was the go-between with the tribe. Then he left us for several weeks when he married Meena, while his replacement, Ishtol, stepped in.

There was no future sign of movement. Our travel plans and search for our forever home remained on hold. We had to sell the caravan, so our weekend retreat was also gone. Even though we felt isolated, we discovered that Isame and Gemel took us to the tribe's village several nights a week. There, we visited the healing waters and had lessons from the elders. We also contributed to life in the village, attending ceremonies and celebrations and telling stories around the fire, but our nightly forays were rarely remembered when we awoke. That feeling of being stuck and alone continued. My sense of belonging was at a simmering point.

I had no new information to share from experiences or journeys with the tribe apart from my dream time. Life seemed to pause. Every time I tried to hit the start button, it paused again. 2020 flashed into 2021, then 2022.

Life didn't stand still. Online studying became my thing. Herbalism, Forest Bathing, Foraging, and Holistic practices to begin with. All that would be useful for our healing retreat. We never lost sight of the forever home we both envisioned, set in acres of forest with a stream, waterfall, and healing spaces for people with life-limiting conditions.

At the beginning of 2022, I joined writer's groups to overcome my fear of visibility and enhance my self-belief. I committed to a daily writing practice, which helped with the recall of dream time forays and past lives. I knew my story could awaken minds and hearts to untold mysteries and ancient wisdom. It was my gift to the world - sharing knowledge from eons of time and space travel with my star brothers and sisters.

Oon'ch-illia

III

Identity

*I hope you have enjoyed my journey so far.
What follows now is a series of short stories offering
more insight into my search for self and the
connection with Mike and our tribe through the
adventures and learning we have had together.
Accompany me as I step into my role as healer, seer,
and teacher.*

28

Angels

Many things have I found, planted by my tribe and hidden in unusual places - discovery games to test my intuitive skills. On Christmas morning, 2014, Mike and I set out on a woodland walk. Our destination was a bird sanctuary for stillness and solitude. We picked our way through the overgrown branches and over the gnarled root system. Layers of leaf litter hid such death traps. Finally, stepping around boggy puddles, we arrived at a bird hide: the perfect place to enjoy sherry and a mince pie. Our arrival heralded a gentle pulse of energy. The air shifted, and Mike quietened. As I looked on, a lightness appeared across his forehead, and with an intake of breath, his body shuddered.

When Jheneeka became tribal leader, Teela replaced her as our regular visitor. I had little prior knowledge of her. For most of her childhood, she had been ensconced in a room next door to Isame. She suffered from childhood diabetes, and it took time to regulate her insulin. Activities with the tribe had been curtailed, but she hadn't remained idle. The elders had prepared her for a future role. When her health improved, she became Jheneeka's confidante and an active member of the tribe. The girls' closeness was palpable; sometimes, it was difficult to tell them apart. As Teela grew in strength and confidence, she also developed a thirst to push herself to the limit and engage in risk-taking activities. As Jheneeka's right-hand woman, the role of a teacher was assigned to her. Standing in as a leader was also expected. Her freedom was curtailed, and she didn't take kindly to either role.

It took several minutes to distinguish who my visitor was, which amused Teela. She was training as our new gatekeeper and liked to keep us on our toes. She enjoyed special occasions when gifts and different foods were on offer. Her joy and sense of fun were palpable. More spontaneous than Jheneeka and often excitable, she was also mysterious this time.

"Hi, nice to see you again. Are you up to something?" I asked.

"Who am I?" she whispered.

"Teela," I offered tentatively.

She giggled and did a hearty jig on the spot.

I scanned the area around us to ensure nobody was about. We were alone, but all the same, I enticed Teela into the bird hide for a Christmas tipple. She is partial to a tot of something.

We hugged, wishing each other a happy Christmas, and Teela gave an overview of our tribe's daily activities. They don't have the same traditions but join us in ours. Now, at Christmas, they are all given a day off to share food and stories around the campfire, and their events are all-night affairs. Teela has been allowed the day off with her brave.

"My brave stands there...he's happy to see you," she said while pointing at a delve by a tree. "He's come to help; you have to find something."

Then, jumping off the seat, she pulled me after her.

"What is it?" I asked while following her gaze toward some trees.

"You find it - I'm going to say hot or cold."

Oh no! Her tone turned serious, so I realized this might take some time. She often copies the time I hid a birthday gift for her in our house. Teela likes to do things right, so I wondered how deeply buried the surprise might be.

I set out on my search around the trees and shrubs and then moved towards her brave. His presence was intended to put me off the scent, so I headed back to the first location. All the time, Teela was shouting: "cold, cold, warm, warmer," until I was upon a dip between two trees.

"Warmer" she shouted. I homed in on my quarry using all of my senses, like a dog sniffing the ground. Then, I reached down to brush some leaves away.

Teela shouted: "Warmer - very warm - hot."

My fingers scraped deep into the earth, and I pulled up a smooth, cold object. As I brushed away the soil, it revealed a tiny white opal angel.

"It's beautiful - thank you," I said, reaching for a hug.

"There's more," Teela announced.

I went in the opposite direction, trying to sense where Teela and her brave had been.

"Cold," she shouted.

I was wrong there, but I asked, "are you sure?"

"Of course," she pouted. Then laughed and shrieked, "cold...colder."

"Keep the noise down," I pleaded.

"Still cold," Teela whispered.

I made a broad sweep of the area and kept one eye on her. She giggled.

"You know me too well," I said as I hovered nearer her brave.

"He's over there now," she pointed and laughed. "Still cold."

I headed towards a deer path and passed under a fallen branch.

"Warmer...getting warmer," Teela whispered into my ear, and I felt her breath on my neck.

There were two sticks strategically placed, so I moved them away and reached down into the soil.

"Hot...hot," she bellowed into my left ear.

I picked up another angel; this one was larger and speckled brown. I later learned it was a brown sunstone. I cleaned and inspected my treasures in the sun.

"They are beautiful...where did you get them from?" I asked.

"Later," she insisted. "There is still one more to find." Teela glanced at her brave, and I thought she had gotten bored and given the game away.

She must have realized I'd clocked her, so she said, "yeees...warmer."

Her gaze settled a yard from his feet. Then, she cried, "yeees...there." She pranced towards him as we reached the spot together.

"Hot?" I asked, looking at her brave and laughing.

"Whaaaat?" she mouthed.

"Am I hot finding the right spot - or is your brave hot?" I asked.

She looked puzzled, then pointed to the ground. "Yes, hot here."

She didn't get the joke until I explained, and then she doubled over. A bit overdramatic, but she got there in the end. "Yes, my brave is hot," she shrieked.

I reached down to the spot and dug up another small crystal. It was a lighter brown and sparkled. Later I identified it to be a golden sunstone.

"Is that it now?" I asked.

"Yes, done now. My brave is leaving, but he's coming back for me soon," she said.

She formally introduced us, pronouncing his name, Jasfa. I am known for struggling with their language's complexity and long names. For ease of speaking, they shorten them, like nicknames. I speak their language in the village, but it's lost when I'm not. Mike sometimes slips into their words. Any interactions we had with other tribal members sounded familiar to me, but it frustrates me that they have a good grasp of English, yet I lack in their language.

"Bye, Jasfa; thank you for visiting and helping Teela. It's lovely meeting you at last," I said, reaching up on my tiptoes to kiss his cheek. Then, I sensed his light fade.

We returned with my third gift to the bird hide. I inspected all three and placed them in a safe space in my walking bag, and then we shared a mince pie and some coffee while Teela chatted about her plan for the day.

Jasfa returned but remained at a discreet distance.

"We're going now...for our picnic. Asda woman has packed some food for us," she serenaded her words with hugs and slowly faded away.

Mike's body shuddered. When he opened his eyes, he asked, "Has Teela been?"

I showed him my gifts and shared the adventure of finding them. He was intrigued when I pointed out where I discovered them and how.

"I'm so pleased Teela came, and you had such a good time. They are better than any present I gave you, then?" he quipped.

"Well, they are special...they are from all of the tribe...I feel so blessed and loved...but of course, I love your gifts too...these are just different...and it was fun to find them in that way."

29

Shifting

My first understanding of time and body shifting, other than tribal members merging with Mike, was when I was told about 'Asda Woman,' who was Old One's sister. When we lived in the caravan, we often shopped at Asda. She observed and followed us, unbeknownst to us.

Asda Woman merged with an old lady who was close to the end of her life. She reveled in her role as a 'secret shopper.' She bought many strange things, anything she liked the look of. The braves in the tribe often visited her for unique items for their romantic picnics. They wanted to copy our ways, as we were avid picnickers. We chose tea and toast, sandwiches, crisps, and cake, with mince pies at Christmas. Their picnics were more elaborate and eclectic. They often had fizzy pop, marshmallows, tinned corned beef or spam, and a selection of sweets, which accompanied their fresh catch of the day.

After Asda Woman had passed away, there was one occasion when an old man at our local shop stopped me. In his hand, he had a packet of chicken casserole sauce mix. He asked me what ingredients he needed to buy. I looked at what he already had in his basket and walked the aisles with him for the remaining items. He thanked me with a toothless grin, and I passed on by. A strange sensation lingered. Did I know him - was he testing me?

Later, I asked Teela about him.

"He's one of three now in training to take over from Asda Woman ... I don't think he'll cut it," she said.

Since then, their shopping forays have progressed to other stores. Eventually, another female elder passed the test to become the new Asda Woman. She's the go-to person for picnic treats but also knows what to buy to make healthy meals.

30

Merging

The pressure on Mike's body and mind has sometimes been too great for him to bear. I have often been ignorant of the impact on him when various characters enter his body to communicate with me. It became more apparent when an ancient one chose to converse and only managed to stay a few minutes. Jheneeka arrived soon after to tell me why.

"Higher vibrational beings mess with daddy's internal wiring and DNA...everything's moved around...Isame is correcting it now," she solemnly informed me.

"Will he be, okay?" was all I could think to ask, shocked by the news when I had been so excited about the visit. Instead, I crashed back to earth with a feeling of guilt. I didn't fully understand but could hazard a guess how such visits could prove dangerous. So, from then on, only Old One would enter Mike's body as a member of the 'Ancient' crew.

Over time Mike has described the different sensations he experiences with each person that merges with him.

"With Old One, heaviness presses onto my chest, then a whoosh of energy assails me, and I'm in the village looking around. With the girls who come more regularly, it is a delicate process, but there is a significant difference between them. They slide in and push me gently out or to the back, where it's like I'm dreaming; I catch snatches of things."

Mike is often tired and disorientated when he returns. If he has been to the village, he may be given tasks to occupy his time, rest or converse with someone. He often merges with the body of Vormash, a warrior of the tribe, who has agreed to the process. On his return, I recount what has happened in his absence and share the conversations/learning I have had.

Oon'ch-illia

There have been long periods when we have had no visitors due to the state of Mike's health. He has asthma and has had several bouts of pneumonia. So, the tribe are mindful they do not impede his life any further.

We had both agreed to participate in our individual roles before entering these lives. Mine, as a seer, is to recognize a need and when to act. I plan and prepare, then Mike does the dirty work, as I see it, and I do the mopping up. Mike is the eyes and ears on the ground, the go-between, and the warrior when needed. He allows me to be present with those I meet or to immerse myself in remembering or shifting between the veils of time.

When Mike allows others to use his body, we receive direct interaction instead of channeled, ensuring quality control of information as my mind would struggle to cope with the rapidity of information entering in thought forms and symbols.

We have termed the merging process *Episodic Ethereal Symbiosis.* It is a union between light and human beings that mutually benefit both. It is episodic for Mike since the individuals arrive for short periods to teach or share time. Within the tribe, each light being has merged more permanently with a member of the tribe. When they visit us, the human travels within their ethereal body in the presence of their light-being counterpart. The two-for-one offer becomes three-for-one when they merge with Mike. His body becomes their vessel for communication, while his ethereal body is free to travel to the tribe's village, or he rests.

31

Near Tragedy

A relaxing early morning dip nearly ended in tragedy for Mike, who was always ready to please Teela. The eager visitor begged to show off her gymnastics in the pool, whose sprints across the pool turned into handstands until panic ensued.

"Ahhh," Teela shouted as she bobbed to the surface, gasping. I reached Mike's body in a few strokes, and my teenage lifeguard skills kicked in. I dragged him to the poolside. Teela had left his body, but I sensed her panic and tearfulness beside me.

"Dulaa, please get Isame," I shouted, then scanned the doors and for cameras, mindful that security guards and paramedics could rush in at any time. My next thought was, am I being careless for not shouting for help?

But I didn't allow panic to take hold and shout 911.

Within minutes, Isame attended to Mike's body, and I began calming a hysterical Teela. Imagine the scene: a stocky six-foot man is heaved half out of the water by an invisible force from behind. His eyes are closed, and his breathing is labored. Then there is a loud crack in his rib cage.

Even though Isame had control of the situation, my heart pounded in my ears as Teela sobbed beside me. The cracking and groans from Mike made me gasp as sweat and chills played a tune on my skin.

"Isame doesn't need me freaking out, too," I thought.

After fifteen long minutes, I helped Isame drag Mike out of the pool and into the Jacuzzi.

"We need to warm him...five minutes. His diaphragm and sternum have been overstretched...the last time his body was thrown underwater. He is healing now," Isame said.

Oon'ch-illia

Teela couldn't look me in the eye but said, "It was the last handstand; I should have stopped. I did too much. It's all my fault...I could have killed daddy."

Isame then took the remorseful yet relieved Teela back to the village while Mike returned to consciousness.

With a jolt and then a wince, he asked, "What the fuck just happened?"

32

Terrible Two

Ishneah is Sashma's daughter. When she was very young, she loved to spend time with me. She was always excitable and pushed the boundaries to the limit. Her intelligence was sharp. She wanted to learn as much as she could in a short time. Her bravery held no bounds, and she had a curiosity and desire to entertain.

I thought Teela was the risk-taker, but she had a competitor. Ishneah was the only one of the girls who chose to have a picture taken of her light-being self. It took me a while to decipher the image, which was in black and white. However, I was blown away by her beauty when I saw her clearly.

Unfortunately, it wasn't long before another youngster in the tribe led Ishneah astray. They conspired to have a test of their abilities within Mike's body. Unfortunately, it was timed when we, and the tribe, were all distracted.

We viewed our permanent home a month before our wedding and then drove around the area. I soon realized Mike wasn't in charge of the vehicle, which speeded up.

I shouted, "Whoever this is, you must stop...pull over NOW."

The car was pulled into a gateway I'd pointed at. Ishneah confessed. "I'm sorry we were only having fun...I didn't think you'd mind...I just came in...we're excited you are getting a new house...we like it. My friend wanted to meet you."

She pointed back at her friend, who bounced up and down, looking at herself in the mirror.

"You must go now; I need to speak to daddy. Look...a tractor wants us to move...go now...get daddy back, quick," I instructed as the tractor driver glowered at us.

Mike returned too quickly, but I insisted he drive on

even though he was confused. We stopped further along the road in a lay-by to discuss what had happened.

As he wound down the window to gulp some air, Mike exclaimed, "Bloody hell! I was booted out. I didn't know what had happened to me. Was that Ishneah?"

"Yes, she had a friend with her, who I think egged her on. We had no control and were going too fast. I felt strung out. So much for a nice drive to think about things."

"Well, that can't happen ever again. Where was Teela? Isn't she meant to say who can come and when? It was dangerous and stupid." Mike ranted.

"I know. I don't feel I want anyone from the tribe to come now. We will have to speak to Teela or Old One when we get home." I suggested.

Mike started the car. We were both lost in our thoughts, feeling like pawns in a game. As soon as we were through the door, Teela arrived to apologize.

"The girls will be punished...severely. That will never happen again. We are all angry with them. I took them away when daddy returned. We saw him wander by the lake...he was confused. I was mortified...it's my fault...we have no idea how they got through...Old One says she is too smart...I promise it will never happen again."

I said, "They put our lives in danger...we were both shaken up. How could they sneak in undetected? Who was that other girl? We don't know her, do we?"

"No, she has been quiet in the past but befriended Ishneah and then encouraged her to steal. She will never be allowed through in her lifetime. Jheneeka and Old One are considering their punishments...it will be severe." Teela said sternly.

Mike seethed quietly, then spat, "Good, they deserve harsh punishment...my body feels violated...I dread to think what they could have done next."

We didn't see Ishneah for some years after that. Both girls were given hard grafts deep down in the cave, where no one else ventured. In time Ishneah was given more meaningful roles, but her friend remained defiant. All the dirtiest jobs went to her. They soon grew up. Ishneah was repentant and wanted to make amends. Her friend's willfulness was monitored, and access to knowledge of our world was denied to her forever.

Ishneah is now a well-respected member of Isame's healing team and has helped many people. We forgave her weeks later and questioned her about the harsh measures metered out to her.

When I next spoke to Jheneeka about it, her response was, "The punishment had to be tough to ensure they or no one else thought it was acceptable to play with your lives and not respect you in that way."

When Ishneah visited us on her next birthday, she hid. She was unable to look me in the eye, and when she did, her apology was profuse. It took several visits over many years to convince her she had been forgiven soon after the event.

33

Hybrid Child

Hibi shares my birthday. She is a special child; the only hybrid conceived by a native girl and an off-world visitor, who integrated into the tribe. Her mum, Keela, spent one of her birthdays on a walk with me and shared her concern about wanting a child with her brave, Gambatar. He had arrived in the village about eighteen months prior with a group of centurion warriors to support the tribe in battle.

There is a vicious tribe from a faraway planet that has plagued the Shee'masha'taa People (our tribe) for eons of time. Old One knew another attack was imminent and had a device that could provide protection, especially off-world. It could also communicate with ancient ones from the council of tribes. The centurion people answered the call for assistance against those; the tribe named the *bad ones*. A bloody battle ensued, with much loss of life and injury. That story appears in the next chapter.

After the battle, Gambatar and another warrior stayed behind, and the rest returned to their planet, way beyond Orion's belt. Gambatar had been a guard for Jheneeka, and the other warrior remains Old One's guard. Keela's relationship with Gambatar flourished, yet they believed blessing their union with children was impossible.

While we walked, Keela shared a recent discussion she had with Isame.

"Isame asked, "is your love for Gambatar strong? Are you prepared to be childless when you are bonded? I told him yes if that is how it is meant to be. He then told me that there might be possibilities. But he would need to speak to Gambatar's medicine men."

I rarely got to spend time with Keela. She is the tribal inventor and engineer. Her duties were all-encompassing until she met Gambatar. She had learned by observing our world and found solutions to many problems in the village. Gambatar's presence in the tribe added value with his strength and his weapon, a sort of lightsaber that can blow up rocks, drill into the ground, and terminate attackers.

As Keela and I spoke of their predicament, I gave her hope. I told her about adoption and then IVF treatment. Her light sparkled when she returned to the village, keen to talk to Gambatar and Isame about the viability of IVF. Isame arranged a consultation with Gambatar's doctors. He learned about the biological differences and problems Keela may experience carrying a hybrid child. After many discussions, Keela returned to speak with me several weeks later.

"We have decided to go ahead. Isame will do the IVF treatment with the remote assistance of a doctor from Gambatar's tribe. Of course, there are risks, but we are well prepared. Thank you, White Bird; I will always be indebted to you," Keela said. She hugged me tight, then slipped away.

The procedure went well, and long story short, Keela became pregnant with Gambatar's child. It was a fast pregnancy, and Keela required more protein to nourish herself. She visited our home on at least two occasions, searching for certain foods. Once, it was a cucumber - don't ask me why!

There were so many unknown factors to such a birth. So, a day was planned for induction since the child was large. The day of my birthday was chosen in honor of me. Hibi's complete name (Cawhibimuoon) is a portmanteau (blended) word created from the names she knows me by (Cathryn, White Bird, Mummy, and Oon'ch-illia).

She was born into a healing pool of water and had many physical features quite different from the tribe, even compared to Keela and Gambatar. As a result, she was a source of confused interest for many.

Hibi grew very quickly, physically, and intellectually, and is now a strong member of the tribe in all respects.

Oon'ch-illia

At the time of writing, she is a beautiful young adult at just five of our earth years. In infancy, she developed spines on her back and hard bumps on her temples. The spines receded as she grew, but she spent more time in the water, where her color changed. She has many gifts and abilities that are unique to her.

Every time Keela visits me, she says. "We are so grateful, White Bird. If it was not for you, for what you said on my birthday, Hibi would not be here."

34

Bad Ones

I woke in a panic. My neck and chest were damp, and my nighty was disheveled. I caught my breath and looked at Mike, sitting upright, his eyes wide, staring ahead.

"What's wrong...what's happened...are you alright?" I asked him. I turned, face to face, looking into his eyes, but it took a few minutes for him to focus on me.

With a huge intake of breath, there was a whimper, and tears welled in his eyes.

"He's gone...oh no...I'm frightened," a small voice said.

I hugged Mike's body to me. I needed to know who this was. It certainly wasn't Mike, but where was he? What had happened to him? My heart skipped a beat. I had a sense of foreboding, so I required information, but I knew my visitor was in a state of shock.

"Can you tell me what is happening...is he in the village?" I asked.

"I'm sorry, it's Keela...they sent me away...to be with you...to stay safe...I should be there, helping them...the bad ones came...they are all fighting now...he, too (Mike), is fighting...some have been killed...many injured...it's bad...I'm so frightened...some of the women are coming here...we must protect them...others...we must pass on to the light...will you help me?"

We began chanting words to help the dead return to the light. All the time, my heart raced, and my mouth was like sandpaper. I could see through Keela's eyes the battle raging on. Flashes of lights destroyed people on both sides, and the 'bad ones' kept coming. They attempted to infiltrate the cave where the old, young, and infirm were hidden.

Between receiving the dead and sending them on their way, Keela gave details of the battle. I knew what was happening to every family member and friend. Many were now injured. Old One and Isame were also fighting and moving the wounded to the cave to be attended to. All the 'warrior' girls, apart from Keela, were also fighting. It tore her apart being a spectator rather than the heat of battle with them, but she had been assigned to assist me.

The battle raged on with more deaths and injuries. The onslaught lessened as the centurions from a far-off planet arrived and deployed their precision weapons. The warriors were few, many severely injured or exhausted, so they welcomed reinforcements.

Keela screamed, "He's coming for you...we must stop him...Mammy...stop him...he's going to kill you."

"Nooooo...be gone." I repeatedly shouted at the top of my voice, commanding the 'bad one' to leave. Gemel had arrived behind him and pulled him back as I shouted.

I am confident I did much more than shout, as did Keela. Our combined light prevented him from entering Mike's body. The vibration emanating from us resonated with the village to get the help we needed. The 'bad ones' had retreated apart from that one determined soul in his last-ditch attempt to take out the protector of the tribe.

I later learned I had alerted the tribe of the imminent invasion. It had been expected for some time but had arrived sooner. As 'Eyes in Sky' (protector of the village), one of my most important roles is to keep a vigilant watch from above. I had forewarned them in my sleep, and the tribe prepared as best they could. With foresight, Old One had requested help from his friends on another planet. They had catapulted their craft through Orion's belt to reach earth in just enough time to save the tribe from slaughter. They had followed the defeated 'bad ones' back to their craft and blown it up so they could not summon back-up from their planet.

Keela and some of the women stayed with me while the injured were attended to in the village, including Mike. So, we continued to pass the dead, including the 'bad ones,' to the light.

Cathryn Mahoney

Since time in the village is different from ours, it wasn't long before we received news about the severity of injuries and were given a headcount of survivors. Those I was closest to in the tribe all had injuries, although not life-threatening. But we lost many brave warriors and some of the women who came out of the cave to fight or take care of the injured.

Mike had been gone for ninety minutes of our time. The battle had raged for hours in the tribe's time, and Mike stayed for nearly a day afterward while the healing waters speeded up his healing. When he returned to his bed and me, his injuries were scars, but recuperation was still needed.

A few days later, Teela updated me on the events of that day and told me it would take many moons for them all to grieve and heal.

35

Crocheted Bag

On a cold post-storm January morning, we ventured out to one of our special places - a coastal stream within a woodland glade.

A few days previous, Mike had stopped along the motorway to help a flustered young woman change a tire. He suggested she take a break from her journey and escorted her to the next service station. Then he realized her mother and grandmother were in the car. As he bid them a safe journey, the grandmother said:

"I have an important message you must pass on to your lady. You will find a container for her. Within it will be an adornment for her finger, gifts from a bird, and parts of a plant. You will know what each item represents when they are visible. Have a speedy journey now and pass on my love to her." She said as a farewell. As he neared home, an owl flew past. He sensed it was the wise old woman.

There was no doubt we had been guided to Saltburn Gill. The coastal stream flowed fast and deep from days of heavy rainfall, but we climbed down the bank towards the shallows. Mike was overcome by an urgency to search for something in the water. Before I knew it, he was downstream, digging his hands deep into the streambed. Then, with a look of glee, he fished out an object. It was soft and bulgy.

"I just knew it...I had to look ...something or someone was telling me...go over there." Dripping wet with his hat askew, Mike grinned and jiggled.

"You'd think you had just won the lottery," I said as I washed the object in the stream. It was a small circular crocheted bag with a pull-tie seal at the top. But unfortunately, it was soggy and difficult to open, so we left that surprise till we got home.

Cathryn Mahoney

When we opened the bag, there was a ring, a feather, and some rosebud petals and leaves. They were placed on the mantelpiece to dry out. I now use the crocheted bag as a medicine pouch. It has the pattern of the Fibonacci spiral on both sides in seven shades of blue with two brown inner rings. It had been made especially for the objects and to use in my healing work. I have often wondered if my gran made it, being an avid crocheter.

Mike remembered the ring was the one he had given me in several previous lifetimes, and it was time to return it. The feather was from Old One as a reminder of his eternal presence. The rosebud petals symbolized my gift to humanity, which is agape love. The leaves represented change and transformation. They offered reassurance as to the progress made along my spiritual path.

36

Quartz Stone

We traveled to the west coast of Cornwall in January 2017 to hunt for a unique megalithic quoit stone. It was just our luck that we chose a weekend that followed torrential downpours. Our rented cottage was hidden down a country lane, cut off by the floods. We drove around in circles as darkness descended until, in a panic, we ignored a 'No Entry Flooded Road' sign. We collectively sighed when we realized the turn for the cottage was before the flooded area.

The days remained wet and windy, and we came down with horrendous colds. Yet, our mission stayed firm in our minds, even though the prize was elusive till our final day. We got our bearings by car, and we took photographs of the sea and rugged rocks during the brief periods when the sun peeked out. While we dodged the heavy rain, we were drenched by waves over breakwaters.

Our prize continued to evade us. We drove around country lanes and down pot-holed farm tracks but could not locate the quoit stone. We knew it was in a farmer's field beyond one of the hedges we had driven past. Then, Mike's phone signal returned to life at the eleventh hour. Daylight had dimmed, and I was ready to admit defeat. At last, we had the coordinates that had evaded us until that moment.

As we climbed in desperation over a forbidden gate, our feet sunk deep into cow pats among the frozen earth. I flailed about as I followed Mike the short distance toward our target and pushed aside my fear of being shot for trespassing. This was our only chance to connect with the mystery held in this spot. The moon peeked out behind a curtain of heavy clouds and lit up the large quartz stone. We prayed to God for our prize bearing witness to us. Darkness and light aligned to present us with a magical occurrence for the briefest of times. All our angst had been worthwhile.

Celestial brilliance highlighted cup marks, delves, and starry grids, illuminating ancient language for Mike to decipher. It would assist us on our journey at some future point. We sensed the importance, but our understanding of it had to wait.

I wore a thick ancient bangle on my wrist from a previous Roman lifetime. I took it off and placed it within a central cup mark. An internal key turned and unlocked the code to the starry grids, only visible in the moonlight.

When we returned to our cottage, Mike's first mission, when warmed through, was to sketch the star grid from memory. He then hid it away for safekeeping for many years to come. Its message would be revealed to us when the time was right. We felt honored and humbled and prayed for a safe journey home the following morning.

A few months later, a small quartz stone appeared. It was one I'd noticed hidden behind the quoit stone but had landed softly on the ground outside our caravan. We knew it was a gift from the creator to remind us that one day we would share the secret message of the star grids contained within the megalithic stone.

Update - September 10th, 2022

The morning began like most mornings, where I made breakfast, ready to take upstairs to share with Mike in bed. While waiting for the toast to pop up, I heard banging from above. I ran upstairs to find Mike slumped naked across the bed. As I reached him to check his breathing, I stood in a pile of grit. On opening the curtains, I saw Mike's feet and hands were caked in soil. Gently I roused him and encouraged him to take deep breaths. Then, I got him to the shower. When he opened his clenched hands, he revealed four stones in a dirty palm. He had old wound marks on his legs and face and said he ached all over.

Oon'ch-illia

When I got him settled back in bed, he produced a piece of paper with his writing on it. Before we read it, we studied the stones; then he told me what had happened.

The largest stone was an inch strip of granite, which Mike termed the keystone. There was a smaller strip and two round stones.

"The smallest one is for you to rub with your thumb," he said. "Like the other one you've got."

Mike had been sent on a mission back to the quoit stone we visited in 2017. He had been prepared for it for several moons. We knew that this event was imminent and would coincide with the harvest moon. It had shone brightly for two nights, each of which I had been restless due to the anticipation of what could happen to Mike.

On his safe return, I was curious, yet relieved Mike had survived his ordeal. I was grateful to him for completing the task that fitted another piece of the jigsaw into place. Mike had dreaded it, but now it was over, and his wounds had begun to heal. The traumatic memories also lost their hold as he talked and let his tea and toast get cold. Then he slept while Barbara stepped into his body to complete the details, which she plucked from his mind, and we explored Mike's written words together.

First, Mike had to find the keystone hidden under the ground. When he landed naked on the field, he arrived amidst a battle. He cut his leg on something sharp but began digging to find the keystone hidden under some slate. As he reached the quoit stone, he stumbled after receiving a grazing musket ball wound. Amid the noise and chaos, the keystone traced the starry grid within a hazy moonlight. The stone spoke in tune within lines of gold and silver. It proclaimed the following words and images on the night's moon: (These are transcribed as Mike wrote them.)

The sky rains rocks. There is summer frost and plague. The angry sky makes a fire mountain breathe clouds over the land for more than 16 moons. Skies will close, then skies will open with anger when many cry. The king will die. Rivers and waters retreat to the rivers in the sky. The embraced star will rise and be seen. The stones of the land will cry out warnings to deaf ears and blind eyes. Hyperboreans will huddle together. People of Mulfra to be aware of stone people. Listen to the voice of the returning water from faraway places. Returning life to where once life was not.

Mike remembered: "The gold lines took me up above. I saw death and destruction around the world. It was all muddled up. People were fighting with others from different eras. Some of the ones fighting by the quoit stone were primitive but fighting well-dressed soldiers with muskets. A great fog surrounded the earth, and all the waters had been sucked up. They became rivers in the sky. A comet exploded, and then a volcano erupted, sending ash around. In one part of the world, there was a plague; in others, was drought and famine."

Barbara offered the following details: "Many historical events collided, and Mike was seeing them all together. Most of what he saw was around the year 540. It was when king Arthur died in a battle with another king. When the meteor exploded, it showered the earth in stones. They set off volcanoes. It was the one in Iceland that Mike had seen. The Hyperboreans are an ancient civilization from the North. They, too, suffered. The people of Mulfra - this is the future event the man up at the stones (*Hob on the Hill*) told you about when he said - the year 2043 will bring a threat, but do not worry about it." (*See Chapter 38, Creating History.*)

"The embraced star is Saturn, visible in your night sky. The gravity from it will help the water beings to come." (*See Chapter 57 Update of September 8th.*)

In my research, I discovered records of the volcanic winter of 536 when a mysterious fog plunged Europe, the Middle East, and parts of Asia into darkness, day and night—for 18 months. It was believed to have been caused by a volcanic eruption in Iceland that spewed ash across the Northern Hemisphere early in 536. Two other massive eruptions followed, in 540 and 547. And, in 541-543, the Plague of Justinian spread rapidly, wiping out one-third to one-half of the population of the eastern Roman Empire. [4]

---

[4] Why 536 was 'the worst year to be alive' | Science | AAAS

Cathryn Mahoney

37

Stepping Up

On a country walk in 2015, we came across a standing stone high up on the North Yorkshire Moors. We had been searching for the 'Hob on the Hill', a special place we had been guided to find. The Hob is a 'Bowl Barrow,' a funerary monument from the Late Neolithic period to the Late Bronze Age around 2400–1500 BC. The standing stone is raised several feet above the ground, surrounded by various smaller stones.

From that discovery, we tapped into previous lifetimes when Mike and I had met on the moor. I was drawn there as a seer, healer, and teacher. Mike, in different aspects, watched over me. He endeavored to keep me safe and to support my calling. In doing so, he had lost several lives upon the moor or thereabouts. When he perished, so did I, or was moved on by Old One.

'Hob on the Hill' remains a sacred place for us both and our supporters. It is a regular meeting place, and I have visited stones in the vicinity and further afield across the moors to offer healing and guidance. The Hob is the main stone I use as an altar to address the crowds of people who arrive from different times and places on and off the earth. They arrive from all directions, and some are beamed down, all to be together in one place for a specific reason, to hear me speak. At the time of writing, there have never been people present from our current time, but all those present are alive and have shifted in time and space, apart from one or two who exist in life between lives.

I am not visible to the crowd until I step up to the altar, where there is a cup mark to place my metal tankard for offerings and a place to rest my stick. I do not see those present with my human eyes, but Mike does and acts as my communicator, but when I address people and listen to

175

them, my higher senses connect with theirs. I am Cathryn,
Oon'ch-illia, and White Bird, all as one.

During the first visit, we spent time tuning in to the
vibration of all the stones. The energy was the strongest
at the Hob. We found a secluded hollow nearby that we
had used as a resting place in previous times. It was a
perfect vantage point for the Hob. We could see all around
but were hidden from view.

During our second visit in December 2016, we were
told that some of our followers from previous times would
arrive, and I was expected to talk to them. The prospect
daunted me. I didn't know what to expect or what they
hoped to hear.

Halfway up the moor, I sensed Mike shifting and noted
an old man had joined us on our walk toward the Hob.

"Hello, Miss, may I walk with you," the man asked. His
gait was labored, and his back hunched. I slowed my pace
to match his.

"Yes, I'm pleased to meet you. May I ask your name?"
I asked.

"Of course, Miss...I be Albie. On my way to listen to
the lady speak...this will be my last time ... soon to meet
my dear wife...I miss her so," he told me between breaths.

"That's also where I'm going. I'm happy to have your
company," I said, but wondered if Albie knew it was me,
he would hear. I was also concerned that Mike agreed to
this man stepping into his body. Where had he gone? I
needed his support when we got to the top.

As if he were reading my thoughts, Albie said, "Don't
yea worry, lass...I will leave you when we are there...your
man will return."

We continued walking in companionable silence until
we reached the hollow. Mike and I had planned to rest
and wait until we knew what came next. Instead, Albie
asked if he could stay a while. As we chatted, he told me:

"I miss my late wife; we had so many happy times together. We traveled these yon moors and many other parts of the land. She heard you speak often."

"Ah...so you know it's me then. I don't remember other times, but I sense them. I don't know what I'm meant to do or say," I confessed to him.

"You will know when you step up to the stone, lass. See that groove by that rock? When you leave this space, rub your stick three times against it." Albie said, pointing at a jagged stone at the point where I planned to step out of the hollow.

We shared a flask of tea and mince pies. Then Albie said, "I must leave yea lass...find my place in the crowd ... they are gathering from far and wide."

He scanned his arm around the moor, then stepped out. He turned back to tell me: "Your man is coming back to you now; his energy will keep you strong...remember your stick now...aye...I'm looking forward to hearing your words...bye love." With a peck on the cheek, he departed.

Mike returned to his body, but I watched where Albie had gone. He turned, looked me deeply in the eyes, and said, "I'll soon be joining m' wife; I'm so happy."

At the Hob stone, I addressed the people who were present. Even though I could not physically see them, I certainly sensed them. Mike could see them and relayed their responses to me. I shared spiritual lessons and offered my understanding of divine love.

Mike whispered quietly in my ear, "I can see Albie in the crowd...oh wait...his light has just risen...he's left his body."

We announced to the gathering Albie had passed away and asked them to join us in a time of silent reflection. Then we asked if those standing close to him could return his body to his home. I was surprised when they seemed to know what to do.

After the people left, a young girl and her mother approached me.

"Can I talk to you and give you something from my mummy?" the little girl asked.

"Of course, thank you for coming to see me. What is your name?" I asked as I held my hand out for the gift she offered.

"Rebecca...I'm nine...I'm so happy to see you. Mummy is too...this is from us," she said as she handed me a coin and poured some liquid into my cup. "You must drink it, mummy says. It will help you...give you more energy."

Her mother nodded, and I drank it. Then thanked them both for attending and for their support.

While walking back down the hill, Dulaa said: "58 people were present and were from different times. They left satisfied, and all hoped to return. Well done, White Bird."

Our next visit was in late December 2017, three months after our wedding. Halfway along the journey, I picked up a stick that I knew belonged to Albie. Just before we reached the hollow, he popped into Mike's body.

"Hello love...it's good to see you again. I'm so happy now I'm reunited with my wife...we are both fine. I will be up there listening to you, lass...bye for now."

Mike and I followed the same procedure as before but were told to expect more people. I had also decided this time to do a group meditation followed by a question-and-answer session.

While I was addressing the people, Mike whispered, "there are twice as many people as last time, and some seem from the future."

The meditation included a remembrance of Albie, which was well-received. Many questions were asked and successfully answered. However, two questions regarding future events were challenging to respond to:

"Do you think Trump will be re-elected in 2024?" (*He was in office in 2016, and we didn't know Biden would win the election in 2020*).

Cathryn Mahoney

"Do you think Texas will break away from Mexico and return to America?" *(In 2016, Texas was still an American state).*

As the crowd faded, we were approached by a young girl and a couple of other people offering gifts, including one of the people from the future. The headcount this time was approximately 263. The meeting proved successful. We advised those gathered that we would return sooner, in less than a year.

We returned ten months later, in October 2018. Dulaa guided us in choosing an appropriate time. He organized the event with the elders of the tribes who attended. They required a week's notice, as many traveled from much further afield.

I felt unprepared as we had gone through a difficult year due to our travels to North America. We did not anticipate the change in the weather. It had been warm, but the moors had their own weather system. A gale blew when we reached the top. My anxiety also strengthened.

"There are many more people waiting to hear you talk," Dulaa said.

That didn't help. I also sensed there were people from our current time. That would certainly distract me. But the time couldn't pass soon enough, even before I stood up.

"There's loads more people than last time," Mike said. "Even some from the tribes we met."

No wonder I was nervous. The experiences in North America had been amazing, but they also shook us up. To have tribal members listening to me talk when my nerves were frayed didn't help. As soon as I opened my mouth to speak, the wind blew hard and whipped my words away.

I faltered, but Dulaa and Mike, both saw me hesitate.

Both nodded and said, "They can hear you, carry on."

To cap it all, two farmers turned up to repair a nearby grouse shooting hide, which certainly put me off my stride. So much so that I asked for a break from speaking.

Oon'ch-illia

I requested that the crowd talk among themselves to get to know each other. I later learned that was the plan all along. At the time, I thought I had let them down. I had given in to my own insecurities and fears from the past. Memories of being hounded by landowners who distrusted my intentions flooded my senses.

I recomposed myself and then led those gathered into a short meditation followed by a question-and-answer session. There were many questions I could not recall due to my anxious state at the time, and I ended the meeting sooner than I had wanted because we were both cold and hungry. Three of the people who had spoken asked to give me gifts. Mike went into the crowd to receive them. Then a young native girl with her mother and grandfather came to speak to me. My attention was limited, so I apologized for not giving the best of myself and left.

I was reassured by Dulaa and Mike afterward that I had done a brilliant job. Yet, I couldn't take on board their reassurances. Self-flagellation took firm hold. Mike got angry, and we fell out. It overshadowed the whole event.

When we returned home, Dulaa told us, "There were approximately 646 in attendance from many times and cultures. The time you afforded them to mingle will be useful in their futures and will potentially avoid conflicts and wars."

The young native girl who approached me introduced herself as, Running Eagle. She became a brave warrior in her Blackfoot tribe, and we had visited her memorial in Montana. Running Eagle had given me a gift on the moor, which we discovered on our return home. Mike had seen her take a leather bracelet off her wrist. She wanted me to have it as a thank you, as she held me in high esteem and aspired to be just like me when she grew up. We also received one dollar, one shilling, and some leaves and heather from a couple who followed us up the hillside.

I later learned that Mike had been chastised by some Ancients among the stones.

He said, "I'm not allowed to return there till I apologize to them and ask for their forgiveness."

That was because he had shouted at me for judging myself. It was a learning curve for us both, and we wondered what would transpire next time. Did we have the courage to return? Especially since the numbers and diversity of those attending seemed to grow.

As it happened, we did not return to the Hob for some time due to several events. In 2019 I had recurring mobility issues with my feet, and Mike had breathing problems. We had been in North America for May, and our recovery time was protracted. To top it off, my Auntie became ill and died that August. In January 2020, we were both unwell, and then the Pandemic hit.

Another meeting was arranged for my birthday in April 2020. The Ancients worked with Dulaa to gather people and brought them to a field near our home. We believe there were 523 in attendance at that time. It had been a very difficult process to get them together. Many had been brought through a portal. They had a narrow time slot from arrival to return home. It was a juggling act due to the differences in travel times. There were people from times past and future and some of the tribespeople we had met in America. In addition, there were beings from other planets. Some travel times were equivalent to several of our years. I told them we were grateful they had chosen to visit with us and spend time with the others present.

At that meeting, Mike and I discovered that each person's level of awareness, the time and place they came from all affected how they saw us and our environment. Some saw us as we were in our current time, some saw us how we appeared to them in their time, and some saw us in our light bodies. On this occasion, our time together was limited to twenty minutes of questions and answers. Dulaa assured me that they all left happy. It was more productive than I would ever realize. We were enabling new connections for peaceful understanding and alliances. I gave them assurances we would gather again by the end of 2020 at the Hob on the Hill.

By the end of October, tier systems were introduced to manage the pandemic, which still curtailed social activities. Fortunately, we could travel within our own county of North Yorkshire, but my mobility wasn't good, yet we made tentative plans to return to the Hob on the Hill. We agreed on December 20th, 2020, the last Sunday before Christmas, and the day before the winter solstice. Even though there were no local travel restrictions, we had to contend with floods. With that in mind, we had a practice walk in November. It was difficult underfoot, but we achieved it. I remained optimistic about the date we had set.

When the day arrived, I still had doubts about my mobility, and my pain levels were worse than the previous month. I was also nervous about other people out on the moors since the number of local walkers had grown during the pandemic.

It was a difficult walk in cold, wet, and windy weather. When we arrived at the stones, instead of having a hot drink and snack, I wanted to get on with it. First, Mike gave me a quick overview of the layout of the crowd; then, I addressed our visitors. I spoke of the 'plague' and how it affected countries worldwide. It was a history lesson, for some, about their future, and for others, a reminder of past events. Finally, I encouraged people to greet their neighbors and connect in love and peace. A few people asked questions, and then we left them to mingle.

We witnessed many new and old faces, and a group from Scotland, some Picts. One of them asked: "When will you next visit our land?"

"Thank you for asking," I replied. "We look forward to returning...but it will likely be another two years because of the plague."

Mike and Dulaa later told me there were about 800 people present. On leaving the moor, the return downhill was so painful I thought I wouldn't make it at one point.

Cathryn Mahoney

The evening of the Summer Solstice - June 2021 marked our return to the Hob. Many of the same people were in attendance. First, we updated them on current events.

Then I decided networking was more advantageous for all present. It was a relaxing, sociable event, with some questions answered to the best of my ability. Since we had been socially isolated for over a year and had little contact with clients and groups, I felt inadequate in my abilities. Even spending time with our tribe had lessened. I had become insular since my focus shifted to writing about our travels in North America and preparing to write this book.

Dulaa reassured me, "Their coming together is the important thing...you are making that possible...bringing so many to this place...creating a place and time of peace and harmony...it means more than you may ever realize."

38

Creating History

I stepped up to the Hob Stone once again. Mike said he could see beings appear from a cloud and others materialize in front and around us. Various tribes and cultures dressed in an assortment of colorful garments.

I greeted all present and said: "It's a beautiful sight to have you all here connecting for the same reason. I'm pleased to see familiar faces and new ones. In our time, today is June 19th, 2022. The summer solstice is near." There were a few gasps.

"Today, I will try something new. Please mill around and connect with someone not of your tribe or people. Pair up, look into each other's eyes, deep into their soul, and connect with the heart. If not in a pair or you do not want to pair up, mix in small groups. Look with soft eyes around the people in front of you; look at their aura - energy fields. Do this until I ask you to stop; afterward, you can share your experience."

There were people in front and all around us. Mike timed a minute for silence, then indicated they could talk and share with one another. Then I asked for questions or feedback. There were communication difficulties with language and marked differences between races and cultures. Many found it peaceful, relaxing, and pleasant; some found it uncomfortable. Nevertheless, they were all grateful to each other for the experience.

Questions:

A member from a species that cannot get close to a neighboring species because their skin gives off an enzyme that attacks that of the others asked if that would change over time. Both groups were present but stayed far apart.

I asked, "Do you both want to connect?" Both groups nodded.

"Well, anything is possible if you want it to be. Many species adapt and evolve in a changing environment."

"Where there is a will, there is a way," Mike added. "Perhaps there is some technology you can find to help you. Maybe a space suit?"

I responded: "Mm, something to think about. There could be another species that can help you create something to help. Collective consciousness is a powerful thing. What if you project the same thoughts to the universe that you desire to meet in the way I've suggested today?"

A woman, who Mike described as simply dressed and appeared to be from the 1700s, spoke next.

"I've read about you in our history books."

I whispered to Mike. "She must be from the future."

"There were times you wanted to give up but kept going. What made you keep going until you achieved what you wanted?" She asked.

I responded: "Yes, I have felt like giving up many times recently."

"One of the dates I read was 2022, and 2019 was a bad year for you too." She reminded me.

"What year are you from?" I asked.

"2107," was her response.

"My faith in the creator," I replied. "My love for humanity, my husband and tribe; it's not just for me, for everyone. I honor those who have supported me in all my lifetimes. That is what I am here to do; I cannot, will not turn away from it." I spoke with conviction and volume, so all could hear my words.

A man spoke next. He said: "In a few years, you will read about the year 2043 being one of threat. If I told you now not to worry, would that help?"

"Yes, we will remember that, thank you," I told him.

Oon'ch-illia

I hadn't realized many people were standing behind us. A man in front pointed to a very tall and stocky man behind us who had his hand up to speak.

Mike said, "It's difficult to describe his attire. It's silver and white. He has what looks like oxygen tanks front and back. I can't translate...Dulaa, can you help?"

Mike spoke Dulaa's words: "He's from a faraway place. He's heard it said you've been through many times in this world and others. How much do you understand about earlier travels and the worlds you've been on? Does it stay with you, or do you have to use a different part of your mind to recall it?"

I answered: "It's in my distant consciousness that I bring to the forefront. I haven't remembered until recently, from my dreams and in my writings. It's been pushed back; memories are deep in consciousness in a place of safety, and I'm now bringing them forward more."

The man responded: "Keep practicing."

I then asked the crowd to chat among themselves for a while again. "This time is important for you to connect with one another." I reminded them.

Mike told me more about the people in the crowd as they talked.

"There are so many colors of clothing and skin - silver, white, black, and colors in between. We've not seen a crowd this big before...there must be at least 1500 here."

He looked to Dulaa for corroboration. Dulaa said: 1831 beings present from many times and places on and off-world."

I wound up the gathering by thanking people for attending and engaging with one another. I encouraged them to linger for as long as they could after we departed.

My parting words were: "Remember how you have felt during this gathering. Remember this occasion and its importance to you and everyone here. Go and teach others and encourage peace, love, and respect among your own tribes and neighbors. You all believe and want the same things; that is why you are present here at this gathering. It is important and heart-warming that you have chosen to be here and taken the long journeys to arrive together. We are grateful to you - for us and for everyone here, what each of you has committed to."

I offered a time of quiet reflection to conclude, but a man stepped up to the front of the crowd. Mike said to me:

"This man would like to speak openly...he's an authority figure!"

I knew he was an ancient one and told him I was grateful he wished to speak.

"I want everyone to know - everyone here today has made history together. This is deemed the point when things changed in towns and cities and countries and places in this world, beyond this world and beyond worlds. This is the point in time it all boils back to. The ancestors and the future generations of many people will remember this time. I want everyone to know, especially you." The man said, looking straight at me.

I asked his name and the year he was from:

"The year 2316, Mike said. "Do you want his name in his language or ours?"

Both, if that is, OK?" I responded.

Mike repeated what he heard from the man:

"I will be unable to repeat it in his language. It's a very still noise he makes - I can't decipher it. Noise travels from him, a feeling, not a sound. In our tongue - Slola NaMamba. From within the Eskimo galaxy. The planet will be discovered in time."

"Thank you for your words that reinforce the importance of our time together, that everyone is contributing to make it a significant time in history," I said.

I asked if there was anyone else who would like to speak before we departed. Another man raised his hand and made us laugh by saying:

"Well...it's been worth the time and effort being here if we are going down in history for it. Something to tell my grandchildren and the ones after. I've heard of these meetings...they have been life-changing for those I've spoken to. I will take back my own experience, and in my heart, I know it will have a greater impact on the people I speak to. I'm very grateful to you."

A crescendo of excitement reverberated around the rocks.

"Please shake hands or hug each other and leave when you feel it's the right time to do so. Please know you have our love and that of our tribe. We bid you farewell," I said as my parting words.

Mike reported his observations: "There's a sh-ing sound...people are leaving...lights are going up...and some are fading away. We're fading to them. There's a young girl approaching. Hello sweetheart. What is your name?"

"Jashwa"

"How old are you?"

"In your years?"

Mike nodded.

"Eight."

"Who are you here with?"

She pointed behind her, *"my grandmother. She has been many times and it changed her life. She hopes it will be the same for me."*

Jashwa touched my stick. I put my hand out, and she reached out to put her little hand in my palm.

"Thank you for coming to see me, and thank your grandmother for bringing you," I said as I pecked her on the forehead and waved at her grandmother. Then, they, too, disappeared in front of my eyes.

IV

Belonging

*On our travels, we rediscovered many special places
where we had been before, within other timelines. The
familiarity of places sometimes struck us dumb,
made us weep or brought forth a fit of giggles.
There has always been a subtle sense of knowing, which
heightened our senses and emotions. Often,
we felt bereft on leaving, and sometimes, when we
touched base, we didn't feel pulled to return. But, once
we had reconnected with the essence of our presence
there, we sealed it in, just like an animal marking its
territory.
We have visited many places, often in secluded locations,
where we have either shifted between
times or received visitors from other times or
planets. Such visitors have shared knowledge and
wisdom with us or offered guidance on our journey.*

Oon'ch-illia

39

Homelands

Weaving across the lake, we cut across the wake of passing boats towards the distant mountains. An hour had passed, yet we were no closer. Despite the two-hour slot and being only meters away from the restriction zone, we refused to turn back. A rocky outcrop denoted an invisible barrier at the natural bend in the lake. As we reached it, the peak of a majestic mountain came into view.

"Yeeeees, that's it," we hollered in chorus. It was the first view of our tribe's mountain home. With no viable access to their cave, we could only ogle from a distance and capture the image to retain in our memories.

It was a bittersweet moment as we bobbed in the idle boat, floating closer to the rocky shore.

"We have to keep away from the rocks; what are you doing?" I asked Mike.

"I know what I'm doing. We have visitors. Look in the forest. They are coming to greet us," Mike said as he pointed into the trees while keeping the boat in the shallows.

"Who's there?" I asked him.

"Sashma, Jheneeka, and Teela...ah...I can see some of the other girls...wait...they're all here...there are more appearing among the trees...I think some of them are coming onto the boat...I'll have to keep it still," Mike said, astounded to see so many of the tribe.

"Is it safe?" I asked as Jheneeka, Teela and Sashma climbed aboard to announce they wished to honor us with a Binding Ceremony.

"Reach into your right trouser pocket and bring out the objects," Sashma asked Mike. From his previously empty pocket, Mike retrieved several leaves, a stone, a small yellow flower, and a small cone.

"Hold each other's left hand," Sashma asked just as Old One appeared.

Speaking softly in his own language, Old One bound our wrists together with a pure white silk scarf. His words serenaded like a gentle breeze and lulled us into waves of deep peace. Then he placed a hand over our joined hands.

Sashma asked Mike to throw the leaves into the water and repeat after her: *"let our love grow as the leaves, supporting those who are important to us, aging slowly as the seasons pass."*

Then, she asked me to take the stone, throw it into the water, and repeat: *"may our love be as deep as the waters, may our love be as solid as the stone, and may the stone sleep in the waters of deep love forever."*

Sashma asked us both to look at the yellow flower and repeat the words: *"let the flower be likened unto the sun. May the days bring us light and beauty. May our love and actions be an example to others. As the sun moves across the sky, may our lifetimes be as long and beneficial to the earth and its inhabitants in all the ways we can."* Then Mike threw it into the water.

I held the cone and threw it into the water after repeating Sashma's words: *"let this seed represent the seed of wisdom and growth within us both. Bound by love for all day until the long night comes of separation, as one waits for the other."*

We were mesmerized as Old One sang a beautiful chant. It was a subtle, haunting melody of modulated tones. After a short silence, the whole tribe, those on the boat and on the shore, sang in unison to express their happiness at our union. The rhythm between the boat and shoreline filled the air until silence reigned. Then, the tribe faded deep into the forest, followed by Sashma, Jheneeka, and Teela, who congratulated us with a kiss. Old One, as usual, was the last to leave. He expressed his joy and love for us in his familiar way, with three taps on the head for Mike and three gentle pats on my cheek, while saying, "I love you, my child."

40

Endurance

"For many days, we have traveled to get the soldiers off our scent. My people grow weary, and each day the sun darkens, we yearn to return home. Our plan to hide in the caves near our hunting grounds is thwarted. We make a hasty retreat, leaving many belongings behind. The soldiers are a day behind us. Their determination is to be admired if they were not after our blood or to remove us from our homelands. Our friends, the star people, come to our aid. They plan to send the soldiers in the opposite direction.

With our path cleared, it takes two more revolutions of the sun to arrive safely home. Then, with our tepees erected and food and water supplies restored, we can breathe and settle.

As the light shifts at the end of each day, I find solitude on my chosen rock deep within the trees. I commune with the Great Spirit and ask for peace and good fortitude for my people. They have suffered enough. I have learned from the Old One of the star people that white soldiers have annihilated many tribes. Everywhere on these great lands is the smell of death and sadness, for what? Greed. Is there not enough land and bountiful resources provided by Mother Earth and Father Sun? Old One and the other chiefs I have communed with say it will never be enough for the white man until we are no more. We have signed their papers to preserve only small areas of our lands, but they go back on their word. I must keep my people safe, but my heart is heavy; it is only a matter of time."

Narrated by Tuekakas (Old Chief Joseph)

Cathryn Mahoney

We had learned about the plight of Chief Joseph and his band of Nez Perce from Carney, another visitor from our tribe. She had spent time with us on part of our journey at Wallowa Lake, Oregon, and introduced me to Wahluna. We sat by the lake where Wahluna told me of her meeting Tlasca, a Blackfoot warrior, who was standing beside her as she spoke. She told me the story of their betrothal and their demise that night when a monstrous creature had taken them into the depths of the lake. Despite this, their union had brought peace between the Nez Perce and Blackfoot tribes.

After chatting with Wahluna and Tlasca, Carney asked me to perform a ritual to rid the serpent from the lake. I repeated the words Carney spoke. It was an incantation. While reciting it, I smacked my hand three times in the water to command the serpent to leave.

A few weeks later, we read a news item about a dead lake creature washed up on the shore of Bear Lake in Utah. We wondered if there was any connection. Was it the same monster swimming between lakes? Was there a cave system that connected them?

I later learned from Old One about his promise to the Shoshone Chief, Washakie. Our tribe helped his people escape slaughter from a non-allegiance Blackfoot tribe. Washakie told Old One that some of his people had also been taken by the Lake monster, so Old One promised to rid the lake of it.

I understand that is what I had done in May 2019, but I stepped between the veils into 1870. While talking to Carney, I also visited Old One in the mountains above Wallowa Lake. He took me on a journey, shifting through time.

Although I hadn't been aware of the shift and my time with Old One till several months later.

When Mike returned to his body, I gave him a brief overview of Wahluna and Tlasca's visit. He appeared to have no prior knowledge of them, so I did not tell him that he had once been Tlasca. That surprise would come later after I had time to ponder it for myself. So instead, we shared some quiet time by the lake.

"We've been here before to see the stars," Mike said. "It must have been in our sleep. Do you remember?"

"There is some distant memory, but it is hard to recall, but I sense you're right," I replied.

Then we walked on and headed up the hillside along a forest path. As we entered the forest, we arrived at a large flat boulder. During the day, I struggled to walk. Despair and fear still permeated the land and appeared to immobilize me. However, I asked Mike to help me climb on top of the rock. As I settled, a sense of peace within the breeze wrapped subtle shifts of rainbow colors around me. Mike observed the color and light play on my physical body and connect with my etheric body. A butterfly landed on my shoulder; with it, pure bliss filled me. I recognized the energy of Old Chief Joseph speaking through the butterfly. He said, "thank you for visiting and resting here for a while. This is my rock of peace and solace. I begged the Great Spirit to save my people. My heart was heavy when I came here...but then it lifted...I knew all would be well. We would all meet again."

I smiled at the butterfly on my shoulder. It was an inner smile as my eyes were closed. I felt him all around me like he was sitting on the rock talking through me.

"Thank you, Chief Joseph, for visiting to share your thoughts with me...I can feel how tortuous life was for you then. The responsibility for your people weighed heavy on you...I love you, always have, and always will," I replied.

As I climbed down from the rock, I did not want to leave. I felt pulled back as if I wanted to fly away with the butterfly to where Chief Joseph returned to, a place not of this world.

41

Mountains Call

The mountains of Southern Oregon and Northern California hold great mysteries hidden within the rocks and peaks shrouded in mist. At every turn, I sensed being watched and scrutinized. Not in a threatening way but with curiosity and awe. There was a sense of returning, once again, to homelands.

A particular mountain track drew us deep into the forest of Chinquapin Mountain. We drove as far as possible, weaving between fallen trees, but as soon as we left the car, Dulaa alerted us to danger.

"A bear sniffs close by; it's picked up your scent. I will divert it. You may proceed," Dulaa said. Our dutiful guide and protector disappeared into the trees to send the bear off in a different direction.

We were wary of putting too much distance between ourselves and the car. Luckily, our destination was a few meters away. It was a large rock on a grassy bank above the track. Mike gave me a leg up so we could both sit atop it. I settled into a well-worn groove and connected with the essence of Old One. When Dulaa returned, he told us, "This was another of Old One's meeting places with the Ancient Ones."

I bathed in their essence as well as my own memories of my feet upon the land. The energy of the forest, mountains, and lakes swept brushstrokes of subtle colors across my body, leaving feathery imprints within my auric field, and activated connections within my consciousness.

Imagine electric circuitry flashing as each connection is made. It traveled for miles in each direction across Oregon to the North in Washington, and the Northeast reconnecting with Montana and Alberta. To the East, it reconnected with Idaho, Wyoming, and the Dakotas. And, to the west, connected with the coastline, and South into California.

Dulaa then broke me from my reverie, my state of bliss and remembering.

"Can I introduce you to my new friend, Chief K'Kyum," he asked.

We both sat up straight upon the rock, smiled, and nodded. "Yes, of course, welcome, Chief K'Kyum; I'm sure I recognize your name," I said, and then looked at Mike for clarification.

Mike shrugged and then looked to Dulaa to enlighten us: "Remember, my friend was the guide for that woman in your group, the one who fell. We gave her a message from him."

"Ah, I know now, of course," I turned to Mike and said, "Can you remember...what was she called? Mmm...it was...Pam."

"My friend and I have chatted much since that time ... he much admires you, White Bird, and wishes to join you both along this part of your journey. Is that acceptable?" Dulaa asked.

"Yes, of course it is," I turned to Mike for agreement to my response as a formality.

"What about Pam? Are you no longer with her?" I asked of the Chief.

Chief K'Kyum said, "after you had told her about me, her reaction did not suit me...she has taken a different path ... I am now befriended by your tribe and may stay with them awhile if they will have me."

"Old One has insisted you stay if you wish, my friend. White Bird, may we walk ahead for a while and meet you by the vehicle?" Dulaa asked.

"Yes, of course, we won't be long," I assured him while Mike jumped off the rock and started taking photos of me on it.

Pam was a lady in our spiritual group at Saltburn. She often regaled us with her visitations. She sensed she had a Native American connection but was unsure from which tribe. Towards the end of the course, Dulaa suggested he could visit a spirit guide connected with each person within the group. They were so excited as they awaited what they believed to be channeled messages. In fact, Dulaa had spent days and weeks going back and forwards in time and space to visit the guides he had identified. It had taken some time to gain their trust as to his intentions.

Chief K'Kyum from the Yurok tribe had been watching over Pam for many years, guiding her spiritual growth. Unfortunately, after receiving his message via Dulaa, she disregarded it. He realized it was time to move on to another chapter of his life. With Dulaa's encouragement, he returned to his homelands briefly, and his visit to us coincided with that.

We returned in haste to our car after I slid off the rock, and Mike caught me in mid-flight.

"Right, are you ready to run...so the bear doesn't get us?" Mike teased. Thinking of the distance between us and the car and a bear that could jump out from behind a tree, we half-ran before collapsing into our seats.

When Dulaa joined us, I asked: "Where's the Chief going?"

He replied, "Off to visit his people...he'll pop in from time to time to watch your progress along the journey."

Back in the car, Mike negotiated the log-littered track and then stopped sharp.

"What's wrong?" I asked, following his gaze toward one of the logs.

"Can you see it...it's camouflaged...see...there, it just moved," he pointed excitedly out my passenger window.

"Ah...yes, the lizard...I see it now. It's strange, though; I sense it's Chief K'Kyum, but it's not him; is it Dulaa?" I asked, with a grin in the rear-view mirror.

I looked over at Mike as I shrugged, "I think he's just shapeshifted. Was he not walking along waving at us - then shifted in space? Can he really do that, Dulaa?" I asked.

"What do you think, White Bird?"

I huffed, then smiled, "Here we go again, as always - work it out for yourself, White Bird," I muttered.

I think Dulaa felt sorry for me. He thought a moment, then said: "You will see him a few more times on your journey and in different forms."

On another mountain road, we drove up the hairpin bends towards the peak of He-Devil Mountain.

"Where on Earth are we headed?" I asked Dulaa.

"Keep driving until you sense when to stop," was the reply.

We hit snow and logs across the road, so there was no choice but to stop. After Mike negotiated an eight-point turn above a steep slope, we returned to a lay-by near a rocky outcrop.

"I sensed this was the right place," I said as I tugged Mike towards a ledge with a view across Hells Canyon. It stole our thoughts and held us suspended in space. Our essence, just a hazy imprint, lingered on the mountains across the way from when we met with Old One and his brother, Old Chief Joseph.

A twin tree and the colors of flora and fauna then kept us enthralled until Dulaa interrupted us, "You have a visitor, be ready; he is an ancient one and has waited a long time to see you again."

We were introduced to Chief Smohalla. His essence was like a favorite scent. Deep love radiated from his heart to mine. I felt the urge to wrap my arms around him but restrained myself as I listened to his words.

"Greetings, dear ones. I am delighted to have your acquaintance again. It is a long time since I have been in my homelands; it is good to be back."

"Thank you for your visit. This feels like such a special place to us. Have we met here before?" I inquired.

"Oh yes, many happy times here and elsewhere. In time, you will recall." He said, with a glint in his eye. "Do you have any questions for me before I depart?"

Cathryn Mahoney

I remain certain to this day that for those next few moments, Chief Smohalla wrapped his light around us and took us elsewhere. I have no recollection of our questions and the answers. Yet, after his departure, deep peace and joy prevailed.

"I don't want to leave here," I said as I hugged Mike, and he agreed.

When we eventually returned to the car, I noticed a delve in the earth where I'd seen a quartz stone.

"That's unusual. Did you see that stone when we arrived," I asked Mike.

"Mm, I wonder where it's gone?" he shrugged.

"I can feel an invisible thread pull me as if tugging at a memory. Whether in the past or future, I don't know." Mike looked bemused at my words then we laughed in tandem. Magic hung in the air.

42

Friendship

Within fifteen minutes of walking the Sac and Fox Trail alongside the Cedar River in Iowa, we felt a sudden pull to return along the path. Four deer watched our movements with interest from the safety of the trees. Then, Mike stopped short.

"What's wrong? Company?" He asked Dulaa.

I sensed tension sizzle between Mike and Dulaa. They consulted with one another in the tribe's language.

In front and to the sides of us appeared a group of warriors.

"They're Sac & Fox. Their leader wishes to speak to White Bird," explained Dulaa.

Dulaa asked their intentions, then said: "I am to introduce you, White Bird, to Chief Wapello and his warriors." He panned an arm around the group that surrounded us. "Chief Wapello insists he must speak to you alone, White Bird."

Mike stepped in front of me, but the warriors stepped toward him with their weapons raised.

"I'm OK...I can go alone," I reassured him.

I walked several steps to greet the Chief. I had a sense of inner peace, not unlike the feeling I have with Old One. "Greetings...thank you for visiting...I am honored by your presence and that of your warriors...it is good to see you again."

"Greetings to you, Peacemaker; I desired to be in your presence again. We are grateful to you for your love, wisdom, and guidance. Please accept two of the animals," he said while pointing at the deer who watched and waited among the trees. Then, he ushered two warriors in their direction.

"That is very kind of you...but please, no, our journey

Cathryn Mahoney

does not allow...we are unable to accept your gift," I said instantly, to stop such slaughter on my account.

"We will leave you to go on your way...until the next time...farewell." The Chief summoned his warriors, and they faded away along the path.

I remained calm and was overjoyed by such a reunion. Mike, on the other hand, had begun hyperventilating.

"What on earth was that about?" he asked Dulaa.

"The Chief knew White Bird as the Peacemaker. He didn't recognize you as Hiawatha. He just saw you as White Bird's brave." Dulaa replied. [5]

---

[5] In other lifetimes Mike had merged with Hiawatha, the Orator for the Great Peacemaker. I had merged with Jigonhsasee, known to the tribes as the 'Mother of Nations,' and Gemel had merged with the Great Peacemaker, whose tribal name was never allowed to be spoken by the people. All three had been instrumental in devising the 'Great Law of Peace,' which brought together 5 (and many years later) 6 tribal nations: The Haudenosaunee/Iroquois Confederacy.

43

Victorian Visionary

As I partook in an early morning stroll, I saw no other soul along the sands. But I was torn from my reverie by the gulls' insistent cries as they dipped and dived into the gentle waves. Such a special time of the day as the sun rose above the horizon with streaks of orange and pink. I enjoyed the quiet, connecting with each grain of sand while sensing the warmth in the air easing the aches in my joints. Then, I quickened my step, remembering I had an important rendezvous with Henry by the pier. I knew he would already be there, awaiting the construction workers, despite many calls on his time. And, of course, I would give him my customary scold to remind him of his wife and children.

The previous night was wearing. So many people had gathered for healing and potions. But a warning came to finish early, leaving many disappointed. The ones who wished me harm were drawing closer each time. Gemel had advised me to find a new location, but I wasn't ready to leave the town.

Henry was a great pull on my time and my affection. This was the third, and I knew it would be the last time I could advise him. So, I picked my way through the pebbles up the beach to the lower promenade. I saw him waving his top hat like a child rather than the important businessman reviving a humble seaside town. He greeted me with a bear hug, lifting my feet off the ground. His gratitude for my presence was palpable. Then, he grew serious, updating me with the finer details of the works in progress of his pier construction. Out of his suitcase, he produced the plans for the hotel and houses, which were in various stages of development.

"I'm sorry to rush you. I must catch the train in thirty

minutes. I have an important meeting at the Houses of Parliament," he said.

"What about your family? I hope you are not leaving them behind again," I scolded.

"No, I'm taking them with me; there is no need to scold, not this time anyway," he laughed.

However, he was keen to speak about another matter before his time with me ran out.

"I need to talk to you about what happened last time we met?" he said.

"Of course, I guess you have lots of questions...it was certainly interesting...where would you like to start?" I asked him.

"Well...I need to know where you went...one minute we were talking...I turned to my desk, and you were gone. I sat for a few minutes with my arms wrapped around my head, thinking I had gone mad...then when I looked up, you were standing in the same spot as where you'd left. How do you explain that?" Henry shook his head but had a grin on his face.

No wonder he was insistent we met so soon. Although I could not explain it at the time, it also confused me.

"It was a shock to me, too, when you told me what had happened. I spoke to Gemel about it. You remember me telling you about him, don't you?"

Henry said: "Gemel? Ah, yes, I recall him now. So, did you go somewhere with him? Why did you leave when we were discussing such important matters?"

I placed my hand on his arm. "I'm sorry I did that; it was rude of me...I have no control over when it happens ... Gemel and Old One had to take me with them there and then...believe it or not, you will benefit from what we did in time to come."

"Can you tell me more...where you went and why?" Henry frowned, looking more confused than ever.

"I went a little way into the future...Gemel said my essence needed to be placed there...It will help you to be successful with your plans for the town ... that is all I can tell you. I feel your frustration ... I feel the same way but cannot give more information. It is vague for me, but I know it will serve us both well in the years to come. Old One reassures me that I will know when it happens. Our visits will be no more, Henry. The way I know you ... I'm certain you will be forever grateful to me. We will keep each other in our hearts." [6]

---

[6] Henry Pease (1807-1881) was a director of the Stockton and Darlington Railway Company, MP for Durham South (1857-1865), and founded the Saltburn Improvement Company in 1859. He was responsible for the development of Saltburn-by-the-Sea, North Yorkshire.

44

Reminisce

Swathes of the lush forest had been wiped out by the construction of Grand Lake, so there's nothing grand about it except its volume that once fed the Miami-Erie canal.

We searched the barren lands for a thicket of white and red oak that still exist but is now hidden behind the town. Finally, after a frantic search, we found the 47 acres of Baker Woods State Nature Preserve, all that is left of the historic homelands of the Kickapoo, Shawnee, and other tribes.

Our discontent was soothed away with the warmth of the spring day with the company of birds singing and dancing butterflies along the 1.3-mile loop hiking trail. Our senses were on overdrive, with vibrations of light, sound, and movement stopping us in our tracks. Then, Dulaa asked, "What do you feel?"

"I'm drawn to these trees ... I want to touch each one," I told him as I proceeded to hug the grey-mottled bark of the largest oaks.

"Each of these trees was planted by a member of our tribe ... can you name who planted which?" Dulaa said while walking between the trees.

I stepped up to each one and named them correctly. Then, a bit further along the path, Dulaa stopped us again as he stepped between two oaks and asked, "who planted these trees?"

I walked up to the one I was most drawn to, and Mike moved toward the other. We named them as our own, and Dulaa said, "yes, you are correct."

At another group of trees, Dulaa asked, "White Bird - which one of the larger oaks resonates with you?"

A rush of emotion assailed me as I wrapped my arms around a silver trunk.

"You helped Chief Inkpaduta plant that tree. He was

Oon'ch-illia

like an uncle to you. We befriended his tribe and spent time with them here. You were only a small child then. The tree represents your bond. The trees surrounding it were planted by some of his tribe and ours, working together as one."

"It's remarkable the trees are still here; have they been protected?" I asked Dulaa.

"Yes, the lady this woodland is named after protected it. She listed it as historic land in her will ... to be kept as a nature preserve. It also has Old One's protection."

A circle of trees drew our attention. Misty figures danced and laughed around a campfire in a beautiful wildflower meadow. A brief glimpse of a happy time for Chief Inkpaduta and his band of Santee Sioux. A respite from their journey across the Great Plains towards another battle. [7]

---

[7] Chief Inkpaduta escaped capture following the Spirit Lake Massacre of 1857. He traveled across the Great Plains, where he met Sitting Bull. Together, they fought in many battles, including the Battle of Little Bighorn. Like many notable chiefs who evaded capture, he died in Canada.

45

Kinship

The beloved, mystical Mount Shasta pulled me into her heart and into a tight embrace. A song of time and space and distant cousins from faraway lands.

I may have stayed away. The acrid taste of commercial spiritualism almost kept me from Shasta and her twin, but the deep pull for reconnection was reignited when I flew over her shrouded peak. The eyes of the ancient ones followed our journey. They tugged at my heart. My longing intensified. I knew the time was right for my presence again—a reunion with our kin who reside within the caves.

The spirit of the peak drew us up to the snowfields, where we could marvel at her majesty. Her meadows were hidden for another occasion, but an open glade further down the slope was green again with mounds of melted snow. The wind whipped hail against the car. It sang a haunting tune to keep us in suspense as if the icy air had frozen us. As an eerie stillness descended, I looked at Mike but asked Dulaa, "We are not alone, are we?"

"You have visitors. They are among the trees waiting. I must go talk to them and ask their intentions."

Dulaa stepped out of the vehicle and disappeared into the forest.

"What do we do now? Who do you think they are?" I asked Mike.

"I think we are meant to wait here until Dulaa returns; then, he will instruct us. I sense they wish to talk to us but are wary," Mike said as he peered through the misted window.

Dulaa returned, saying, "You must follow me. If you meet them halfway, your visitors will step out of the trees."

Oon'ch-illia

I held tight to Mike's hand, hesitated, then hurried. A warm breeze assailed me then I stilled as I sensed the presence of our two visitors. I followed Mike's leading body language - and recognized that our visitors awaited introductions.

"Hello, we are pleased to meet you, thank you for visiting us," I said.

Dulaa drew forward to interpret for us. "This is Helena and her brave, Ch'Garik. They are pleased to make the acquaintance of White Bird and her brave."

"We are honored to be here and to meet you both. Is this your home?" I inquired as I spanned my arm toward the mountain.

Before they answered me, Mike asked our visitors, "Can I describe your appearance to White Bird?"

They agreed, and as Mike talked, I conjured up the details, seeing them clearly in my mind's eye. Their white garments from head to foot. Helena's blond hair and icy blue eyes. Ch'Garik stood attentive by Helena's side without saying a word. On the other hand, Mike had become our interpreter, with Dulaa stepping aside. The conversation flowed. I felt a strong connection to Helena, like a sister's vibration. Our likeness in thoughts, actions, and roles seemed identical.

I asked Helena questions about the information I'd read about sightings in the vicinity.

"Are you the woman that some people have seen? Are you a Lemurian?"

"It is time for you to know the truth. There are many beliefs here. Many sightings. My cousins, the Arameans, have misled humans. Spiritual seekers have been led down many wrong paths. It has skewed the history of this ancient place." Helena said.

"I'm not surprised," I replied, "But I am sad to discover again the truth is hidden within distorted stories. Is it my place to speak out and correct that? Or do I plant silent seeds by my presence? Is that my purpose here, to scatter them behind me along the right path for others to find?"

Her smile and her hug farewell, for now, gave me the answer.

The wind and hail returned as we stepped back into our vehicle.

Dulaa asked, "Did you hear that?"

We were light-headed after our time with Helena and Ch'Garik.

"We have found others just like us...all my doubts and beliefs about misinformation being spread were well-founded. I hear singing in the wind and feel such joy in my heart. Do you?" I asked Mike.

Mike bear-hugged me, and I sensed the grin on his face.

"I'm so impressed you translated Helena's words. She spoke so fast in that strange tongue," I said into his chest, then pulled him into a smooch.

Dulaa interrupted us: "What you hear is the mountain celebrating your return and your reunion with Helena...this is only the start."

46

Leadership

His hand held mine like a vice, scared to let go in case I fell, as we picked our way around the deep holes in the ground. With one false move, they could have quaked and swallowed us whole. Our destination was only a breath away. Success or failure sat on a knife's edge.

The cave was within sight, and Teela encouraged us on. We stepped into the aqua shimmer of Old One's protective shield while Teela grabbed my other hand, urging me to follow her deep into the cavern. Mike and Dulaa took up the rear. When I looked back at them, the entrance to the cave had closed.

The passageway took us into a crystal chamber. We descended further. A waft of warm air stopped us and suspended us in time. A moment later, we arrived at a familiar cavern. The deep hot spring awaited our arrival to cleanse away the fear and shadows of the time we had just left. Isame was in attendance. He instructed us to strip and step into the water. Mike held his hands out as I slid into the blissful feeling I know so well, stepping into Isame's healing pool.

It is my nightly retreat spa from the rigors of human existence. I have stepped into it, thousands of times. It is also where I recharge my light body before merging with another human, which feels like I'm selecting an outfit from an ever-changing wardrobe—then stepping onto the stage as a new persona. With each one comes unique challenges but in them all, a similar role. I'm fighting for justice, educating, and encouraging change.

The lifetime I had escaped was yet another battlefield of good against evil. My only crime had been preaching my beliefs to those who wished to be healed. But the squire had assumed it to be the devil's work and ordered his men to destroy me. He didn't want me to encourage the common people to know their own minds. It posed too great a threat to his existence.

The moors are so wild and unforgiving for some but have given me the means of escape on many an occasion, since we know the rocks and cave systems intimately. Old One created a vortex in many strategic locations for our safe return to him.

The Challenge

We arrived deep within a valley of the Yorkshire Dales, having avoided Storm Desmond. The land was soaked, and the air was dismal.

I ranted as we donned our wet weather gear. "Why on Earth have we chosen to do this challenge in December? I will never know."

As with all the places we have visited on our unique spiritual journey, this one was no different in that we had to find a specific location. Today it was Douky Cave. To find it, we had to navigate the moor avoiding mine shafts, fences, and drystone walls. My map reading skills had to be up to scratch for this one.

Wrapped up in our thermals and waterproofs, we headed up the hill into the breeze and drizzle. The first hurdle was getting through a locked gate through a farmer's field, hoping we didn't get shot at. Next, we zigzagged across several moorland fields and realized we were on the wrong side of a six-foot drystone wall. After climbing over it and another two, we were soaked through, battered, and bruised. By this time, the wind howled, and horizontal rain lashed.

"So much for thermals and waterproofs," Mike said.

"Why have we gone the long way round?" I replied, pointing down the hill at a gate much closer than where we came in.

Mike shrugged and then rushed ahead when he noticed a group of stone cairns ahead. They were once an ancient settlement. Perched atop the hillside, they looked majestic and were an ideal spot for their dwellers to survey the valley below.

"I can sense the memories of hundreds, if not thousands of years of activity here," Mike said. He had become nostalgic, as if he had returned home.

Despite the cold and our soggy boots, we took our time to explore and absorb the energy of the place. Then I got my bearings. I led us along a ledge at the foot of the cairns and into the valley. I sensed this was the right direction to the cave.

Within fifteen minutes, we found a hole in the ground. There was a way down over precarious wet and mossy stones into a tiny entrance.

"This can't be it...I don't think I can get down there, and it's so dark and dank." I almost spat my distaste for attempting it and dithered, unsure whether we would be expected to enter the cave.

After some debate, we compared the hole to pictures I'd found during my research; I concluded, "this can't be Douky Cave."

I asked for some guidance from the tribe, so Teela arrived with a desire to help. However, she could not confirm if it was indeed the right cave, which surprised me. And, since all three of us were - *not feeling it,* and Dulaa decided to opt-out; I decided to carry on with the search.

Teela suggested, "go up there...I think it's further up the hillside."

We couldn't have got any wetter, but with each squelchy step, I did wonder if we should abandon the expedition. Instead, we continued to climb higher. When I realized we had just walked in a circle for the past hour, I was ready to quit. Then, hail set in. Our faces stung, so we sheltered behind a wall, compensated by a flask of tea and mince pies. That helped me to switch on my logical or more likely, intuitive head.

Cathryn Mahoney

"If we go further over this hill, we may fall down an open mine shaft ... let's go a little further this way...look...I can see a hole; let's check it out," I said to Mike.

"No - stop, it's a mine shaft," Mike gasped, then turned pasty.

"What's wrong?" I asked him.

"I'll tell you later...let's go...we need to go down now." He said between shivers.

The light dimmed, so we began to descend the hillside. I struggled with my feelings of failure as I navigated the treacherous land. I had been unsure what to expect if we had found the cave, but it seemed I wasn't going to find out, anyway.

I shouted to Mike over the wind, "I'm sure that was Douky Cave we first saw...but why didn't Teela know it?"

When we arrived back at the cairns, I reassessed the situation. "Let's retrace our steps where we went before to that first cave," I said.

It only took us ten minutes to arrive at the dank hole in the ground. Then, I found the article about it on my phone and recounted what it said:

"Douky means damp, and this cave is very damp. So even though it looks treacherous, there does seem to be a way down."

However, we decided not to investigate further, as it would have been just our luck to fall. We decided it wasn't meant to be.

Dejected, we descended the hillside and across the fields. After taking a more direct route, we were back in the car within thirty minutes. We had made a meal of the trek up it, which was typical of us. I felt numb, and it wasn't just from the cold. Tears dripped unhindered and warmed my face.

"Don't get upset; we found it the first time around ... it's typical of us not to trust ourselves ... maybe that was the lesson?" Mike said.

"I feel stupid and don't even know why we had to go there...I feel like I put us through hell up there," I replied through my sniffs and shivers.

Teela welcomed us when we returned home and helped us get warm and fed, although I shunned her fuss. I had failed the tribe by not reading the signs we were given.

"Why did we have to go there in the first place," I asked her.

Teela got upset. "I was no help; I'm going to go now."

"You did your best...maybe I didn't listen...or we were stopped for some reason," I reassured her.

Teela departed dejected as Sashma stepped into her place.

"You both did well...better than you think," she said.

"What? We can't have. It was a disaster. Anyway, why on earth did we go there? Nothing happened," I pouted and moaned like a stroppy child. I had hoped to go into the cave and travel through a portal into my tribe's village but didn't realize I remembered that from another time.

I recalled a story Jheneeka told me when Old One had taken her to Mount Shasta. He had taken her through a portal into another time and place. I didn't know I had also done something similar myself - I was to learn about that while writing this book.

My insides twisted when Sashma said, "the journey was about the challenge of doing it and not actually about entering the cave and shifting in time."

Tears welled once again, and then acid burned my gullet as Sashma added, "Teela was encouraged to direct you away from the cave because you found it too soon. There were further challenges to complete. I will explain the reason to her, and she will understand."

Sashma reminded me, "In previous lifetimes, you used the cave as a place of safety and gave healing to people at the entrance. In those times, the cave wasn't as damp and offered solace and peace away from the demands of others. It was also a place you often went to commune with the Creator, looking toward the stars."

She continued: "Mike lost one of his previous lives by falling and being swallowed by the earth. He had dreamt of such an event, which is why he was nervous about walking near the mine shafts. Your challenge was to demonstrate the caliber of a leader, that you wouldn't give up under difficult circumstances. Mike's challenge was to show he would follow and support your leadership. You both did very well. The whole tribe, and especially Old One, were joyous when they heard of your achievements."

47

Moors Healer

On a different moor, in another time, we walked along a rocky ridge leading to the shelter of a valley. There, we found an old desolate watermill. An engraving on the wall indicated it was built in 1811 by William Strickland.

We later discovered that his son Emmanuel was the curate of Ingleby Greenhow, a small village in a nearby valley. He was so keen to spread the word of God that he inscribed 'Hallelujah' in Hebrew on the Cammon Stone. He also added the inscription on the wall of the mill and others on a sundial within the grounds. These were written in Hebrew, Latin, and Greek. They proclaimed: *"Rejoice evermore. Pray without ceasing. The Fear of the Lord is the beginning of knowledge."*

Before descending to the valley floor, we'd visited the Cammon Stone high up on the moor at Rudland Rigg. As I placed my hands upon the stone, I reconnected with it, and Dulaa confirmed it was one of my regular meeting places in times gone by.

The worn stone steps down to the mill led us back in time when a face materialized at a bedroom window. I gasped and realized who the woman was. Our eyes met. Hannah Strickland was observing the beauty of her vista, or had she sensed our presence? I witnessed her contentment and knew that for her, it was her second summer staying with her cousin, William.

I had snatches of memories - merging with her on numerous occasions in this very place. As companions, I assisted her role as healer and teacher up on the moor at Cammon Stone and down in the next valley at Kay Nest. In addition, she had illicit meetings with our mutual friend, the local farmer Joseph Trowsdale, who Mike merged with. So, you could say it was a four-some!

My eyes were diverted away from the window by the presence of Joseph. He was sitting on the bottom step and upon his right arm were two white doves. He smiled and waved with his free hand. He'd suffered much in his life, so we were pleased to see his contentment and the look of love on his face as he smiled up at Hannah in the window.

Then, an invisible force pulled us towards a small derelict outbuilding. I remembered a small girl Hannah had befriended; they often chatted there. I sensed the child had been Teela, creating a link between lifetimes for me to remember. Then, she appeared and instructed Mike to collect a souvenir from the building. It was an iron pin from the stanchion.

"For your new home," she said.

Oon'ch-illia

48

Shining Light

For many days and nights, the people cowered within the circle of rocks. They were an unusual group of travelers from three separate tribes but were united in fear and for safety. Their respective destinations were many moons away. One group's journey through the mountains was towards the setting sun. Another group would follow the same route and veer east across the plains. Lastly, the third group was headed toward the rising sun. It was a fortunate meeting for all, as each group was small, with only two warriors each. Hunger and tiredness had weakened old and young. Now, their focus was on survival while they waited it out.

Within the pitch-black sky, searing lights endlessly rained down around them, followed by a brief period of quietness that offered silent hope. Then, it began again, crashing into the rocks above their heads. Time was running out, and exhaustion had set in. Whoever their aggressors were, the people prayed to the great spirit that the onslaught would stop. Were they attempting to wipe them out or simply make their presence known?

Then, a quiet period extended for the longest time, but the next shock was a golden orb that appeared before them. They feared that all was lost and prepared for their extinction. But a stillness descended around them. Fear kept them frozen, like stone people fixed into the earth. Then, a feathery touch descended upon each of their hearts, and slowly they lifted their heads. They scanned the space around them as a soft voice murmured, "follow me."

They didn't move till one brave soul spoke. It was one of the elders, a man with leathery skin and a shrunken statue. His time on earth drew close, so acceptance of his fate brought courage. He asked, "is it safe to proceed?"

"Follow me; we are here to escort you home – you are safe now."

Then, a host of angels drew forth. Human-like forms appeared through the golden light. "It is time to go – please follow us – we will protect you," – one of the light beings beckoned.

Hesitancy stalled them until they left the cover of the rocks one after another. As they followed, a pulsating light coming towards them stopped them in their tracks. It was different from the burning fire lights and shifted from a glow of icy blue to lagoon green, then a soft sunset sheen of feathery strokes.

The pulsating light spoke with a feminine voice. "Hurry along; my light will assist the weaker ones."

She became tangible and glided with male attendants on either side. Behind them were two huge warriors who carried unfamiliar weapons across their torsos.

A river halted the journey. The ferocity of the rapids paralyzed the group from moving forward until she of the light insisted, "you must cross the waters to reach the mountains ahead." Consternation reverberated among the people, some falling to the ground in despair.

"Going forward will end in death; only the strongest will survive," a tribal elder proclaimed.

Through the light, another bipedal figure appeared, but its size and facial features were not of this world. It shimmered an aqua glow. The voice sounded like the crescendo of storm clouds.

"I offer you safe passage," it bellowed. She of the light drew circles of rainbow lights above the heads of each group member, and their thoughts stilled. Then the light beings and the two warriors transported them across the river. The people appeared to float above the rapids and were deposited on the opposite side. Like sleepwalkers, they followed on foot to their journey's end, apart from several children and elderly ones who had been carried along as if on invisible stretchers.

Oon'ch-illia

In a short time, they entered a cave, which opened into a vast cavern. It was lit by the light of two new light beings who greeted them. A fire had been built, which burned bright, and then food and water appeared before them. They were instructed to rest upon the soft furs spread out across the ground.

For many days and nights, the group rested while their wounds of mind and body healed. A familiarity and peace descended among them. They began to talk, share their tales, and ask questions of their rescuers. A few hardy souls ventured outside the cave to bathe in the hot spring waters and feel the sun's warmth upon their skin. Their female rescuer accompanied them. She shared her knowledge and wisdom during their close discussions. The old man who had ventured forth ahead of the group asked her,

"Are you the ancient sky woman...from beyond those stars?" he pointed into the darkening sky at the seven sisters. "I have heard stories about you from my elders; they have seen you fly...are you she...the one who flies?"

The woman smiled, became a golden sheen, and lifted off the ground. Her arms became expansive translucent wings. Then she transformed back into human form. Her hair was long and black - straight down her back. She had a lithe youthfulness and was strong and sleek like a female deer. Two ocean blue opals sparkled from her face - within a sheen of sunlight on tanned skin. But her form blurred as she drew near, entrancing the observer with her golden light that soothed the soul.

The man thanked her for showing them and said, "They were right...can I tell them I have seen you fly?"

"If they ask," she replied. "There are many mysteries and much beauty within this world as in other worlds beyond this place. Please reassure the people they are now safe to continue their journeys."

As spokesperson and encourager of his people, the old man asked them to prepare to leave the cave. Within two more days and nights, they were ready. The light being that assisted them across the river reappeared, offering safe passage as they began their journey. They remained in awe of the enormous presence. After bidding farewell to the ancient star woman and her companions, the people were scooped up within the aqua light and disappeared into the new light of the dawn. The group separated to continue their respective journeys, each group returning to their tribes with such mysteries to share.

49

St Catherine

After traveling 300 miles to a southern English coastal town; we began searching within a mixed-leaf woodland. I knew our quest was to find something hidden there. In addition, it would offer a deeper understanding of myself.

We stopped and tuned in to the energy of the earth and trees and knew something was about to happen.
We rested on a fallen branch in the middle of a clearing encircled by trees.

Mike said, "Someone has just arrived." Then, in a pulse of light, Sashma merged with Mike.

After a gentle hug and a few words of greeting, she led me to a dense area of leaves and moss.

"There is something buried here that you must find," she instructed.

Down on my hands and knees, I searched among the leaf litter.

"Delve deeper into the earth," Sashma suggested.

My fingers touched a small round object, and I pulled out a coin. When I cleaned and inspected it, I knew I had held it long ago and planted it there. It was old and worn, not of our coinage.

Sashma told me how I was linked to the coin.

"It is connected to St Catherine of Alexandria from 282 AD. She once visited here ... you merged with her. Ley-lines are running through the land beneath our feet ... can you feel the energy?"

She took my hands, and we stood in the center of the clearing, tuning into the ley lines beneath us. I felt a vibrational pulse like electrical currents passing through underground wires.

"Ley-lines are used for travel between other times and places. They connect you to the time when St Catherine traveled here…stand firm upon the earth and feel her energy course through you…remember that time."

My daily path is unusual yet familiar, with its undulating hills sandy from the coastal land. Meetings with local folk who speak a strange dialect, my understanding of their language tested at each place I go. They are interested in where I originate, but some are suspicious of my intent. My light shines bright for some. They have followed me from sacred sites to monuments and feel the energy beneath our feet. On our travels, I explain the earth and starry grids and how I shift in time and space.

It is dangerous to stay in one place for too long. My warriors keep me moving on and are watchful of those who gather around. Some clamor and others wait patiently as I administer words of comfort and a laying of hands. Despite the dangers, I give my time freely. There are so many people in need wherever I go. They offer shelter and food in return and pray to Christ for my safe passage.

While in England, I spend time with scholars and church elders as well as humble folk. My name becomes known upon these lands. I'm asked to remain in many places but remind all who ask that my time here is transitory. I am a messenger of the lord and a weaver of the grids to enable safe travel for all who follow in my wake.

My essence is all I must leave behind as a reminder of my presence. Time, distance, and space collapse through the energy portals of the grid. I am here and there momentarily, an imprint left, and I am back in Alexandria, or among the stars so bright, they shine my way home.

50

Nine Minutes

The frozen lake cracks and groans at the edges. Life returns in the dapple of the sunlight, and insects revel in the tiny pools of water. Ice crystals shimmer and bubble as they break away, revealing streams of moss and algae. Sounds reverberate around the mountains. The constant movement beneath the lake, of life breathing once again.

We rest a while on a rickety bench. Our eyes are drawn towards the sentinel high above us, a statue on the rugged mountainside. There is heat around his chest. Upon the highest peak, seven golden columns of light flash as one then disappears. Stillness descends from the mountaintop.

Whooping cries echo within the trees. We are not alone. There is no fear, only peace. Our tribe is close. The veils are translucent; perhaps we could hunt with them if we choose to. Yet, instead, we stay to pay homage to Old One and his visitors and hazard a guess at their discussions.

Our world stills. It's frozen in time for nine minutes of peace and solitude.

Within a shift of light and air, movement recommences. People pass on by; their chatter disturbs our peace. We send our message of 'farewell' up to the mountaintop and continue our walk towards a waterfall that is slow to melt. A tinkle and chime of water over rock and ice draws us close to smell the life force that has broken free from hibernation.

Barbara joins us for a while. Our assumption about the nine minutes was correct. Time stopped to allow us to reflect on all we had achieved on our travels across the states.

"There is nowhere...nothing else to find – you have completed it all." She informed us while dancing on the spot.

"We are ready to go home...but have three more days. What do we do now?" I ask but try to hide that I feel dejected.

"It's up to you...rest...explore...we are all proud of you, White Bird." She announces within a beam of light and then vanishes.

Later that day, we learned the significance of nine minutes. It gave us access to all three worlds at once (the upper, middle, and lower worlds). To experience it in time, space, and 'beyond both' in all three worlds: hence the nine. It introduced us to the experiences of the tribe when they travel in time and space and in time between times.

51

Glastonbury

A tinkle drew us toward the spring. It bubbled down the stone wall and into the ancient rock channel to feed the pools of healing waters, in which we paddled and meditated.

The iron-rich water is believed to have flowed for 2,000 years from its underground source beneath Chalice Well.

I connected to the water's energy. Chimes alerted me to their presence among the trees, and I became aware of stillness as the voices of people drifted away. Then, I inhaled the heavenly scent of blossoms and felt a shift within.

I'm dressed in a long flowing gown and feel the weight of my hair cascading down my back. I'm in the water, transfixed by the floating blossoms, and then my reverie is broken by the thrush's song. I talk to it in its language. It lands upon my hand as I step out of the water and walk with it towards a holly bush. We talk more; then, I place my feathered friend on its favorite branch. My purpose is to visit the well, to place an offering for the safe return of my love. He is fighting in the crusades.

I found myself standing out of the water next to a holly bush. Then, I heard movement beside me. It was Mike, lifting his hand towards me. In his palm were several ancient coins.

"Where did they come from?" I asked him.

"They were in the water. I just found them. A sudden glint caught my eye, like an apparition," Mike replied.

As we walked around the garden, we also inspected the coins. Two of them, however, were so small and worn that it was difficult to decipher what they were.

Cathryn Mahoney

"I think we will have to use the magnifying glass when we get home," Mike said.

I ruminated over my daydream as we walked, but my breath was taken when we reached the well. I looked at Mike and got a sense of praying for his safe return.

After a few deep breaths to center myself, I asked him, "do you sense anything here?"

"There's something, but I can't say what," he replied.

"I had a vision when we were stood in the water. I was praying for your safe return. I'm certain we have both been here before," I said.

"Mmmm, really, nothing surprises me now."
Mike gave me a piercing stare. Then, he looked deep into me. "Your eyes have changed color again," he said.

"Have they? I was wearing a long chiffon gown of heather and pea green. I was young with locks of golden hair. I had a conversation with a song, thrush, can you believe that? Then I was praying for you...you were away fighting in the crusades...I'll have to work out what year it was, and who we were...do you recognize anything about it?"

"Can't say I do...interesting though...there's certainly something about this place," Mike replied as he surveyed the garden and watercourse behind us. "Let's visit the White Spring next and see if we sense anything there."

Oon'ch-illia

52

Mercy Mission

Whispers of change engulfed me as I stood upon the moor top. The air was now cool with a damp mist. Moments before, the skin on my bare arms burned from the heat of the midday sun.

As I scanned around me, I noticed the grass seemed saturated from days of rain or melted snow. The new shoots and wildflowers had disappeared. Then I realized my body was clothed in a thick heavy sack-like garb. My legs were enveloped in the same material forming a long skirt and apron. My foot attire was heavy lace-up boots thick with muck. As I felt around my head, my fingers found a wool shawl. Underneath it hung long tendrils of dirty, matted hair. Then, I fingered my face and felt leathery, pock-marked skin. I looked at my fingers next. They were gnarled and caked with dirt. I was surprised to find a small golden ring with three pearls tight upon the small finger on my left hand. Suddenly, my right hand grasped tight on a staff. I sensed my body was shrunken, and my crooked shoulders forced my face parallel to the ground. I began to walk, and pain shot up my legs with each slow step.

"Bloody Hell! What has happened to me?" I shouted in despair. I had been walking, enjoying the unusual heat of an April day. My mind had been lost in the silence all around me. Then the world went dark, and my body fizzed like I had been plugged into an electric socket. My heartbeat pumped laboriously as if I was almost dead, and the weight I carried dragged me even closer to the ground.

I soon realized where I was heading when I saw the standing stone ahead. It was calling me toward the people who were gathered. A renewed sense of purpose urged me on, but gaining speed was difficult. Then, suddenly, I was further along the path, walking confidently, even though my withered body and the cold, misty day remained the same.

A figure approached out of the mist. I recognized him immediately. I felt it was Mike's essence, but it wasn't in his body. Instead, it was that of my good friend, Albie. The 'shift' had brought a younger version of him into my line of sight, not the old man I knew in the time I had just left behind.

Albie addressed me as Alice and escorted me towards the gathering crowd. It felt strange being the older one who needed a gentle guiding hand. We chatted about the task before us, and I mentally prepared myself before meeting the young couple who urgently required my assistance.

My healing hands vibrated, and a tremor ignited my senses as I approached the stone. I placed my staff in its special groove, then removed my ring, placing it in the waiting delve. Albie had brought my metal cup. He placed it on its holder upon the lower shelf of the stone for the offerings.

A hush descended around those gathered as they watched my movements in expectation. I sensed they all desired comfort and healing, but this was a special mission. I asked the lady I had come to see to step toward me. I scanned my hands around her body and then asked Albie to lay her to rest upon the healing stone. He placed his fingers in the pool of water by her feet and sprinkled droplets around the perimeter. Then, I asked the crowd to remain quiet, to sit and observe, while I tended to the lady and her companion.

Kneeling beside her body, I pulled lights down with my hands and placed them in her. She squirmed, sighed, and then stilled. As I worked, my hands became smooth and line-free, then turned translucent as I morphed into a golden orb. The crowd gasped then stillness descended once more.

Oon'ch-illia

I heard Albie's soothing words in the distance, reassuring those present that all was well. He then asked the lady's companion to join us around the stone. I wrapped my light around him as he stood at his lady's feet. He shivered and then dropped to his knees. Albie positioned him with his head resting upon his lady's stomach. Albie moved her arms to encircle him. A circuit of light traveled through and around them as my hands wafted down violet light.

The midday heat roused me. I realized I had dozed off against the stone and had been dreaming. A shiver ran through me, and when I opened my eyes, the view was misted. Then, a shadow skirted before me, which brought my attention to the present moment. I remembered the couple and the crowd, but they were gone now. The mist had cleared to reveal the vibrancy of new growth across the moors. It was peaceful and quiet.

Perhaps, I had been dreaming the whole time. But then, I felt a movement nearby. It was Albie, but he was much older. He reached behind the stone and drew out my metal cup filled with old coins and sprigs of heather. Then the golden ring with three pearls was placed on the small finger of my left hand. He reached a third time and retrieved my wooden staff from its resting groove. He placed it in my right hand. I stood up with its firm support upon the ground. Wildflowers wafted their scent, and I heard a blackbird serenade from a neighboring stone. Skylarks hovered over the heather and bracken. They were excited, like a crowd witnessing a magical scene.

Albie said: "Your dream was a 'shift' in time. You were called on, and you obeyed. It was no more than five of your minutes. You helped the couple greatly. You even had time to talk to the crowd and gave one or two healings. Why do you think you got the offerings? And you were gone for one hour, fifteen minutes in that time."

I had no response. I stood and stared at him, trying to take it all in.

53

All Seasons

For some strange reason, for my birthday in 2016, I'd set plans in motion to complete one of the quests set by our tribe. It wasn't a long walk, but it would stretch us with two hills to climb. The destination was my focus, as was our picnic. But doubts loomed when snow began to fall. I dithered and shivered as I laced up my boots. And, huffed and puffed.

"Perhaps we are daft even considering this today?" I mumbled, but Mike was determined to continue despite his lack of sleep.

"I want to do it; you've sown the seed. There's no going back," Mike countered.

"Why are we always being tested? Other people don't put themselves through things like this," I continued to mumble under my breath as I donned my thermal hat and gloves.

We set off up the gentle incline and were soon soaked through. Then, the snow turned into driving horizontal sleet. I moaned up the slope until breathlessness silenced me at the steepest point.

The sun appeared as I reached the top, and I unzipped my coat. "This is more like it...maybe it's not so bad after all," I said with a grin.

The sun warmed us as we hiked across the moorland path. As we were getting into our stride, we reached the steep descent leading to our destination. A large rock by the stream looked inviting and was ideal for our picnic. We settled and opened the flask, but the sky darkened after a few mouthfuls of tea and a pork pie. Huge flakes of snow carpeted the ground. With it, Teela appeared.

"Isn't it beautiful?" she asked while twirling around.

"I guess...it does look pretty. Maybe we can walk along the stream?" I pointed ahead and led the way.

Like a nimble mountain goat, she climbed down the rocks towards the stream. I hesitated and looked back along the path.

"That's far enough. What are you doing?" I warned her while stamping my feet to keep warm.

She didn't respond at first. Instead, she searched the streambed.

"Ah...you'll see," was all she mustered.
She went out of sight behind a rock, and all I heard was: "Yeeeessss! Found you."

I stumbled down the rocks to the stream, where she washed something in her cupped palms. "Look at these."

She lifted her hands to my face, and I peered at some old coins—a half-crown dated 1896 and some pennies dated between 1891 and 1936.

"How did they get there?" I asked her as I looked more closely at each one.

"They were put there for you to find, but I wanted to help for your birthday," she said radiantly.

"But why? Who put them there?" I asked as I turned to warm my face in the sunlight. The snow was melting around our feet.

"All I know is they were placed there by your gran and some people you have healed. She loved it here. You often came here when you were Hannah to have private time with Joseph. See that rock up there? You bathed in the water and canoodled on the rock." She giggled.

Dumbfounded, I reflected on what Teela had said, and as we walked to our picnic spot, I asked many questions.

"Can you feel it?" Teela stopped and asked.

"Feel what?" I searched around me for an answer I knew she wouldn't give. I had to find it for myself. Was it in the rocks, the plants, the stream, or deep within the earth? As I pondered, I sensed belonging. Then realized that, yes, I had been present here many times in the past.

Recalling that memory years later, I sensed subtle shifts in time coinciding with the weather changes. The trees and vegetation were abundant as I returned uphill from the stream. Lilting melodies of the birds stopped us in our tracks. As I looked down at the stream, the earth was sun-baked. The gravel under our feet was sandy, whereas an hour previous, it had been soggy from days of rain, not a mere snow shower. I looked across at the rock within the stream. There, I saw Hannah and Joseph bathing naked. Sunlight highlighted the radiance on both their faces. Mike and I reveled in their sensory experience for the briefest moment. Then, we walked into rain and howling wind across the moor top. It disturbed our shared reverie.

"Whatever next?" Mike looked to the sky and asked as if speaking to God.

"What an odd day. We've had all four seasons; all we need now is thunder," I replied.

At that exact moment, a clap of thunder reverberated around the moor. It stopped us dead. Stunned, we looked at one another and then laughed.

"Time to go...get warm, have some rest, then we've got a lovely meal to look forward to, methinks. Happy Birthday, my darling," Mike whispered into my ear as he hugged me.

54

Jemina

In 1348, I lived a short life as a peasant girl called Jemina.

"My cottage be in the shadows of the great castle. Many a day, I wander through the woods and down the stream to the sea on the scour. I am gifted with sight and 'ow to use 'erbs. The light of an angel fills me. My friend, Oon'ch-illia. She taught me the knowledge to help many who ail. It's secret work. I have my hidey holes in the woods and meet folk by the waters. Many dangers close to the manor. They hunt me like a fox - rumor-mongers - the good for nothings tell the tots I work for the devil."

In 2017, Mike and I visited Mulgrave Woods in North Yorkshire. As we walked alongside East Row Beck, Mike halted. "See here, there was a bridge…"

He froze mid-word. "I'm trying to help Jemina escape. They're on us. I'm shouting to her…run…she turns and smiles at me. She's gone now. Where is she…they struck her…she's in the water…Aww."

He doubled over, gasping. "I'm going to be sick…need to go."

I pulled Mike away from the stream, and within a few minutes, his breathing regulated, but he said:

"My head's banging…my heart's beating so fast. They struck me…everything went black. We both went in the water…it was in full flow…we were washed out to sea."

Half an hour earlier - on a walk up the valley, we both felt a strong pull to walk down to the stream. We sensed being there before, so we sat for a while by the water. Butterflies fluttered close by, and then, we noticed a swarm of flies hovering.

"Odd how they are circling us. Wouldn't they normally bother us?" Mike asked, intrigued by their behavior.

The flies kept their distance from us.

"They are showing respect. They honor you." Dulaa said.

"It seems so, but it's unusual. I feel such peace here, do you?" I asked Mike.

"I love it here - look at the butterflies dancing around our heads." He said with a sigh.

Oon'ch-illia

55

Queen of Scots

In 2021 we traveled to the Scottish Highlands for our fourth wedding anniversary. We were relieved and a little nervous about traveling since being locked down to local journeys for the past 18 months. Our wanderlust had been dampened. Plus, the nine-hour journey was more daunting because we both suffered from colds despite the forced social isolation - but at least it wasn't COVID.

As always, a specific mission took us to the middle of nowhere. But doubt rumbled in my guts. Did we have the stamina for the walk I'd planned? Our destination was the 'Bone Caves' at Inchnadamph, Sutherland, where I hoped to recapture memories and leave my imprint once again.

The Scotland journey was also crucial for Meena and Dulaa, newlyweds who fell in love after meeting at Dunino Den. Mike and I were guests of honor at their bonding ceremony. Now they planned to escort us on parts of our journey.

Meena wanted to introduce Dulaa to her relations, so at Garry Bridge, Killiecrankie, the newlyweds left us and shifted into the time when her relatives were alive. Later, on the journey, they also planned to visit the Culloden Battlefield - the site of the Jacobite Rising of 1745 since Meena is of both Pictish and Jacobean origin.

The summer weather had packed away its sunglasses and heralded Autumn with cold winds and showers. Great weather to cabin up, but since I get cranky if I'm unable to explore a new area, we agreed to lazy mornings followed by short outings. I encouraged Mike to drive around the coast on the first day. The next day we spent the afternoon in ancient woodland and on a private beach, where we were introduced to Jacob, one of Meena's ancestors.

Cathryn Mahoney

On our Anniversary, we trekked into the caves. It was a cold day sprinkled with sunny spells and brief showers. We managed a slow, gentle climb up the mountain valley. Towering rocky hills surveyed our movements along the dry riverbed. Then, we reached the steep incline that led toward the entrances of several caves. As we stepped into the middle cave, I entered through another time.

The electric shock reeled me as I shifted, and I found myself deep within a spacious cavern. Light streamed through an aperture, so I followed the misty shaft of light through a winding passageway. It ascended to an exit shaft. My body was light and agile and garbed in tight-fitting furs. As I stepped into the light, I turned around and saw Meena following me. I knew her as my faithful servant but also my friend and confidante.

A Legacy

The cave had been our home for many moons, just the two of us. Apart from the two warriors at the entrance or in the valley below, on constant watch. I looked forward to the occasional visits from Old One but never to his news. The battle raged with much bloodshed; he told me. I punched the rocks and howled like a wolf after remonstrating with him. "I must go to fight with my brave and my sons...my people need me there. No use hiding like a coward in this damp hole."

Old One's appeal to stay put was like a dagger to my heart. To him, the Stone of Destiny was more important for me to protect it at all costs. My mission was to ensure it reached its destination. I was stuck, unable to return through the vortex to the Emerald Isle or travel south into the land I'd found myself in.

Many distances had been traveled on foot and across the waters from my homeland of Egypt since the exile. My people and I faced great challenges along the way, and during that time, I bore four beautiful boys.

Oon'ch-illia

"Why are we never left in peace?" I prayed to the Great Spirit to save all those I loved.

Then, I stepped back through the searing light of the cave entrance. Through the narrow neck, I reached the dip where I rested but dreamed of happier times with my husband. I watched the sun setting over the mountains, as I did most days. Then fingered the ledge above my head to retrieve my bangle and extra weapon. These were my protection every time I left the cave. I inhaled the fresh air deeply. It was cold, so I tightened my cloak and moved out onto the ledge. The warriors noticed my movements and accompanied me down to the riverbank. I wished to bathe in private and commune with my husband. Our connection was strong within the deepest part of the spring. So, I lay down in the soothing waters and reached deep into my heart to hear his voice. He was battle-weary but would not admit defeat. I asked to join him, but he, too, persuaded me to stay put. "You must spare your life; you have an important task to complete," he reminded me.

I returned to the cave a reluctant dweller, climbing deep down into the cavern of my prison.

On the next full moon, a golden light shone through the passageway. It was Gemel. As I looked at his face, I saw grief etched there. I fell to my knees and prayed to the Creator. Gemel took me to the battlefield in another land. I discovered the extinct body of my gentle giant lain among some furs. There were torn bodies with blood and guts strewn across the rocks, turning the river red. These were my people. They had accompanied us across distant lands and had survived great trials. Only to have their lives taken in a place they had lived for many revolutions of the sun. Their lives had been taken instantly because we had the tenacity to call the Gaelic hills our home. The Tuatha de Danann had gathered many tribes with one mission in mind, to see to our demise.

Cathryn Mahoney

There was no time to grieve. My sons were fighting for their lives. Gemel and I joined them, and our lives were savagely taken within several hours. My dying breath to my sons was to take the Stone of Destiny I had secreted away in the cave to its rightful royal place. No more fighting, I pleaded; they must fulfill my mission, which was our purpose upon the new green lands. They must forge new lives upon another foreign soil. It was now time to turn their backs on destruction, to tread a path of light out of sight of the aggressors.

Old One came to me in another lifetime and told me my sons had fulfilled my bequest. Somehow the Tuatha de Danann were satisfied once my death was announced. They retreated and allowed my sons, their families, and followers who had survived to move on to their new lands.

The history books name me Queen Scota. My mission was always the Stone of Destiny; to provide the seat of power to enable future generations to live rightfully upon the land. The Creator's love permeates the stone with peace and unity - so that all life is honored instead of constant bloodshed. If only that had been the case!

56

Healing Mission

I felt a rocking motion and an insistence to take deep breaths to lull myself into sleep. Then, from beneath me, a wave of blue light lifted me out of my leaden body. Within the time it usually takes me to step out of bed, I had shifted from my room to the tribe's cave. Mike followed in my wake. Our companions on this occasion were Sashma and Gemel, and as soon as we arrived deep inside the cave, Mike and I knew the purpose of our visit.

Sometimes, we go for healing in the hot springs, and on those occasions, Isame collects us. But, this time, it was our turn to be the healers. A warrior and a child lay by the pool, being attended to by Ishneah, who seemed to be waiting for our assistance.

"Isame is still off-world, helping the beings who have succumbed to an unknown virus," Sashma said. "It isn't deadly, but they do not have the knowledge to deal with it themselves. Ishneah is out of her comfort zone. Can you help her?"

I inquired about the ailments and remedies that had been applied so far.

Sashma said, "they both need some of your combined light. It needs to go deep. The warrior fell off his horse. We have dealt with the cuts. Can you reset his dislocated shoulder? The child fell from a tree and cracked her head. She was unconscious for a while and then sick when she awoke. She is dazed, and her memory has been affected."

We got to work manipulating the shoulder, selecting the appropriate lights, and placing them within the injured areas of the warrior. Then placed lights around the head and back of the child. Attendants from the tribe carried them back to their rooms to care for them, and we promised to check on them before we left the village.

Out in the light, we stretched and breathed in the air, so fresh and invigorating. The mountain air is pure and free of any pollution, unlike back home. We observed the activities of the village. Everyone was busy undertaking their roles and responsibilities, but two small children ran up to us, asking for cuddles. We were grateful not to be mobbed this time, as all the other children were at their studies or working. So, we took the little ones by the hand into the shade of the sprawling oak by the lakeside.

"Please tell us a story," they cried in unison.

Mike told the first story, and then I told them mine. They were captivated when I regaled them with a journey in our motor vehicle, and I told them about our grandson, Jack's love of football. Then, the children's mothers came to collect them, so we visited Keela. She was attempting to construct a refrigeration system within some rocks underground. Mike offered a suggestion, but I looked on, proud of her ingenuity. After all, she had constructed a greenhouse, a watering system, underfloor heating for the rooms of the cave, and other quality-of-life inventions to help the tribe.

It was soon time to return to our bodies in our beds, so we checked in on our patients, who appeared to be healing well. Ishneah promised to call on us if our assistance was needed again. Then, Gemel escorted us home. The pull to stay was great, but we had to return to face another day of life in our chosen time.

57

Birthday Surprise

In April 2022, I turned 61, significant since I was born in 1961. To celebrate my birthday, we revisited a favorite place, Lastingham, a village in the North Yorkshire Moors with many walking paths and a wonderful pub.

Several months earlier, I had reconnected to a special pine tree by the stream. It was one of many areas across the moors where I had a history. The connection with Lastingham ran deep but repelled me, as times had been hard.

The scenic view from Lastingham across the moors offers beauty and stillness, whereas the village offers history, both dark and light. Memories of a harsh life fade insignificantly compared to the majesty of the rolling moor and the comfort found by my favorite tree.

Life was cruel; survival was for the strongest and most resourceful, eking out an existence in barrenness and poverty, while the richest in society reaped the benefits of those who sweated and toiled at their farming and servant work.

I merged with both sisters, Catherine and briefly Jane, in 1791-1793. They were young women of the village from hardy stock, but the demands from others stretched them to breaking point. I merged with Catherine while Jane was still a child. Her resilience and love for humanity, animals, and the natural world enabled her to hold no bounds in what she could achieve. It was her endeavors to help others against all the odds that drew me to her.

Catherine sneaked through the houses to the valley whenever she was able and followed the stream up onto the moor. Before the ascent, she spent time at the pine tree that somehow appeared as if overnight the size of two tall men, one standing on the shoulders of the other. She often connected to the tree for solace or sat on the large

Cathryn Mahoney

boulders in the stream on warmer days and cooled her feet. That was where people in need often found her. They knew it was safer there than in the village, where eyes and ears were always alert.

She offered strange but comforting words and healing for their heart, body, and mind ailments. Those who knew her recognized the wisdom and love she had to give, but her family and the rumormongers saw her as simple and mad, except for Jane. As soon as Catherine was married and moved away, Jane was more than ready and able to allow me to step in.

The first time I returned to Lastingham a few years back, my energy tuned into the harshness of Catherine and Jane's lives. I picked up on the fear and need for an escape from the village. I did not visit the valley and the tree, but as I looked down towards it from the moortop, I sensed the solace found there. It was the darkness that I felt on that day that kept me away until more recent years. Since then, I have reconnected with the pine tree and discovered Old One had planted it there for me. There are markings where I have often stood back-to-back with that tree and merged my energy with it.

Two months before my birthday, I merged with it again, and this was my experience:

As I linger by a favorite tree, it calls to me - a pounding in my heart. My body freezes, feet sinking deep into the ground. A hefty pull tugs me backward as if on a recoiling spring. Within its grip, I'm pulled, and my feet come unstuck. I'm drawn back-to-back with the tree. A calmness descends and transports me down, down into the earth through the root system, down deeper into a cave system so dank it takes my breath away. Panic has no place here - stillness speaks my name.

A beam of light I have become. Burning a path through solid matter, a destination mapped out, within the speed of light, whoosh, I'm gone. I cannot say where. Only dark and light exist.

Oon'ch-illia

I'm a shooting star that flashes through a velvet sky, then past a golden moon in a turquoise sky. I witness the setting sun that hides beyond darkened clouds. I am a firefly as it hovers within an olive tree.

Another flash of light in the darkness, and I am deep within the sodden earth, beneath the ocean floor, along the bottom of a riverbed, and up into the chamber of a pyramid.

I return to witness my tribe in ceremony and watch spellbound as their bodies sway in motion, connected by shimmering golden threads.

There are echoes of other times and places. Stories are sung while bodies sway in tune, a harmony so enchanting. Heartbeats synchronize as one while a ball of fire floats among them. It touches each head with a flash of light. One by one, they fall to their knees in gratitude. Their mouths become still, now their hands sign their words, within an ecstasy of belonging.

Old One's gentle touch, an eagle's feather signals - rise. As eyes lift unto the sky, light beams down. Then within a flash, a multitude of visitors arrive.

Ancestors show the way within the silence. Light vibrations dance among the crowd. Orbs of translucent lights flicker, sizzle then flies away to join the sparks from the fire. Shades of reds, oranges, and gold harmonies bring those present out of their trance. Time to welcome their guests with unspoken language. Thought forms of images and emotions flit among the crowd. From race to race, custom to custom, a reading of perception and form is understood in an instant.

Young ones play with free abandon. Old ones sit cross-legged beside the fire. Food of all varieties is passed around. There are teachings about the stars and life from faraway places. With a common language of faith, the tribe pays homage to the ancient ones. With a nod from each one present, a chant resounds; "We give thanks to one of many names...for our light...our food, our shelter...the rivers of gold...the sands of time...the skies of many colors...for creating it all."

I rest deep within the cavern. The last thing I'm aware of is my tribe singing. The portal of my return spits me out. I'm an orb of light, not one but two merged as one. With my back against the tree, my breath quickens, and my heartbeat races. A flicker of movement signals that I am back.

It's no wonder I chose to return to Lastingham for my Birthday. To spend time merging with my favorite pine. Its branches reach far across the stream, and its roots rise from the ground as if to tap the shoulder of passers-by.

My desire to be out all day led me to plan a walk double the length of our usual ones. By the time we reached the tree, we were weary and doubted we could complete the return journey.

"Do you think we should call a taxi after lunch? I don't think I can walk all the way back." I asked Mike as I put my back against my delve within the tree.

"I'm sure we will be fine once we've rested and eaten," Mike said.

I loved his optimism and knew I had to complete my mission. I called to the tribe we had arrived as I connected my roots with those of the tree deep into the ground.

As Mike settled on the sandy bank to listen, I watched him. His head tilted left, with an ear cocked and his eyes glazed over.

"They are coming from every direction," he indicated with a sweep of his arms.

I sat beside him to watch and wait. I knew the tribe would visit to wish me a Happy Birthday. I was uncertain if it would be a few or all of them. Who knew at that stage?

"There are so many of them...they are coming from across the moor and over the brow of the hill...even other tribes...Oh! I can see some who come to the stones. That woman from 1972, the little girl with the long blue dress, and that man from the future who asked us a question about Trump. I'm sure there are as many as last time," Mike told me, his brow furrowed.

"I think there are five hundred or so," I replied. I meant it as a question but said it with such certainty that Mike nodded in agreement before he told me more.

"They are nearly all gathered now. Old One is going to speak. No, hang on, it's Ishneah; she is upfront. I must tell you what she says... 'Happy Birthday, White Bird. We have gathered here today to sing you a song, but before we do, we all want to thank you for all you do for us. Each person here has been touched by your kindness. You have helped us all in some way. We all love you and are so happy to have you in our lives.' Ishneah has stopped speaking now, and they are all going to sing. They are doing it in their own languages, so Ishneah will translate, and I'll repeat it to you."

They sang as I listened, sensing the tune and melody. I smiled and acknowledged all those within the crowd as Mike repeated their words. When they finished, there was a shimmer as they departed in small groups. The tribe was the last to leave. Old One remained and approached us to thank me personally.

There seemed more than met the eye, but I listened as he told me: "I'm so proud of you, my child...you did well today...enjoy the rest of your day." I received his usual three pats on my head and breathed in his essence to regain strength for the return hike to the car. I knew he had already topped up my light before his departure, but my need for his love is a drug I crave.

Then Teela appeared with her back to the tree. She announced, "this is a special day because you are 61 but not in the way you think...you will find out soon why this one has been celebrated by so many whose lives you touched. Are you going for food now?" Then she shrunk into a tiny dot of light and popped inside the tree.

I was too tired and hungry to give recent events much

thought until I downed two shandies and ate my fish pie. Jheneeka arrived to share some time over the meal but evaded my questions. I left them for another time. After all, I had several miles to hike before the day was out.

The following week she returned for her own birthday treat and had surprises in store. She told me Mike had got up one night and written information an ancient one he calls Zero had given him. Jheneeka directed me to the piece of paper hidden among Mike's work. It was full of numbers, words, and symbols. That one sheet gave a full explanation of the missing link. I knew something magical had occurred on my birthday, and now it was being explained to me by Jheneeka. Then, when Mike returned to his body, we explored and digested the information together.

I had shifted to another time and place. Along with 61 representative tribal leaders, including 32 ancient ones, we toned a vibrational frequency of 22281 Hz as a call to some water-based beings on another planet. Apparently, it had been a remarkable achievement that I had held the tone for 19 minutes, and on one breath.

For the life of me, I can't say how I managed that, but I'm pleased I played my part. I later learned from Old One that I had been prepared for the event long ago. It had all been planned and synchronized. My age was the number of participants with me, and I had lived for 22281 days on Earth by the time we did the toning. The total number of people present that day equaled the Love Frequency of 528 Hz. The purpose was to seek assistance from beings on a watery planet within the Constellation of Caelum to shift the earth's vibration to the 528 Hz frequency.

Update - September 8th, 2022

It was a relief when storms brought much-needed rain following the summer heatwave and droughts worldwide. On the evening of September 7th, a stillness descended as sheet and fork lightning lit up the darkened sky above our home. Overnight the rain deposited large droplets of water filled with the 528 Hz vibration. As I stood barefoot on the grass facing Southeast, as I do each morning, my body was filled with pure bliss.

Since encircling our new home during the summer weeks, (see Part 5), my body sways and is pulled in its direction. This morning, as I swayed, a presence pulsed above my head and told me, "It has begun." I centred myself and thanked the ancient one present and the beings who answered our call. The earth felt still. It sighed in relief, not only for being replenished but for the gift of 'love' sung within the water it drank.

As I sat having breakfast in bed with Mike, we listened to the joyous song of the robin, our mutual gaze upon it on the highest branch shifted to the aura around the trees. They breathed and expanded.

"Can you see the clouds of gratitude released back into the atmosphere?" Mike asked.

"Yes, there is a subtle shift of peacefulness around us, and I feel it within me. I wonder if anyone else will notice it?" I replied.

V

Accomplishment

Sunday walks through the Spring and Summer of 2022 took us to new but familiar locations. In a woodland glade, we had a visit from Old One. He said, "White Bird – feel your essence here. Use your stick on the ground – find the spot where it is strongest. Now, connect with your essence here. Collect it. Some will stay here, but you can now take it with your stick and plant it wherever you choose. The locations chosen will form a circle. In the middle of it will be your new home."

Oon'ch-illia

58

Begin West

On one of our favorite moorland walks, we took a new path through a forest we had visited twice before. We both sensed that was where we would find spruce trees hidden away behind the pine. I was searching for new spruce tips to make some syrup.

Mike said, "we need to go down this way. I feel a strong pull to go further into the trees."

I was unsure if he meant the Spruce tree we stumbled upon or what happened next.

Halfway along the path, he insisted, "this way – to these trees."

We dodged ant hills and stepped over branches and stumps to reach the oldest tree.

"Here – yes, you have to put your essence right here," he said.

I stood and connected. It didn't feel very strong, but Dulaa confirmed I had done well - the essence had been planted. My instinct had taken us to the forest, but I hadn't expected to find the first location that day. We continued the walk to connect deeper with the forest. I sent my radar out around the vicinity. We both felt satisfied and collected a bag of Spruce tips as a bonus.

When I surveyed the map later, I gasped. There was every chance we were circling a house we both liked. It fitted the one we had both envisioned—an L-shaped house with outbuildings and a cottage. I had pictured the layout of the rooms, the gardens, and the expanse of land. But the house in question had recently been on the market and then sold. We didn't have the money for it then and were unsure we could ever afford it, but we still knew it was meant for us. We have prayed to the Creator for our ideal home and healing retreat for years. Were we getting closer?

59

Go East

Two valleys east of the previous location, we found an ancient woodland where I was drawn towards a copse of trees and the foundations of a small house. It had been the home of an old Norse woman named Bamara. The locals said she was a witch as she had remained the same old woman for many generations. They hunted her down and attempted to kill her several times, but an ancient visitor from Scotland had placed protection around her until it was her time to die of natural causes.

I sealed my essence with my stick deep into the earth of her home. The energy was intense – my body swayed back and forth. I felt deep love and respect for the Earth and sensed eyes watching and ears listening. The spirits of the woods were pleased.

Mike disappeared down some rocks to the stream and returned with a tiny stone.

"The old lady wanted you to have this. The groove is from her rubbing it as she did her spells." He told me.

Bamara's spirit witnessed my essence planted at her home, so to honor the event, she left the stone as a token to mark my return to the woodland glade. As I rubbed it, I knew it would help me manifest our desires.

When I looked at the map, our new home was smack in the middle of this and the previous location.

"Yeees," I shouted to Mike. It must be that house." So, I used the map and my intuition to plot our next visit to the area. We decided to go south.

60

Then South

Our southerly point was in the woodland beyond a church. We stepped across the dry stream bed, the same stream that ran alongside our future home. Then, Mike rushed on like a mountain goat up the hill into a deeper part of the woods.

He stopped and shouted, "here."

I stood on the spot, and my body swayed. I nearly fell forward, so I steadied myself with my stick. As I tuned in, I sensed two young girls playing nearby, then running up the hill.

When I had sealed in my essence, Mike told me, "Two young girls are here. They like it here. Do you feel them?"

"Yes, I've seen them playing. They were having a picnic with their mother up there," I pointed to a clearing above.

"It's a happy place," we said in unison.

"I think maybe I merged with one of them or visited them here," I said, then looked to Dulaa for confirmation, and he nodded.

Later that day, I wanted to find the next location. Since we were downstream of the house, we needed to go north. I drew the circle on the map and located a place upstream. We drove as close as possible to the new site. Then, we went down a farm road, across hedges, and over several walls to get to the stream. Mike tried wriggling through a hole in a wall, but bracken and a steep drop stopped him in his tracks. It reminded us of our time at Douky Cave. Doubt set in, and it didn't help that Dulaa had abandoned us.

He hadn't gone far, but we didn't sense him, and it certainly wasn't a good omen. We both felt frustrated when we could not find our way. It felt so close, but I knew I had pushed it. Trying to find two locations in a day probably wasn't the right thing to do.

61

Head North

On July 3rd, we did a scouting expedition by car and then walked a short distance into the forest of our first foray. Among a group of ancient trees, I found an additional location to seal my essence, which felt stronger than the first time. But it didn't fit into the circle. I asked Dulaa why that was, and he said, "it will all make sense. You are creating other connections."

After another unsuccessful attempt to reach the stream at a northern point on July 10th, we returned on the 24th but stopped a mile short of the previous attempt. Mike felt pulled to a stream that ran parallel to the one I wished to visit. A large bird of prey flew overhead as we crossed the moor. I was certain it was a red kite, rare in North Yorkshire, so I suspected it was an ancient visitor. The Ancients Ones often appear as hawks and eagles, but occasionally new ones arrive in different birds. They like to shapeshift into large birds so we can see them, and they prefer an aerial view. Old One and other elders of the tribe appear in this way, and sometimes tribal members take the form of crows.

The path we took petered out, so we forged through thick heather, bilberry bushes, then tall bracken as the bank sloped down to the stream. Mike was like a bear tracking a scent. We slipped across mossy rocks into the stream, then Mike pulled me up through the bracken onto the opposite bank. His radar pinged, and he found his prey - several large rocks, which were an ideal place to rest and stop for lunch.

Mike named the two largest rocks - Flat Rock, and Pillow Rock. "People came here for healing. And it's a place where the ancients meet," he explained.

Oon'ch-illia

We sat upon Flat Rock and tuned in to its vibration. Mike looked to his right at Pillow Rock. It was identical to a single bed with a pillow at the top.

"I need to lie down there. I can feel the energy coming off it, but let's have lunch here first. I love it here and can feel the energy pulse up my legs. Can you?"

The longer I sat on Flat Rock, the more I felt attuned to the energy, but Pillow Rock had the strongest pull.

"Am I to seal my energy here?" I asked Dulaa.

"What do you think, White Bird?"

I knew I shouldn't keep asking him. He wasn't allowed to help.

Mike said, "I can sense where you need to be, but let's see if you find it first."

A strong gust of wind blew. Mike asked, "did you feel that shift? Someone is coming. An ancient one, I think."

He looked to his left and right. "Ah, he is talking to Dulaa. He wants to speak with us."

I watched Mike listen and nod. "The ancient one says, "why were you looking over that way? I was right here. He is happy to see us. We have done well. By the way, he is about 7 ft 4 inches tall."

"Hello, thank you for your visit," I said. I didn't ask his name but knew he was a new visitor. I looked up, noticing another bird of prey overhead. The ancient one said, "that is my companion."

"Is this a place I gave healing?" I asked our visitor.

"Yes, many times. Three in particular: 1316, 1514, and 1638. Many came to you here with injuries from the farm, diseases, and other illnesses. Some came from a hamlet down there." He pointed to the left, downstream.

"Some walked along the water. Some came across the moor top; others came across the moor from behind us. Your brave and your warrior, not this one (pointing at Dulaa) but the other one."

"Gemel?" Mike asked.

"Yes, Gemel, he stopped them from getting close until you were ready for them. You laid them on that rock

(Pillow Rock). You had a soft matting for them to lie on. The children lay on the pillow and the adults full length. Sometimes you placed a child with their mummy on Flat Rock. The people arrived at the bottom of this hill by the stream and were told to fan into a single line and wait for you to administer to them. Would you like to know about one of the dates? What happened?"

"Yes, the first one. Whom did I merge with?" I asked.

"It was a lady you knew many times and by different names. One was Brenice Smithy. There was one time you stayed all day and night. You constantly healed apart from one short break. You stored the light in your palms in a short stick and retrieved it when needed. It was a hot, windy day like today. Do you know there was a time when it was hotter than your recent hot weather - when the temperature went above that recorded since records began? It was in 1540."

"That's interesting," Mike said.

"Returning to my story. When you finished someone's healing. Your brave told them to wait by the water for five degrees of the sun, in case they had a bad reaction, then they could leave. If you had worked inside their body, then they had to wait for fifteen degrees. See that stone down there?" The visitor pointed at another large stone several yards away. "You spent the night there in front of a fire. A group of men arrived, led by one in uniform. They called you a witch and planned to kill you. When the uniformed man approached you, a large rock rolled and killed him. The others fled. Two weeks later, the men who wished you dead had died of a disease. No one dared face you after that, apart from those who desired your help."

Mike and I were stunned. Then, I asked our visitor's name and where he came from.

"Do you mean in this place or where I traveled from?"

"Both," I replied.

"In your language, I am Calgalory, but my language is like a breeze of air. I'm from Eskimo. Here, I like to spend time at these rocks with my brethren. I like to visit other places. I like Helmsley and this area."

"Didn't we meet someone from the Eskimo Galaxy? Was it at the Hob when we last talked to the people?" I asked Mike.

"Yes, it was. Are you a friend of that man?" we both asked Calgalory.

"Yes, he is my companion. I must leave you now. We will meet again."

He approached and touched us on our heads. We both closed our eyes. Then he was gone.

"Did you feel that? I felt like I do with Old One. Deep love. The energy flowed through me and into my gut."

"Yes, I felt it. That was interesting." Mike replied.

After eating our lunch, Mike couldn't wait any longer. He settled himself on Pillow Rock. I took a picture of him and then sensed where I needed to place my essence. I stood at the head of Pillow Rock with my stick deep in the earth. My body rocked back and forwards, then in circles. It got more potent, then I centered myself with my stick and sealed it.

"That's certainly the right spot," Mike mumbled under his hat. He was so relaxed.

"Phew, I can feel it pulse through me."

"Can I lie there now?" I asked. I relaxed and felt the energy course through me as I laid my head on the pillow.

We didn't want to leave. It was a special place indeed and so hidden away.

"I sense we need to go that way," I said to Mike as we prepared to leave. "Calgalory said people came upstream that way, see by those trees, we need to go back that way, then we can get out of the bracken quicker towards the moortop."

At the stream, we found an old stone bridge. "Well, this is easier than where we crossed earlier," I told Mike. He was taking pictures, capturing the reflection of the trees in the water, and caught an ethereal shimmer on his camera.

Once we reached the top and looked back down at the

rocks, they seemed tiny. We felt a sense of achievement, especially going off-piste. I had allowed Mike to lead and trusted he was tuned in. Despite having to forge our own path through rugged terrain, we achieved our goal, and the best part was that we hadn't fallen out.

Oon'ch-illia

62

North-West

Our next location took us across another moorland. It was a lovely day, with a moody sky and swathes of purple heather around us. We marveled at the view of the valley we had driven along, the rugged hills on three sides, and the forest behind us. Each landmark was familiar.

An invisible thread pulled us along the path. Within half a mile, we reached several cairns. An arrangement of three stones made ideal seats, so we rested and tuned in to their energy. It was familiar, but we chose to walk on. The invisible thread kept tugging.

Dulaa confirmed there was further to go. "There is a limestone wall...you may wish to see it," he said.

"Okay, I think we should keep on the path till it starts down toward the fields. There is another cairn marked on the map – and I think we should see the wall," I replied, and Mike agreed.

We walked for another mile, but the path veered off in a different direction, and there was no sign of a limestone wall. The only addition to our view was newly erected grouse shooting hides.

"I don't think I want to walk much further," Mike said.

He paused near a hide. With his eyes narrowed and his head leaning off to one side, I knew he was tuning in. I sensed the pulse of energy pulling him away from the path into the heather. I followed but was unable to see or feel anything of significance. A few yards from the path, Mike stopped by three small stones. They were lined up at the head of a circular indent in the heather and moss.

"Is this a place for me to connect my energy?" I asked.

Mike nodded as he searched the ground with his stick for the spot. It landed at the exact spot where my stick was placed.

"Guess I already found it," I said. I felt nudged to turn

towards the east, facing the hillside where I knew our new home was situated in the valley beyond. I connected with the land through my stick and tuned in. My body swayed forward several times. I felt pulled in the direction I faced. Mike held me by my rucksack straps to stop me from falling over. Then, I swayed in a clockwise motion. Then, I was pulled backward.

"That is telling you to center yourself," Dulaa said.

I ground myself deeper with my feet on either side of the stick and felt my energy sink into the earth. I swayed forward and then backward a little more. Then, I centered myself. When the energy was sealed, I pulled away.

"Good job," Dulaa said. He then offered bits of history. Memories were triggered the longer I stood and listened.

"In the year 1436, a small circular house stood here. Woodland swathed the hillsides that are now moorland. The three stones represent the three pyramids in Egypt. Across them were laid wooden boards, and in front was a wide arched doorway. Behind the stones, you had a seat where the mound of moss now lays. Outside of the house was a flat stone where people left you offerings. Behind the home stood a watering hole for cleansing and a grave where an ancient one rests."

I stand between the seat and the constructed bed and look out of the archway down the hillside. People approach from three directions toward the house. Mike becomes Arnold, a farmhand who accompanies me. He stands by the offering stone, instructing people on correct etiquette. I am Rosa, an old, crumpled woman, yet my light burns bright within me. Some say they follow the light to find me. After placing their offering, Arnold escorts the first person to the watering hole. He uses a bowl to sprinkle water over them before they enter my home for healing. They lie on the bed, and I go to work. Throughout the day until sunset, I continue healing the people who arrive. Then I rest by a fire with Arnold by my side. Sometimes Old One or Gemel, or one of the Ancients arrive to keep us company and offer guidance in my work. They are precious times.

In my reverie, I felt a deep peace and a connection to the land.

I asked Dulaa, "but why here? It seems like such an inconspicuous place. Even the stones are hidden from view."

"That's why. The energy is special here. The ancients came here hundreds of years before you did. One loved it so much he was buried here." The energy of every person that has been here and all the healing that has occurred makes this a strong energy center."

I picked some heather as we left to remind me of the site. Then, we returned to the path.

"We haven't seen the limestone wall. Have we missed it?" I asked Dulaa.

"It was a ruse. You cannot see it now. The stones are hidden. It was a way to keep you walking until you found the three stones. When you discovered previous sites, you ended your walk, except when you looked for a second one. It wasn't the right time then, but this time is right. You needed to continue past the first site to discover this one," he said.

"So, when we were at the cairn, that's another site for my energy? I sensed something but knew to walk on." I told him.

"That's right, it is time to return to those stones. It's a good place to eat your lunch and rest a while," he said.

We were hot and tired and felt like we had walked for ages. Looking at the time, I was baffled. No more than an hour should have passed, but it had been two.

"Have we shifted in time?" I asked Dulaa.

"What do you think, White Bird? There is much you will remember as the days pass," he replied.

With some relief, we returned to the three stones we had sat upon. Before settling for our lunch, Mike, and I located the spot to seal my energy into. It was where I had placed my feet earlier that day.

I didn't feel much at first, so changed direction, facing east again. I was pulled forward, then back a few times, then I rotated clockwise three times. I sealed the energy deep, then the stick began vibrating. It happened three times, so I asked Dulaa if I should stop.

"Yes, you've sealed it deep; you can stop now," he told me. Yet I stayed another thirty seconds as it continued to vibrate.

"Okay, I think I need to step away now," I said.

Then we stopped for lunch. The familiarity among the stones grew deeper as the vista pulled me further in. The hills, the valley, the stream below, and the stones to my left all called to me. Dulaa stood by the largest stone that had been used as a healing bed. He was conversing with a bird. I called him over to us.

"Dulaa is there anything else we need to know or do here?" I asked, while my eyes fixated beyond him to a smooth flat stone that looked like a chair back.

"This was a place of solace and sanctuary," he replied. "You loved it here. That flat stone is where you sat and looked across the valley towards the hills. That stream is where you bathed. You stayed overnight here and made a fire. You sharpened your knife and axe on the grooved stone over there. The knife you used for your food and to cut into people, if need be."

"Whaaat? I used the same knife for eating and taking things out of people?" I exclaimed.

"Remember...White Bird. You had a fire and water to cleanse it," he said.

"I need to sit next to the flat stone again and rub my stick on the sharpening one," I said to Mike, who seemed loathe to leave.

"Don't think I can move; I've seized up. You go over, and I'll follow – Dulaa says I need to be over there too."

I sat in the heather with my back to the stone, and my mind shifted as I connected with Rosa. She loved the land

and reveled in our connection and that of our tribe and the collective of ancient ones. She was loyal and hard-working. In the years we merged, she helped thousands of people. She was known far and wide.

I see the woodland around me and through the trees, the stream. Then, I notice Arnold walk sedately up the hillside. My body is comfortable, and I feel at peace and connected to the land. I sense all my needs are provided for in the security of the stones.

Mike took photos of me and saw the shift between the present and the past. He had a glimpse of Rosa as if from a distance. I sensed being in both times. Then I stood and rubbed my stick along the sharpening stone. The energy in my stick connected with the energy from my knife. I felt warmth in my hands as I wrapped them around it. I sighed as I surveyed the land, the stones, and the vista.

This was one of many places I found contentment. Mike and I agreed it had the greatest pull of all. The energy was peaceful and brought a sense of renewal, whereas the other sites were work orientated. They were places for meeting, healing, teaching, learning, and guidance. There had been other secluded areas for rest and contemplation, but only fleeting. Finally, we found somewhere that provided restoration. The only healing work performed on this site was with travelers who stopped by during the dark hours or early morning light.

A few days later, Gemel visited to discuss my progress with this book. I asked him about the violent death of Arnold. Each time we drove along the valley from our home to the moors, we passed a thatched building that was once the Sun Inn; now, it's a historic attraction. Mike often gasps for air and feels tingles in his hands and feet as we pass by. On the return journey, I sense my heart sinking into my stomach and have a vision of him hanging from the rafters.

I asked Gemel, "Was Arnold killed because he was associated with me? Can you tell me what happened to him?"

"Yes, he was. Everyone knew he was your protector and was loyal to you. Two men from the village tried to harm and then burn you. He stopped them and killed one of them in the fight. The other one went to the lord of the manor and said he had evidence Arnold killed the other man for no reason. The villagers lynched Arnold. They strung him up on the beams of the Sun Inn by his wrists and ankles, then hanged him by the neck.

A few days later, Rosa attended to a young boy. As she gave him healing, the mother told Rosa what Arnold had done and that they had hanged him for his crime. The young boy sat up and said, 'no, that's not right. I watched through the window and heard the man who accused him. He laughed in Arnold's face as he was dying. That shows you, he said, for consorting with the witch. No one will know you were only defending her.' Rosa thanked the little boy and then completed the healing. Afterward, she went to the village and found the man who had lied. She screamed and sobbed in front of the villagers. She pointed at the man and told him to confess. The people turned on him. He confessed and died soon after that. They discovered binding marks on his wrists and ankles when he was laid to rest. The lord of the manor who had sent the men after Rosa also died a few days later. Binding marks were found around his throat when he was laid to rest.

You missed Arnold but continued your work. When you rested against the flat stone, you often saw him walk up the hillside towards you. It gave you comfort."

63

Upstream

We headed to St Mary Magdalene Church, East Moors, with no definite destination. We had passed it many times and felt the urge to visit on this occasion.

On leaving the church, we headed across a field but lacked any sense of direction, and it was getting hot.

"I don't know where we should be going. Today is going to be a disaster; I feel it," Mike said.

"Well, I was uncertain, with it being only a week since our last finds. The forest you suggested, we've agreed, didn't feel right. However, neither of us wants to cross the fields, and I don't feel anything about the forest path where we parked either. What about you?" I asked Mike.

"Nope, I have no idea, but I don't want to go home yet," he said.

We returned to the car, where I retrieved the map.

"Well, we can drive up the road and around the moor and see if we feel pulled anywhere, but it's getting too hot to walk on the moors. Or we can try to get to Bransdale Mill again. It's a long time since we've been there. But I've seen a way we may get down to the stream just off the road that goes through the farms. Dulaa, are you able to advise us?" I asked.

"It will be good to reconnect and help in what you are doing," Dulaa said.

We kept our walking boots on but drove to the moors. We passed a parking spot for a moors track that appealed to Mike, but I said, "It's too hot to do that now. Maybe another time. Let's drive on and see if we find somewhere to stop by the Mill or find the stream."

At a sharp bend, I turned onto the farm road away from the Mill.

"I thought Dulaa said to go to the Mill. I knew you were determined to find the stream," Mike said.

I looked in the rear-view mirror at Dulaa. "But you didn't really say, did you? Is it okay to find the stream instead?" I asked him.

"Whatever you feel is right White Bird," Dulaa said, but I sensed him grin.

After passing through several farms on the narrow road, I stopped at a gateway. "Look, there's the bridge. I knew it. I saw it on google earth. I could see there was somewhere to pull in, and we were so close. This is our stream," I yelled.

"I can't believe it; you've been determined to find it. Let's hope we can get down to the water," Mike said as he got out of the car and headed to the bridge.

"Whaaat! look down there...I can't believe it...no...I guess I can," he shouted.

"What is it?" I asked.

"The flat stone. You know, the one for the offerings for your healing when you were Rosa. I saw it outside the circle where the house stood, and then it disappeared in front of my eyes. I wondered if it would reappear somewhere," he told me.

"How are we going to get down there? It's very steep," I said.

I attempted one route through some trees that took me to a sheer drop, so Mike suggested a descent by the bridge, which we negotiated together. Since the weather had been so hot and dry, we could walk towards a bend in the stream on dry stones.

I stopped and asked Dulaa, "Am I to place my essence here? I wasn't sure if I could do that today. Is this the right location?"

I was uncertain if I was allowed to place my essence in the stream since we had tried twice before further downstream and had been thwarted. My determination sometimes ran away with me, so the tribe sometimes held me back.

"I could not guide you. I know I confused you about the Mill, but yes, you can now put your essence in the water," Dulaa said.

"Yeees, at last, we are really doing it," I yelled to Mike.

"You certainly knew where to come today ... I guess the confusion was to test you would still bring us here," he replied.

"Can I do it here or go further upstream? I feel pulled towards those stones where the water flows the strongest," I asked Dulaa.

"It is fine here, but whatever you wish," he replied.

"How are we going to get up there? We'll have to go through the water, and the stones are slippy," Mike muttered.

"You don't have to go. I'll take my boots off and go through the water. You stay here if you want." I reassured him.

"NO! You'll hurt yourself. I must go with you and keep you safe. We'll go across the stones back there and up the bank, then down to where you want to be." He demanded.

"Okay, I'll follow you, but I was quite happy to go through the water. It would probably be quicker, but I agree, I might fall or hurt my feet." I conceded.

Tentative steps took us across the stream, then up along the bank, and with a slip and slide, we were down at the spot I had chosen. Mike helped me to stand on two mossy rocks. I positioned myself facing East and began to swerve forwards and then backward.

"I can't stop you if you fall, you know," Mike said from the bank.

"I'm okay; my stick is deep in the streambed. I'm being careful." I said as I continued to sway.

"That's enough, White Bird; you've achieved what you set out to do. Well done," Dulaa said.

"But I need to touch the water. I wanted to walk in it, like at Dunino Den. I know. Mike, help me to the bank. I'll put my hands in, instead." I reached for Mike's hand

and was pulled back across. I bent down towards the water and cupped my hands. After four scoopfuls, sending the water charged with my vibe into the stream's flow, I was satisfied. After releasing a white feather into the flow, I followed Mike back up the bank. A movement among some grass caught our eye.

"What was that Dulaa?" I asked.

"Did you see it? You have company. They are watching you," he said.

Further along the bank, we stopped by a tree to pull ourselves up.

"Look, can you see that in the hollow of the tree?" Mike asked.

"No, what is it? I can't see anything." I replied.

"I got it on my camera, I think. We can look at it later. I saw a face." he said.

When we got back near the bridge, Mike took some photos, and we enjoyed the peace and tranquillity until the flies around us became too much.

"Well, I need to carry this stone up. Can you manage to go ahead? Be careful!" Mike instructed as I slipped. Finally, we got to the top, and both laughed with relief.

"We just need to find somewhere out of the sun for our lunch now," I said as the heat hit us upon opening the car.

After half a mile, the farm road turned onto the moor road, where we found an ideal location for our lunch. It afforded us views of the tracks and fields from our previous walks when we attempted to reach the stream. We had partial shade within the car, but we had a cool breeze with the doors open. The views were a bonus to what could have been an uneventful day.

We drove home contented. I even identified a moor track that, next time, would take us Northeast of where we had been over previous weeks. The circle was being formed. Was our new home on the immediate horizon?

Oon'ch-illia

64

North-East

We set out on the track I'd identified along an Old Drove Road as planned. Many a time, I had walked it for gatherings at Cammon Stone or other sites. Our intended destination this time around was no more than 3km along the road. 2km in, we arrived at a batch of large ancient stones. There must have been at least fifty of them lying among the heather. We were drawn to the first group of three main stones within a circle of smaller stones. Mike headed towards one of the stones and searched in his mind's eye for the sealing point. Once again, I had placed my stick ahead of his. When he opened his eyes, he glared at me,

"I guess you don't need me now," he said.

"Of course, I need you. We are in this together. Right, I need to jump onto the stone to do this," I replied.

I placed my stick back on the point, but it didn't feel right. So, I moved to face south-west toward the center of the circle we were forming and placed my stick below me. "Is this, okay?" I asked Dulaa for confirmation.

"If that feels right, White Bird," he said.

The energy pulled me forwards. "Yes, it definitely feels right," I told him.

I swayed a few times, then moved in a clockwise circle four repetitions until I sensed to seal my energy into the ground. Dulaa then asked if I could sense anything else. I pointed. "Did I stand on this stone to talk to people and heal people on that stone over there?"

"Yes, see the circle formed by the outer stones? People stood around the edges, watching, and waiting their turn or listening to you talk. They came from among those other stones up there. They were told to wait there till they were called forward. Can you sense them all around this area?"

"I can indeed. It feels busy, much to do; many calls on my time," I said.

As we walked up the track, I mused, "fancy so many people coming all the way up here to see me. It's such a beautiful spot, though."

"People were accustomed to walking between villages, White Bird. This was their highway. They used horse and cart as well as being on foot."

Along the route were signs of the old stone road, but many parts were covered in hardcore and tarmac for off-roaders, even though motor vehicles were advised not to use the route.

"I'd be surprised if anyone other than farmers and the grouse hunters use this road. I can't see anyone else driving along here, can you?" I asked Mike.

Just as I'd spoken, we saw three 4x4s heading our way. "Well, I guess that proved me wrong. They must be mad driving along here."

Mike laughed, and we continued to a trig marker at the highest point. It afforded views as far as the Vale of York, across the moors in each direction we had been, and to the top of the valley, a familiar haunt from many past times.

I looked for signs of more stones up ahead but saw none. However, I knew there was a second location that couldn't be too far, but I was bewildered.

"Dulaa, is there another location, or is that all today?" I asked, even though I knew he wouldn't commit to an answer.

Mike said, "I think that's it for today unless you want to walk a bit further."

"I think we should. We are not in line with where we were last week. When we are, we've gone too far." Then I asked Dulaa, "We don't have to go as far as Cammon Stone, do we? That's too far up, isn't it?"

"You are right, White Bird, that is not needed for today," he said.

"OK, let's walk a little further. We may find somewhere to sit to have our lunch," I said to Mike.

We reached another track to the left, which I felt pulled to take it. Mike wasn't happy to walk that way as we were heading into the wind and downhill, but after several yards, he said, "look, there's a couple of stones. We can sit there."

We were looking for the best way through the heather when Mike shouted. "Wait, over there is a bigger stone that looks better."

I felt the connection when I reached the stone but was confused when Mike hadn't. I walked around the stone, found a corner facing south-west, and tuned in. Again, I could feel the energy but was compelled to check with Dulaa that it was another location to seal my energy before I did so.

"White Bird, you needed to find this on your own. Trust yourself; yes, you are right."

The vibration began. There was no doubt when I was pulled forward, and then I repeated the four rotations. We then settled on the stone for lunch. Mike was famished after using his energy at the last stone, so we didn't ask Dulaa any questions until after we ate. Each question was batted back to me.

"You tell me, White Bird."

"I feel this stone was my special place to get away from people. I laid or sat upon it and enjoyed the view and the peace. I don't think I worked from here, though. There are two small stones, but they seem to be on either side of the entrance to this stone like it is protected."

"Do you notice anything else, White Bird? Another stone, perhaps?"

"Ah, right in front of me, it's partially hidden. Did I make potions here? Yes, I remember now; I occasionally healed people. It was for the people I chose to bring here. They needed privacy because of their condition or who they were, perhaps the higher classes, who didn't want anyone to know they came to see me. I think there was a pool of water nearby. There, or maybe over there, perhaps behind us. Am I right, Dulaa?"

"Which one? You've said three places. Tell me which one it was," he asked.

I turned around and pointed. "Here, at the head of the stone."

"You are right on all accounts. You needed to find this place for yourself. You have done well, White Bird."

Oon'ch-illia

65

South-East

To celebrate Mike's 65th Birthday, we went for a picnic near Lastingham. We had planned to visit the tree, but on my birthday visit, we knew it wasn't one of the locations to plant my essence. Instead, we walked along a nearby valley.

We headed up a path alongside a stream and up to the moor. Trees of all varieties crowded the stream bank, providing sheltered places to sit on rocks by the water. The scent of the heather tingled our nostrils, and another familiar scent clung to my clothes.

I suddenly realized and shouted to Mike, "It's sage, there's loads of it, look. We've been walking through it, and I kept wondering, what is that smell? We must stop here. Look, up there, we must go to those two trees. There are some stones between them."

There were three small stones. I stood on the middle one and turned towards the west.

"I feel something here. The energy is pulsing through my stick. Am I to place my essence here, Dulaa?" I asked.

"Look behind you, White Bird. What do you see?"

I looked up the hillside and saw a few small stones dotted about. I walked around and then returned to the first stone.

"I'm unsure. I feel something here. Did I sit on this stone and look down at the big boulder by the small waterfall? I'm sure I bathed there, and this place does feel special."

"Look behind you. What do you see?" Dulaa said.

"Ah, it looks like a large stone with a small one on top underneath that moss. I didn't see it." I said as I stepped upon it. I turned to face the stream, but Dulaa said, "White Bird - face the other way."

Cathryn Mahoney

I faced the rolling moor and could see across to where the pine tree was hidden in the valley that ran down into Lastingham. I could sense crowds of people approaching from all directions. Then, I placed my stick firmly on the ground. I felt pulled forward, spiraling counter clockwise until I swayed forwards and backward. Finally, I came to a definite stop and felt my essence sealed. Joy filled me, and a new feeling. Power. I was filled with that unfamiliar sensation. The longer I stood, the more clouds of doubt were lifted, and I stepped into my power and authority. I smiled from within and felt my light vibrate.

"Wow, I bet that feels good," Mike said.

"Mm, it's different from what I've felt anywhere else. Why is that Dulaa?"

"You felt safe here. Many people came to see you from all directions. See the stones up there and over there?"

As I looked to where Dulaa pointed, there were stones all around. "So, I did a lot of work here? Talking? What about healing? Is there a healing stone?"

My eyes were drawn to a flat stone half hidden under the heather. "Yes, I did, there." I pointed and walked over to it.

"Yes, you did. You had students. They sat on the three stones and listened to you while you sat on your stone. You stood and turned to face the moor when people came, and you spoke to them with much authority. When you healed on the flat stone, your three students watched. They were aspects of you, from your past, present, and future, your human incarnations. Do you understand, White Bird?"

"I'm not sure. I think so. Was it Oon'ch-illia teaching White Bird, Cathryn, and Shanah?" I asked.

"I'll leave you to decide," Dulaa replied.

I didn't want to leave the stone, so Dulaa encouraged me to soak up my feelings there.

"Keep the feeling deep inside for when you need it," he advised.

I told Mike, "You know, the tree has lost its appeal. I

think this is our special place now. It feels so tranquil and safe. Why do I feel that Dulaa?"

"You are right. You left the tree and favored this place. You were safer here, and many saw your most powerful presence here. You have come full circle."

Further along the path, we found a large ledge of stone to sit upon for our lunch and reflected on the journey of encircling. A cricket sat beside me as we talked. I was certain it was a visitor listening in, and it confirmed we had achieved completion. What we desired was now within our grasp.

66

Full Circle

We thought we had completed the circle in the summer, but I had a niggle that something more had to be done. On August 28th, we met three ancient beings in a woodland close to home. They told us that our journey was nearing completion, but to help us manifest our new home, they asked us to locate three Petoskey stones and meet them again when they returned within the next three months. They also told Mike that he would complete the challenge of the Quartz Stone, which he did on September 10th.

I cried like a child at the meeting since I believed the ancient ones had set us another challenge. I expected to search for some elusive stones I had never heard of, like how Mike had to find the keystone hidden deep within the ground. Then, I worried they thought me unworthy of the challenge.

Dulaa said, "White Bird, you will find it much easier than you imagine."

The next day I researched and discovered Petoskey stones are fossilized coral from the lakebed of Lake Michigan. Did I have to contact Mike's friend in Chicago and ask her to buy us some? Or should I find an online retailer? Shipping from the states bumped up the prices, and we had to get three pieces, but the size didn't matter. Just as well, since we couldn't afford some of the prices. After three days, I drew a blank and became despondent.

Mike had also been searching for the stones. "Look, we can get three palm stones for £15 with postage. They are in the UK. Should I order them?"

I hadn't seen any UK retailers apart from eBay. I couldn't believe it. "Yes, order them quick," I said.

Three days later, they arrived with a friendly note from

the retailer, and they were perfect. I placed them in my crystal healing bowl to energize them and waited for further instructions from the ancient ones. I couldn't quite believe that it could be that easy.

On October 22nd, Dulaa told us the three ancients would meet us at the High Bridestones on the moors. It was an unfamiliar location, but not far to walk from the road. With the three stones held secure in my medicine pouch, we met them at one of the tallest stones. First, they instructed us to place the stones on indents within the bride stone. Then they wrapped their light around us.

"These stones will help you manifest what you desire and aid in your own healing and that with others," the spokesperson said.

All three put some of their light in the stones to help magnify their potency. Then, they reminded us we were close to the end of our journey and our patience would be rewarded.

They said, "there is one more to do, another location to place your essence, but you will just stumble upon it." Then, they praised Mike on his success with the Quartz Stone and reminded us to remain strong together and not fall out. They then said, "A Robin will become known to you from Sedona."

I thought they meant a bird, but they explained, "A person who will contact you and be important on your journey."

They embraced us and bid "farewell, until next time." Then, they were gone.

At the previous meeting, I had been upset before we met the three ancients because the sole of one walking boot was coming apart, which had added to my emotional state when I met them. When I returned to the car this time, both soles had come away from the boots. "Why on earth is this happening? We have amazing experiences like that, and then something bad happens. I can't afford to get new boots. What am I going to do? I can't even go walking on the moors now." I ranted. Mike got angry at me, so it was one of many magical experiences where we fell out.

The next day, Mike said, "I got an email yesterday from someone named Robin, who contacted me a while ago. Do you think that's who the ancients were referring to?"

Mike passed me the email, and I contacted Robin. We maintained regular contact and explored together our connection and what it means for the future, which, as I write, is yet to unfold.

Since we had not fully completed the circle around our new home, I got familiar with the three stones, which I used for healing purposes for myself, Mike, and family members. And, we had a couple of forays to the moors. We got closer to our new home than we'd ever been, but fog prevented us from seeing it.

"It's not yet the right time," Dulaa said.

So, we stayed away for a few weeks until, on Mike's second attempt to direct us to another standing stone in an easterly direction, we arranged to go.

I like to get out early, especially in the winter, but we were delayed and didn't get to the moor till noon. I had planned a longer walk, but we didn't have the daylight to complete it. So, we drove on instead of stopping at the intended car park.

"Look, let's drive along the road, and sense where we need to be for the stone, and park on the side of the road. We can't walk far today," I said.

We parked up and trod across the soggy moor. We knew there were several stones dotted along the pathway and were still determining which direction to take. So, we went straight ahead, and after walking only five minutes came to a standing stone. I stood behind it and faced towards the house but didn't feel anything.

"I'm not sure if I'm meant to place my essence here. Is this the right spot, Dulaa?" I asked.

"Stand on the other side up on the stone. Can you see where you would have placed the coins?" Dulaa asked.

Oon'ch-illia

I saw the groove Dulaa mentioned, then stood on a two-stone plinth that lifted my head above the standing stone. I surveyed the valley below and the moor towards Lastingham. I sensed where we had been on the stones by the stream on Mike's birthday. I felt the power that I felt then. It grew stronger.

People appeared from all directions. Then, they stood transfixed, awaiting me to speak. As I addressed the crowd, my light shone bright, and wisdom sprung from my lips. I spoke of where the future lies and the shift between times. I spoke of reincarnation – how life goes on. I said, "I have returned to prove that life goes on. I am here in your time of 1705, but in my time, it is 2022. Can you see the way I'm dressed? Some of you have seen me at different locations and in your own times. Those of you who come to the hob on the hill mix with people from different times and from beings from other worlds, and some from your future and my future. We will meet again on December 8th, 2022, in our time. That will be a momentous gathering. I invite you all to attend. Dulaa and the ancient ones will help you to be there if you choose to gather in a larger crowd and make history in this world.

Today, we have completed the circle to manifest our new home. A place you are all invited to, like the hob, but it will be the most secure place for all tribes and beings to meet at. We come together, unified in love and hope, to complete god's plan for us all as bearers of light and truth. Live your life fully and completely and be at peace with your brothers and sisters. Honor the path that you are on and fulfill your destiny as part of the greater plan. I look forward to welcoming you all to our new home."

The images of people walking away receded, and I looked back at the stone. "Dulaa, do I seal my essence here now? I'm not sure if I feel it."

"It won't be as strong since you have done most of the work already. Tune in, and you will know what to do."

Cathryn Mahoney

I tuned in and then felt the familiar sway. I had been confused about facing away from the house but remembered doing the same on Mike's birthday, facing where the people came across the moor. I placed my stick on a stone beside me and sealed my essence there, swaying clockwise three times, then sealing. I swayed back and forward, clockwise another three times, and then the circle was complete. I was at one with the landscape and able to survey in my mind's eye the circle, and my light vibrated around the moors, connecting all the places I had been during the summer but also during the other lifetimes that I had been present as a healer, seer, and teacher. The land, the trees, the hills, and the water systems all serenaded my vibration 'OOn'ch. As I heard it, I responded. "Yes, I'm ready."

67

Completion

December 8th, 2022

As the first freeze of winter whitened the land, we set out for the Hob Stone as planned several weeks earlier. We had given notice of our attendance and couldn't let our supporters down. The 8th was chosen symbolically, but that remained a mystery till after the event. It was also a full moon, signifying completion, and a powerful time to charge the energy of our gathering, shining our combined light into the universe.

The crowd gathered as soon as we reached the Hob, so we stepped up. First, I thanked everyone for attending and told them it would be our last meeting at the Hob Stone. Then, I invited all to come to our new meeting place that would be on our land at our retreat.

I said, "it will be a safe, welcoming space for such gatherings but also for individual and group healing and teaching sessions."

The atmosphere was of festivity and acknowledgment of our times meeting together and our collective success in raising the vibration of the Earth and the Universe alongside many other groups doing the same.

I then gave an update on what was happening at our current time in history then offered more insight into our future. Then, I asked if anyone wanted to talk about current events in their lifetime or ask us any questions.

Questions:

A man who spoke to us last time was the first to raise his hand.

"You have told us the difficulties you currently face in

your world. I am in 2035. What if I tell you that things get worse? I won't go into any details, but you continue to live well past that time, and the work we do together does make its impact - but are you concerned about what happens in between?"

I replied, "thank you for telling us, and yes, I'm aware that things will get worse in this world before they get better. It saddens me, but that's why our gatherings are so important."

Then a young girl said, "you helped my mummy when you stayed with Mother Migg. You gave mummy some honey from some bees you had. She has not forgotten how much you helped her."

I replied, "I'm pleased I helped her, is your mummy no longer with us?"

"No, she has passed now, but that is why I'm here. I had to come and meet you."

Then a being from another planet that Mike struggled to describe said, "our waters had turned bad, but the spring waters returned. Thank you for helping us. I have been to hear you talk a few times. It was after one of those visits, not long after I returned from here, the waters flowed and purified again."

I replied, "I'm pleased our work here has had an impact, that you have been helped, and life is much improved for you. Thank you for telling us."

Another man from the future, his current time being 2073, said, "I have traveled to and fro through time and have heard much talk of Oon'ch-illia, from the furthermost time to my current one, that you have helped many people, your memory still lives on in hearts and minds."

I replied, "Thank you for your assurances that I am having an impact. I only want recognition so that my name means positive change and peaceful alliances are forming."

Oon'ch-illia

I asked if there were any more questions before we meditated together. There was a round of applause and whooping, and then silence descended.

Before I began, Mike said, "wait, there is one of the ancients over there waving his hand. Both are here. Remember the two black geese that flew over the other day? They are relatives of Old One and have been visiting for a while. The tallest one wants to speak."

"We wanted to be known to you, and we're pleased we lifted your spirits," he said.

"Yes, our hearts felt lifted when you did two flypasts. We had never seen such birds here before and were pleased to learn who you were. Thank you for your presence here. We both feel honored to meet you." I told him while placing my hands on my heart and nodding toward them both.

I began the meditation with a grounding exercise and asked each one present to place their hands on their heart and, with soft eyes, acknowledge their neighbors close to them and then further away. Next, I asked them to connect with eye contact or observe each person's aura if they could do so.

"As you acknowledge your neighbors, heart to heart, feel the energy pulse between and around. Send gratitude to everyone present, the Earth, the elements, the spirits of the land, the higher beings present, and to the Creator of all that is."

I waited while acknowledgments were made, and all eyes were back on me. Then, I began to sway and move my arms around as I toned with my voice to shift the energy to higher vibrations to connect with the divine presence around me. I asked the group to move and vocalize with me if they felt the pull to do so. I sensed ribbons and streams of light connect us all, and euphoria building, then I brought us to stillness and silence.

Mike said, "there's a humming sound. I've never heard that before. It's beautiful."

As the sound faded, I thanked everyone for attending and reminded them we would meet again soon, but in our new surroundings.

A young woman asked, "how will we know when and where to come?"

I replied, "Dulaa will notify the ancient ones who bring you all here, and they will let you know. I am hopeful it will not be long before we can meet again, and I look forward to introducing you to our retreat and new home."

There was loud applause and whooping again. It felt like a party atmosphere - we were in celebration mode together. Then the group began to leave.

Mike said, "they are fading now, but we have some visitors who want to speak with you. Hello, love, I recognize you. You've been here before, haven't you?"

"Is it Running Eagle?" I asked while leaning forward to kiss her. "Thank you for returning. It is lovely to see you again." She smiled, then pulled back to let three more young people greet me.

"Now, we met this young woman in a different place on our travels. I'm sorry, I can't place your name," Mike said.

"White Bird, you have written about me," she said.

"Is it Wahluna?" I asked.

"No, but close," she giggled.

"Sacagawea?" Mike asked.

"Yes, Sagwa," I had to come and visit, and thank you once again," she said.

"Thank you for coming here and for the last time that we meet in this place. We are privileged."

"This is my friend, Tobe. He made the white man smart."

Tobe nodded and smiled. Then the other young man moved forward.

"You're Yorke, aren't you, the manservant that helped Lewis and Clark?" I asked.

"Yes, I am, ma'am," he replied.

"Thank you for all visiting us; we appreciate it. You look so happy."

As I spoke, Mike described how Sagwa was dressed, then said, "they want to do a dance for you."

Sagwa and Tobe did a tribal dance while Yorke swayed behind them. Then Sagwa came to me for a kiss. I thanked them again, then said, "we need to get warm now; it's so cold. We hope to see you all again at our new home." Then they faded away.

I had taken two stones with me to be planted under the Hob Stone. One was the smaller piece of granite Mike had dug up during his nighttime foray to the Quartz stone, and the other was one of the smaller, rounder stones he had collected. I pushed them down deep into the base of the Hob, and they seemed to slide down into the earth. Then I gave gratitude to the Hob and its surrounding stones before we went into the secluded hollow nearby for our picnic. The sun peeped out to warm us while snow flurries danced around. Then we said our final farewells before descending the moor for the warmth of the car.

Later in the day, we asked Dulaa how many people had been present. "888," he said.

"Wow, that was a lot; it seems significant. I need to work out what that means," I said.

The following day I researched and found that 888 related to the 8th and the full date, 08.12.2022. When all numbers are added together, the total is 8. We have also met the people at the Hob Stone 8 times since we started in December 2016. Then, the humming vibration that had emitted from the group while and after I had toned, was on the frequency of 888hz. I found YouTube recordings with a similar sound, and the tone was recommended for attracting infinite abundance and connection with the golden energy of the Divine Source of all that is.

Cathryn Mahoney

I was ecstatic. After the gathering, I had been on a high and recognized the importance of doing it on the full moon to complete the cycle Mike, and I had been on. Not just with the gatherings but bringing us many endings and opening the way for new beginnings with our new home and retreat. All those people present had been instrumental, just as those that had gathered on my birthday to help me make a call to the water-based beings on the 528 Hz love vibration had assisted in making that possible.

To learn that all keys had been turned was reassuring, and now it was time to attract what we had been seeking. I spoke to Jheneeka not long after. She told me that Tobe was instrumental in Lewis and Clark's discoveries. His native name is Tosatocube, which he shortened to Tobe, just as Sacagawea shortened her name to make it easier for us Europeans to speak. I also asked her the names of the two ancient visitors to Old One, whom we met in the village while visiting in Dreamtime. They also shortened their names for us to Duba and Temo. I knew they, like the three ancients we met at the High Bridestones, would be helping us on the next part of our journey. So, watch this space.

Oon'ch-illia

Epilogue

When can I return to the stars? I asked Old One.

"When your work here is done. You've waited so long for your retreat; it's only a step away. Embrace the waiting and consolidate your learning. Opportunities flow toward you. Shine your light into the world without expectation. Vision your new home and land as you have seen it from the air.

You have flown with me across it many times. With a bird's eye view, you have seen the kitchen, the library, the master bedroom, the cottage, and outbuildings that will be your workspace. You have flown over the gardens and plotted where to put your herbs. We stopped to stroll through the woodland and connect with the most ancient trees. You have even decided on the location for your tree house. And, Jheneeka has assessed the land as the most suitable location for our tepee.

Over several moons, you have placed your essence in a circle around those lands and soaked it into the waters. You have sealed it in the watercourse and streambed. If you could see the colors as I do – they are streams of light - yellow and purple hues, which crisscross the landscape. They connect down through the Earth and reach far into the Universe. Trust, dear one. It is only a step away."

Acknowledgements

I would like to thank my husband, Michael Mahoney for his agreement to make public our shared journey. I appreciate the commitment he gives despite all the difficulties he endures to ensure we fulfil our soul's purpose together.

I would like to thank Joseph Williams for his support and guidance in freeing up my intuitive writing skills and giving me the confidence to share my work, and for the developmental editing assistance he provided.

I would like to thank Sean Michael Paquet for editing my final manuscript and designing the book cover. His patience, sensitivity and commitment were a godsend.

I am grateful to everyone who has been a part of my journey, particularly those who have believed in me and encouraged me to write this book.

Oon'ch-illia

Author Profile

Cathryn has devoted her working life as a Therapist, Healer, Support Group Facilitator and Trainer to empowering adults and children affected by trauma and grief related to childhood abuse and domestic violence.

In 2013, Cathryn and her husband, Mike began working as spiritual teachers and healers with the support of their 'star' family, the Shee'masha'taa People. Together, they completed 'spirit quest' travels through North America in 2018 and 2019, and Cathryn has documented experiences of reconnecting with tribal nations.

In 2020, Cathryn began writing about her journey of self-discovery, and her otherworldly experiences with Mike and her tribe. She continues to document learning gained from her travels through the veils of time and space between lifetimes and venturing off-world.

Cathryn Mahoney

Published Books

After 189 Miles Turn Left – Treading the Path of the Peaceful Warriors 'A Travel Journal with a Difference'

Cathryn and Mike spent six weeks retracing the footsteps of their tribe, who had undertaken an epic 200-year journey traveling from Roanoke Island in North Carolina in 1583, across the country, until they disappeared into the Rocky Mountains of Alberta in 1785. It was a peacemaking mission between tribes and European settlers.

Exploring Ancient Wisdom
Between a Rock and a Highway!

Cathryn and Mike traveled through Idaho, Oregon, and North California re-connecting with Elders and Ancients of many tribal nations. Their discoveries were painful but rewarding; immersed in the trauma caused by genocide and tribal displacement onto Indian reservations. Native legends and prophecies also drew them closer to tribal spiritual beliefs and ancient wisdom.

Daily Reflection with Oonchillia White Bird

This book was created from a collection of daily reflections written throughout 2020, based on personal experiences and observations of the role nature plays within the healing process.

Printed in Great Britain
by Amazon

21397263R00165